HIDDEN VALLEY

Annie Seaton

Porter Sisters: 4

ANNIE SEATON

Porter Sisters series
1. *Kakadu Sunset*
2. *Daintree*
3. *Diamond Sky*
4. *Hidden Valley*
5. *Larapinta*

This is a work of fiction. Characters, institutions and organisations mentioned in this novel are either the product of the author's imagination or, if real, used fictitiously without any intent to describe actual conduct.

Copyright © Annie Seaton 2021
The moral right of the author to be identified as the author of this work has been asserted.

ISBN 9798772882276

Also by Annie Seaton

Standalone Books

Whitsunday Dawn
Undara
Osprey Reef
East of Alice

Porter Sisters Series

Kakadu Sunset
Daintree
Diamond Sky
Hidden Valley
Larapinta
Kakadu Dawn (2023)

Others

Four Seasons Short and Sweet
Deadly Secrets
Adventures in Time
Silver Valley Witch
The Emerald Necklace
An Aussie Christmas Duo

Pentecost Island Series

Pippa
Eliza
Nell
Tamsin
Evie
Cherry
Odessa
Sienna
Tess
Isla

Richards Brothers Series

The Trouble with Paradise
Marry in Haste
Outback Sunrise

The House on the Hill series

Beach House
Beach Music
Beach Walk
Beach Dreams

Sunshine Coast Series

Waiting for Ana
The Trouble with Jack
Healing His Heart

Second Chance Bay Series

Her Outback Playboy
Her Outback Protector
Her Outback Haven
Her Outback Paradise
The McDougalls of Second Chance Bay

Love Across Time Series

Come Back to Me
Follow Me
Finding Home
The Threads that Bind
Love Across Time 1-4 Boxed Set

Bindarra Creek

Worth the Wait
Full Circle
Secrets of River Cottage
Bindarra Creek Duo

The Augathella Girls Series

Outback Roads
Outback Sky
Outback Escape
Outback Wind
Outback Dawn
Outback Moonlight
Outback Dust
Outback Hope

ANNIE SEATON

DEDICATION

As always to Ian, my ever patient and loving husband.

You are always there for me.

"Earth provides enough to satisfy every man's needs, but not every man's greed.

Mahatma Gandhi

ANNIE SEATON

Prologue

Darwin - Casuarina Shopping Centre

'Mum? What are you looking at?' Ellie McLaren tried to keep the impatience from her voice as she stared at her mother. At the same time, she attempted to prevent James, her eighteen-month-old son from smearing ice-cream on her cargo pants.

Honestly, it was easier to control a helicopter in a dive than get a determined toddler to do what he was supposed to do.

'James, stop it. This instant!' Ellie snapped as her mother ignored her question, and her son squirmed on her lap, his sticky hands smearing ice-cream over her navy-blue cargos.

'Give him to me, Ellie, and go and get some paper towel from the restroom.' Mum's voice was patient as always, and Ellie wished for the thousandth time she had that same patience.

Rolling her eyes, she passed James across. 'What were you looking at then, Mum?'

A head shake. 'Um. Nothing.' Her mother's voice held a slight tremble. 'No one. Go and get the towel for Mr Sticky Fingers here.' Mum dropped a light kiss on James's upturned face.

'More ice-cream, Nanny?'

Ellie smiled at her son as she stood and headed towards the restroom at the shopping centre. She had to queue to get inside; it was a week before Christmas and the crowds at the Casuarina shopping plaza were large, noisy and impatient. By the time she got back to her mother and James, her little boy had a clean face and was resting his head on her mother's shoulder, his thumb in his mouth.

Ellie's heart melted as he looked up at her with an angelic smile. 'Mumma.' He held his arms out to her.

'Clean hands first, little man.' She gently wiped his sticky hands with the damp towel. 'Now, come here.' Ellie nuzzled her face into her son's sweet-smelling neck and breathed in that wonderful smell. As she always did, she found it hard to believe that she and Kane had created this perfect child.

'More ice-cream, Mumma?' James insisted.

'No, it's time to go home. I don't know about you, Mum, but I've had enough of crowds for the day.'

'Oh my God! Not again, dear God, not again.' Her mother's cry was almost a scream.

Ellie's head flew around and she caught her breath as she looked at her mother. Jagged fear sliced through her and as she gripped James tightly, he let out a cry. Mum's cheeks had lost all colour, her eyes were wide, and her bottom lip was trembling. It had been over three years since Ellie had seen that terrified expression on her mother's face.

'Mum, what's wrong?' She kept her voice even and soft as she stood, hitched James onto her hip and reached out to touch her mother's clenched hand. 'Talk to me. Please.'

'It's happened again.' Mum's eyes were bleak, and her fingers relaxed and trembled beneath Ellie's touch. 'I saw him again.'

'What has? Who?'

'Peter. Your father.' Mum's voice hitched on a sob. 'I keep seeing him. Everywhere I go.' She lifted her shaking hand and pointed to the games shop across the concourse. 'He just went into that shop. It was him. I think I'm going crazy. Again.'

'What do you mean? You can't see Dad. You know you can't.' Ellie tried to swallow her fear. Since Dad's death and the discovery of the truth of his murder, her mother's mental health had improved and for the last year, it had seemed as though her recovery was finally complete. Knowing that her husband hadn't committed suicide had been the catalyst for Mum's recovery. The grieving had started, and Ellie and her sisters, Emma and Dru had made sure that one of them was always with Mum as she worked through her grief. Dru lived in Darwin with Connor, and Emma and Jeremy were still in the Daintree, but they had all been there to support Sandra.

When James had arrived, Mum had eased back into her old self; she was so good with him, Ellie had gone back to casual relief work on the helicopters out of Makowa Lodge where she and Kane had met, while Kane looked after their mango farm.

Thank God, Emma and Jeremy are coming over to the Territory for Christmas. Ellie was no good at this psychological crap. With Emma and her husband both being doctors, Ellie had ready access to good advice on how to deal with Mum on her bad days.

Now Mum's hand gripped Ellie's fingers. 'I'm sorry, love.' Her eyes were awash with tears as she lifted her head. 'Of course, I know that. But I've seen him a few times. And it scares me. I know Peter is dead. I miss him so much I must be hallucinating.'

'The man went into EB Games, you said?'

Mum nodded. 'Just ignore me. I'll go back to the doctor and get some more medication. Or I'll wait and see Emma. She'll be here in a few days.'

'Here, take James.' Ellie pushed her son into her mother's arms. 'I'll go to the shop and take a look around. That should ease your mind. What was he wearing?'

'Jeans and a black T-shirt.'

Without a backward glance Ellie strode over to the EB Games shop and walked through the door. There was a crowd inside, and she stood and scanned the group at the counter waiting to be served. They were mainly young guys, but a taller man in a dark T-shirt at the other side of the display shelves caught her attention as he walked past them towards the door.

Ellie blinked and then stared. He was the same height as Dad had been, and his hair was longer and a lighter blond, but it was the guy's walk that held her attention. The same loose-shouldered swagger like Dad's. As she stared, he lifted his hand and smoothed his hair back with his right hand; the same gesture that Dad had used when he was nervous.

Before Ellie could step forward, he walked out of the shop and disappeared into the milling Christmas shopping crowd.

Chapter 1

Hilltop Nuts - Byron Bay
Thursday - Noon.

Dee Peters sighed as she removed the broken brush from the harvester. A breakage was the last thing she needed today. The brushes needed replacing but she'd hoped they'd last the week out. She jumped on the quad bike and rode across to the packing shed, detouring through the paddock where she'd installed the trial nets under three rows of trees. One hundred metre-long strips of thirty percent density shade cloth were angled down at thirty degrees on both sides of the trunks.

Stopping the bike, she reached down and lifted a handful of soil from beneath the net. Below the thick leaf litter the soil was rich with worms and biological activity. The nets acted like a trampoline and the nuts bounced off and into the middle of the row between the trees, away from the tree roots which then remained undisturbed by the impact of the harvester.

Heading off again, she rode through the trees and across the lush green grass towards the sheds, formulating the argument to present to Dad to agree to her expanding the system from a trial to best practice. The experiment had been a huge success, but she knew to implement the system across the entire plantation would be costly—ten thousand dollars per hectare.

He would argue, but it wouldn't be as much as replacing their old harvester.

Parking the quad bike outside the main shed, she strode across to the workbench hoping that Dad had picked up the new brushes and left them there.

She wasn't surprised when they weren't there; the last thing she felt like was a drive into Byron Bay, but she'd have to go this afternoon. Dad's interest in the property was almost non-existent these days. Mum said he'd had great plans when they had first moved there, but his interest had palled as the property market had taken off, and he'd turned his attention to his investment business in town. Dee had no memory of him ever working the place; he'd always hired workers. Now that she knew what that cost, she wondered how he'd been able to afford it. Dad was always after the quick dollar, and he'd obviously learned quickly he wasn't going to make his fortune from slow-growing macadamias.

Sometimes Dee wondered why she worked so hard; it seemed as though she had been working to get her father's approval—and love—for most of her life. She sighed as she hurried up to the house to get her car keys, but turned at the familiar rumble of the mail van.

'Morning, Dee.' Jenny Ryan, the mail contractor stopped at the front gate as Dee walked over. 'Still muggy, isn't it, love?'

Dee walked over to the driver's side window of the small white van and leaned in as Jenny rummaged through the mail crate on the passenger seat. 'Sure is. I always reckon March is the worst month.'

'Started your first harvest this week?' Jenny passed her a bundle of letters and catalogues secured by a thick rubber

HIDDEN VALLEY

band. 'Dave reckons we're going to get rain from that cyclone threatening the top of the Queensland coast.'

'Yeah, I've kept my eye on that, that's why I've been working until dark to get the first lot of falls up.'

'Not too late tomorrow, though, I guess. You'll be at the awards night, won't you?'

'For sure. Although for the life of me I don't know why the Macadamia Association holds the awards' night in March when we've all started the first harvest of the season.'

'Most of the locals employ contractors to do it these days,' Jenny said. 'You're one of the few plantations that still does their own harvesting. Bob Kimberley still giving you a hand?'

'Occasionally.' Dee preferred to work by herself. She nodded as she slipped the rubber band off and flicked through the mail. Her attention was caught by an official looking envelope addressed to her.

'Anyway, I'll see you there. Dave's the MC for the night.'

'See you, Jen.' The van took off and left her standing in a cloud of dust. As much as she didn't want the rain to come this week, they could do with a couple of light showers to settle the dust.

Dee looked down at the envelope. With a frown she turned it over and looked at the return address. Baker and Baker, Lawyers & Solicitors, Darwin—she'd never heard of them and had no idea why they'd be writing to her.

Turning it over again, she checked the letter was addressed to her: Ms D. M. Peters. *Hilltop Nuts*, via Montecollum, N.S.W.

That's me. She was the only D. M. at their farm in the Byron Bay hinterland. Mum was Catherine Jane, and Dad was Gerard John. Slipping the letter into her pocket and placing the rest of the mail on her lap, she climbed onto the quad bike, drove up to the house, and parked at the gate, copping a spray of water from the sprinklers in the front garden.

It was a perfect day in the Byron Bay hinterland. As it was named, the farmhouse of *Hilltop Farm* was set on a ridge that ran parallel with the coast and Dee never tired of the view from the house. To the east, the sea was a deep blue, reflecting a cloudless sky. Between the ridge and the coast, the lush, green landscape was broken by the silver glimmer of creeks and lakes. These days, the land between the farm was a mix of forest and farmland, as more and more dairy cattle properties were converted to macadamia nut farms.

With a frustrated sigh she walked towards the house; as she got closer, she tucked the other mail beneath her arm and pulled the one addressed to her from her pocket.

Dee ran up the side steps of the farmhouse and threw her battered Akubra onto the table near the open French doors. She looked down at her dusty boots with a frown and decided to risk leaving them on; there was a good chance Mum would be out at one of her ladies' lunches.

No such luck.

'Is that you, Gerard?' Her mother's voice came from the kitchen.

'No, Mum. It's me. I had to come back for a brush for the harvester, and I got the mail off Jenny at the gate. I think Dad's still in town.'

'Have you got time for a cuppa? I want to talk to you.'

'A cold drink would be good. It's hot out in the trees today.' Dee stepped into her bedroom, putting the letter next to her laptop. She was curious to see what it was, but it was more urgent to get into town, and back into the plantation. The letter could wait until tonight. 'I'll just have a wash.'

By the time she walked back through the house carrying a glass of iced water, her mother was sitting on the veranda outside the kitchen.

'Darling, how many times do I have to ask you not to wear those boots inside?' Mum lifted a manicured hand and waved at Dee's steel-capped boots.

'Sorry, Mum. I was only inside for a minute. Wasn't worth unlacing them.'

'I don't know why you have to wear such ugly boots, just like I can't understand why you have to be out on the tractor all day. You know your father can afford to hire workers for the harvest.'

'I know *the farm* can afford to, but we don't have to spend that money. And I prefer to work alone. It gives us more to put back into the net trial next year.'

'Next year?' Catherine's long drawn out sigh spoke volumes; she had not been happy when Dee had taken over the management of the plantation.

Dee knew Mum would have preferred her to be off lunching and socialising every day like she did.

'We're going overseas next year. Probably back to the States. Gerard has some business over there. Anyway, there's no need to change anything, Dee. The plantation was only ever meant to be a hobby for your father, and we knew if he put you in as manager, you wouldn't have to move away to get a job. We love having you at home.'

Dee sipped her drink and didn't reply.

'You know, once you marry Rodney Andrews, he won't want you working on the farm.'

Dee raised her eyebrows as she slid onto the cane chair opposite her mother. 'I didn't know I was marrying Rodney.' She held her mother's gaze steadily and as she put down her glass, she controlled her temper.

'Don't be silly, darling. Of course you will.' Catherine raised her eyebrows. 'You're almost thirty-three years old. It's way past time you thought about settling down, making your own home and giving away this obsession with the plantation. I'm surprised he hasn't asked you already.'

'Well, he hasn't, and if he does, don't be so sure I'll agree. And it's not what you call an obsession, it's my career.'

Mum ignored her protest and gave her a coy look. 'I've seen the way he looks at you. I'm not blind.' Dee's temper fired, but before she could retort, Catherine waggled her long hot pink nails in front of Dee's face. 'I've made an appointment for you at Celia's salon tomorrow. And don't argue with me. If *Hilltop* gets an award tomorrow night—and I'm sure we will—you'll have to be looking your best, and honestly, darling, your hair and nails could do with some attention.'

Dee knew how to pick her battles with her mother, and this was one she could give in to. Draining her glass, she stood and walked around the table and brushed the expected kiss on Catherine's cheek, hiding the anger that simmered as a result of her mother's "expectations".

Home making! That was the last thing she wanted to do. Having a romance with Rodney had never crossed her mind, let alone seeing him as a future husband. He was ten years older than she was, and Dee had been surprised when he had first asked her out to dinner a few months ago. Since then, their friendship had firmed—and that's all it was, a platonic friendship; they usually spent Friday nights together somewhere. Sometimes at dinner, and sometimes to see a local band at one of the pubs in the district. The occasional kiss brushed across her cheek at the end of the night was simply affection between friends. Dee shook her head; Mum's imagination was in full flight.

'Okay, Mother dear, tell me what time and I'll be there.'

'I made your appointment for after lunch. At two. We can go to Byron Bay in the morning and find you a dress and then have lunch at *Panchos*. Your father should be home from golf before lunch, and he can get on the tractor for a while.'

'I have to go to town now to get the parts, and then I'll work late again this afternoon. I should get this fall collected, then Dad won't need to worry about it tomorrow.'

'Good. He's been working too hard this week.'

Dee hid her eyeroll and headed for the ute.

God, what have I been doing? Lying on the beach reading a book? I wish!

But Mum was right; Dee knew she did need to go to the salon tomorrow. It might all be about appearances, but she should get herself glammed up a bit and do the farm proud. A haircut and some highlights wouldn't go astray, but she'd draw the line at a manicure. Rodney had offered to be her partner at the dinner, and he would wear a suit, so a new dress was probably required too. Even though the awards ceremony was held in the corrugated shed of the local distillery, like most other venues in the hinterland it was upmarket, and the ticket had said smart casual dress.

***

By the time Dee came back from town, installed the new brushes, picked up the fall from the back paddock, and put the harvester in the main shed, the last thing she felt like was arguing with Dad about money.

Talking to him when she was tired would be a bad move. She'd leave it until the weekend. With a yawn she pulled the shed doors closed and locked them. When she crossed the lawn to the house, Mum was sitting on the verandah watching the sunset.

'Go and have a shower, put something nice on, then sit and have a drink with me.' Dee frowned as her mother held up a half empty bottle of wine, hoping it was the first of the night.

'Okay, sounds good. What's for dinner? I'm starving.' Dee took her boots off, lifted the lid of the shoebox at the door and put them away.

'Gerard's staying in town so I thought we could do every man for himself tonight.'

Like most nights, Dee thought. Not that it was fair to expect Mum to cook every night, but occasionally would have been nice.

'Okay. I won't be long.'

She stepped into her bedroom, crossed to her desk and picked up the letter she'd put there before she went to town.

Carefully sliding her fingernail beneath the flap, she opened it.

Dee's breath caught as she read. With a frown she read the letter twice before reading it slowly a third time. Her heart rate picked up and her stomach churned.

'To confirm your identity and claim your inheritance kindly make an appointment to attend our office at your earliest convenience,' she read aloud when she got to the end for the third time.

Unbelievable. It had to be some sort of joke or scam. Why did people have to do that? Turning to her laptop she sat on her desk chair, not worrying about the dust on her work pants or the soil grime on her hands.

Family secret. Confidential. Essential that you contact us. Inheritance. At your earliest convenience. The phrases jumped out at her as she skimmed the letter again, her eyes settling on the solicitor's firm: Baker and Baker, Lawyers and Solicitors, Darwin.

Placing the letter on the desk, she opened Google and typed in the name, soon verifying it was a solicitor's office, and matched the address on the letterhead. She shook her head; that didn't prove anything. These days with digital printing anyone could have sent a letter like that and faked an address.

Scrolling through the firm details on the website, her eyes settled on the name of the senior partner. Frank Baker. The photograph showed an older man with white hair looking at the camera, his expression serious.

Okay, so maybe it was a genuine firm and Frank Baker was a real solicitor. Glancing at the bottom of the screen, Dee realised she should have opened the letter before she went to town. It was too late to ring Darwin now.

Picking up the letter, she read it one more time, and then slipped it beneath the laptop.

***

Panchos Café - Byron Bay
Friday. Noon.

Dee covered her mouth with one hand as a yawn threatened. She'd insisted on taking her own car to the Bay so Catherine could go home after they had lunch together at *Panchos*, their favourite café. She'd need the time to think without Mum's chatter. She glanced down at the bags beside her as they sat waiting for their lunch. Town was busy—being Friday, locals who lived in the hinterland had come to town, and the weekend tourists had already arrived—so she and Mum were parked two streets away from the main shopping area. Dee nodded at the waitress as she put their drinks on the table. 'Thank you.'

'No coffee today?' Catherine looked at her quizzically as she picked up her coffee cup. 'That's not like you.'

'No. It's too hot for coffee.' She was preoccupied and wanted to get out of here as soon as she could. They sat in silence for a while, surrounded by the buzz of conversation from the other tables. Tourists filled the café, and their loud voices, a baby crying, and the hiss of the coffee machine, made it hard to have a conversation. Dee put her fingers to her temple; a headache was building behind her eyes; she'd had little sleep last night. As soon as she knew the solicitor would be open in Darwin, she'd gone down to the shed and called them. The confirmation that the letter was genuine had rocked her.

'I'm pleased you picked the red one,' her mother said.

'The red what?' Dee turned her attention to Catherine and tried to stop thinking about the phone call. About what she was going to do. Vivian, the paralegal at the firm, had insisted that she come to Darwin as it was essential that Dee be there in person as soon as possible.

No way. There was a harvest to be completed. Her stomach still churned and she wasn't sure if she could even face the light salad she'd ordered.

'The red dress. It looked beautiful against your olive skin. Don't get highlights in your hair this afternoon. It's better dark.'

Dee stared at her mother. 'Where did I get my olive skin from? Both you and Dad are fair.'

'From my side of the family. My father and his brothers were all dark. It's the Welsh heritage. Your great-grandfather used to tell us it was because sailors came ashore from the Spanish ships wrecked off the Welsh coast. They were handsome men and the local women took a fancy to them and a dark-skinned bloodline came into some of the Welsh families. Poppa could sure spin a yarn. Before we emigrated to Australia, we—I—would sit at his feet and listen to his stories whenever we visited them.'

'I don't think I've ever seen any photos of your grandparents. Or your parents.'

Catherine shrugged. 'You know me. I hate clutter. Growing up in a small house drove me crazy. That's why I like everything clean and tidy. You have seen the photo albums though.'

'Have I? I don't remember.'

'Yes, when you were little, you used to ask to see them all the time. There's one of my grandmother that could be you. Same hair, same olive skin, and the same aristocratic nose.'

'Aristocratic, hey? I always thought it was called a snub nose.'

'More like a snob nose.' Her mother giggled, and Dee felt slightly better.

'I'll have to have another look one day.' Dee put her head to the side. Catherine was being evasive, Dee had no memory of photo albums. 'Why did you only have me? Didn't you and Dad want more kids?'

Her mother stared at her, a frown marring her usually smooth forehead. 'That's just the way it happened.'

Conversation died as the waitress slid two bowls of salad onto the table. Dee picked at hers with her fork and finally pushed the bowl away.

'Are you nervous about tonight?' Catherine asked when she'd finished eating. 'Has Rodney hinted at something?'

'Hinted at what?' Dee was surprised to see colour flare in her mother's cheeks.

'Oh, nothing.' Catherine shook her head and looked away, and Dee narrowed her eyes.

'Have you been talking to him?'

Catherine hesitated too long, and Dee knew she wasn't telling the truth. 'No, I haven't. Your father mentioned something.'

'About what?' Dee sat back and folded her arms.

'You'll see. It's a surprise. And I'm not saying another word. Now come on, if you're not going to finish that salad we'll go to the salon.'

'I thought you were going home?'

'I am, *after* I make sure that you have a manicure before your hair's done. I've booked you in for nails, but I know what you're like.'

'Mum!'

'And you can take that look off your face, Deanne Peters. You *are* having a manicure, a facial, and a hot stone massage before Celia does your hair and makeup. I've already paid for it.' Her smile was crafty. 'And you'll thank me for it all tonight.'

##

An hour later, Dee was lying on her stomach on the massage table, hot stones warming her lower back. 'You're a magician, Fiona,' she said as the masseur kneaded her tight neck muscles and worked her way down her spine. 'Sitting on the tractor for hours leaning forward to see if the harvester's missed any nuts isn't good for my lower back.'

'Or your neck. When I'm done here, you should be feeling more relaxed.'

'I am already.'

Physically anyway, Dee thought. She'd been up since dawn dehusking the nuts she'd harvested yesterday. They'd soon learned after the first harvest that the outer husk of the macadamia had to be removed within twenty-four hours of collection to stop the mildew forming. If not, the macadamias would be ruined because of the musky taste that came from the mould.

Dad had been going to help her, but as usual an important call had called him into the office and he hadn't come back to the farm. She should have known not to expect him to turn up, but it hadn't bothered her; the way she was feeling she would have blurted out what was bothering her. She wanted to process the letter and the phone call for a while longer before she raised it with her parents.

Her father had bought the plantation from Rodney Andrew's father, Cec, when Dee was in primary school. He'd opened a financial services consultancy in town, and when Rodney had graduated from university a couple of years later, Dad had offered him a job, and then he'd turned his attention to establishing the macadamia plantation. The property had been a dairy farm since the nineteen twenties, but Gerard had hired local contractors to clear the land and plant hundreds of macadamia trees. By the time they produced their first harvest seven years later, Dee was in her final year of high school, and Rodney was firmly established as her father's partner in his consultancy at Byron Bay.

Dee had learned a lot in those early years, and she'd loved the work on the farm. She'd never had any interest in doing anything else and had learned the business from the ground up.

Literally.

After school she'd worked on the plantation in the holidays while she studied for a science degree specialising in agriculture and business in Armidale. Her parents had been keen for her to stay on the farm after she graduated, and she'd turned down a couple of job offers at their suggestion. Now she was beginning to wonder why they'd wanted her to stay.

When she graduated, Dee took on the role of manager of the plantation. She loved the work but had been putting in longer hours over the past two years. Effective management was difficult because Dad still had final say about what happened on the farm. Even though she was manager, any decision had to be run past him, and it seemed to be a constant battle these past three months to get him to agree to any of them.

He had been dead against the net trial.

Dee was worried that he wouldn't agree with the system expansion. She knew she had to convince him it would save money in the long term. She gritted her teeth as she remembered that conversation. Was she gullible and naive? Was that the only reason she was working here? Had her parents manipulated her into thinking she was important to the "hobby" plantation? And what was this sudden secret Rodney was going to tell her tonight?

Dee closed her eyes and tried to push away the worry that had been at the forefront of her mind since last night. There was no point planning to go to Darwin until after she'd talked to Mum and Dad. A cold feeling spread through her chest and her eyes flew open. Maybe her parents—and Rodney— had known the letter was coming.

'Relax, Dee. Your back just tightened again.' Fiona tapped her lightly on the shoulder.

Taking a deep breath, Dee tried to think of something pleasant, but there wasn't a lot that came to mind.

Maybe *Hilltop Nuts* would win an award tonight. She knew she ran the best plantation in the district, hobby farm or not. Their yield was high, and the quality of the nuts superb. Plus she was only days away from securing an export contract.

That would show Dad.

She hadn't mentioned the contract yet; she'd wanted to wait until she could present the firm offer to him for his signature, and then she could ask about the nets.

'That's better. I felt you relax then,' Fiona said quietly. 'Take another deep breath and hold it. Your neck and shoulder muscles are still tight.'

'I've been thinking too much,' Dee said as she let out the breath.

Fiona removed the hot stones from Dee's lower back and covered her with a warm towel. 'Take five minutes, and then call me when you're ready for the facial. I've left a glass of iced water for you on the table.' The door closed with a quiet snick and Dee took another deep breath.

But it didn't do any good. No matter how hard she tried to forget it, all she could think of was the final line of that letter.

"To confirm your identity and claim your inheritance kindly make an appointment to attend our office at your earliest convenience."

Their office.

In bloody Darwin. Three and a half thousand kilometres away, a long, long way from the life that Dee knew.

The life she had now begun to question.

Chapter 2
Benton's Distillery – Montecollum.
Friday night.

By the time Rodney arrived at the farm to pick her up, Dee had regained most of her composure. She'd convinced herself that she was getting worked up over nothing; the letter was simply a case of mistaken identity.

Smoothing one hand over her dress in front of the mirror, she frowned at her reflection; the neckline was too low. She turned to the side of the antique hallstand that doubled as her dressing table and rummaged through the various necklaces and beads hanging on the side hook. Finally, her eyes settled on a black tourmaline necklace and she clipped it behind her neck before digging out the matching earrings. As she took a last look in the mirror, a car came up the drive.

She'd brushed up okay.

Her parents had left early, arranging to have a drink at a bar with friends on the way to the function. Dee had arrived back from town as they were leaving, and Mum nodded with satisfaction as she examined Dee's artfully tousled dark curls, her makeup, *and* red nails. Catherine had bought a bottle of nail polish to match her dress and left it at the salon; Dee had given in and let them put on a set of gel nails and paint them dark ruby red.

'I'll be lucky if these last a day,' she'd said with a grin as she put them under the light.

'They're strong and the gel won't chip. It'll wear off and grow out before the polish chips. Wear gloves, girl!' Mandy, the nail technician sighed. 'I'm green with envy. Think of me while you're all glammed up. I'll be home cooking dinner for three tired kids and a husband who hasn't held a tea towel since the day we got married. You make sure Rodney knows how to help around the house.'

'Rodney?' Dee stared blankly at Mandy. 'Why on earth would I worry about that?'

'Your mother said there was—' Mandy put her head down and turned the small fan on. 'You're right to go, now. They're dry enough; they won't smudge but be careful.' She stood and picked up the clean towels next to the counter.

'Mandy? What were you going to say? What did my mother say?'

'Nothing. Sorry, I must have misunderstood.' Mandy looked up at the large clock on the wall. 'You have a wonderful night, Dee. I have to go and pick up the kids from the babysitter.' Before Dee could say anything, Mandy was out the door to the back room, closing it behind her. Dee shrugged and headed for her ute. As she drove home, she wondered why this week had suddenly become so complicated.

By the time Rodney climbed out of his low-slung sports car, she was waiting on the front verandah.

'It must be a special occasion for you to bring the black beast out on our dirt road,' Dee said drily as she walked down the stairs. She usually met him in town because Rodney was precious about his sports car.

'It is.' He came around the back of the car and stopped. 'Wow, Dee, you look amazing.'

Rodney hurried up the three steps and stood in front of her. Her eyes widened when he slid one arm around her back and pulled her in close before his lips touched hers and lingered. 'No, let's change that to "you look stunning".' His voice held a husky note.

Heat ran up her neck and into her cheeks and Dee stepped back feeling a little bit uncomfortable with this new close familiarity. 'Thank you. Mum set me up for a trip to the beauty salon in town.' She looked down at her clutch bag, unsure of this new Rodney.

'I've packed a bottle of champagne and a rug in the back of the car. I'd like to spend some time with you after the dinner. I thought we could go up to the top of Monte Hill and watch the moon rise.' He lifted his hand and touched the loose curls that tumbled onto her shoulders.

Dee folded her arms and stared at him. 'What's going on, Rodney? Mum's full of enigmatic hints, even Mandy at the salon seemed to know something was going on.'

'Sweetheart, don't stress. I know I've taken it slow between us while we got to know each other and you've been busy these last months, but I know tonight is the right time to talk about our future.'

'*Our* future? I didn't know we had a future.' Dee knew her tone was a bit snarky, but she didn't know what he was on about.

'Yes, now that your dad is thinking about selling, I thought it would be pretty good to have the land back in the Andrews family.'

'Dad is what?' Her voice rose in pitch. 'Selling the nut *farm*? I don't know where you got that, but you're wrong.'

'Ssh.' Rodney put a hand to her back and turned her towards the car. 'This is a conversation we'll have after the dinner.' He opened the door and waited until she was in the passenger seat. 'The moon rises about eleven. We'll make sure we're over at Monte lookout to see it.'

Dee sat there speechless, wondering what the hell was going on. She wasn't going to say another word until she figured out what Rodney was up to.

##

'And the winner of the plantation of the year is . . .'

Dee sat at the table between her father and Rodney, her eyes fixed on Dave, the MC, as he held up the envelope. The distillery restaurant was packed. Over a hundred and fifty guests were seated in the large space. White linen cloths covered the tables, each with a centrepiece of sweet-smelling Asian lilies. Silver cutlery shone in the flickering candlelight, and the mood was buoyant. They'd watched a presentation on the local macadamia industry and how the Byron shire was leading the nation in production and quality. Despite Rodney's words going around in her thoughts, Dee was proud to see photographs of *Hilltop Nuts* feature on almost half of the slides. Over the past two years, the property had improved under her management. Rodney's announcement about Dad selling the farm had left her very concerned; it was one more thing to add to her conversation with her parents tomorrow morning.

No, she wouldn't leave it until then. She'd wait up tonight and insist on finding out what was going on, and ask if they knew about the letter from the Darwin solicitor. As Dee thought about the last couple of weeks, she realised Dad had been keeping a low profile and Mum had been edgier than usual.

How could things change so quickly? Last week she'd been looking forward to the first of the harvests, enjoying being on the tractor in the plantation, and keen to see how *Hilltop Nuts* would fare at the awards dinner. Now uncertainty filled her.

Dave pretended to do a drum roll into the microphone. 'Ladies and gentlemen, our 2020 winner is . . . *Hilltop Nuts*.'

With a wide smile, Dee turned to her father, ready to go up with him to collect the award, but before she could move, he was out of his chair and heading for the temporary stage that had been set up for the night. She leaned back and waited for him to speak, feeling a bit left out. It would have been nice to go up to receive the award with him.

Gerard took the microphone. Dee looked over to catch her mother's eye, but Catherine's attention was fixed on the stage. A small measure of gratitude trickled through Dee when Rodney reached over and squeezed her hand. At least someone acknowledged her contribution.

'Well.' Gerard beamed at the crowd filling the room, and Dee looked around. The tables were filled with fellow plantation owners, and the remainder was made up of members of the local Chamber of Commerce and Shire Council as well as townies from the Bay here for a night out and a good meal. 'What can I say?' her father continued. 'Many years of hard work has paid off. I'd like to thank the local growers' association for their support, the council for their ongoing promotion of our valley, and a special mention for Rodney Andrews for taking over the work in the company while we focused on building up the property.'

We? Bullshit, Dee thought.

She waited to see if her management merited a mention, and held her breath as her father shook Dave's hand and then took the silver trophy from the association president before walking off the stage and heading back to the table. Disappointment vied with disbelief, and she plastered a smile on her face as a few of the people sitting at their table looked at her. All the local growers knew who ran the plantation.

A small sigh escaped Dee's lips and she looked down at her hands clenched in her lap. If she was fair, it was Dad's plantation, but the fact that she had spent the past ten years almost singlehandedly improving the yield and quality with the latest technology and new methods of improving the crop, while he'd sat in his office, stuck in her throat. If he truly intended selling, she'd stay in the industry and find a managerial job in the district.

The unfairness of his action and speech—not to mention Rodney's talk of Dad selling—sent tears stinging at the back of her eyes, but Dee lifted her head and smiled, determined not to show how hurt she was as her father walked towards their table. He paused at each table as other growers congratulated him.

A warm hand touched hers. 'Can I get you another drink, sweetheart?' Sympathy filled Rodney's expression, but she lifted her chin and nodded, forcing a smile to her face.

'Thank you, a champagne to celebrate our win would be good. Mum would probably like another one too.' Dee knew her eyes would be glittering, but she would *not* verbalise her disappointment. 'I'll just go to the ladies' room while you're at the bar. Thank you.' She pressed Rodney's hand as she stood, determined to get away from the table before Dad came back. She knew she was likely to say something and this was not the right time or place.

When we get home.

Dee put her head down until she'd crossed the room and pushed open the door of the restroom. Glancing at her reflection, she pursed her lips; her eyes were as hard and bright as she'd known they would be and twin spots of colour almost the colour of her red nails, stained her cheeks.

Crossing to the basin, she pulled a piece of paper towel from the dispenser and held it beneath the tap until it was damp. Lifting it to her face, she pressed the cool paper against her heated skin. Voices came from the corridor as she stood here, and when Dee realised they were about to come in, she bolted for a cubicle and shut the door.

She didn't want to talk to anyone. Maybe she was being precious, but it was hard seeing how little her father thought of her. If she was honest, it wasn't the first time. But this award was an accolade, and anger began to build as she thought about how many times Dad had let her down. They were not an affectionate family—unless it was for show—and she'd often felt unloved when Dad was dismissive of her achievements.

Stop being such a sook, Dee told herself firmly. It's his farm; you're only the manager. But a simple public thank you would have been the right thing for him to do.

Quietly closing the lid of the toilet she sat down and pressed the paper towel to her cheeks again. It would be nice to find a back way out and just go home, but that would be childish.

Besides, her ute was at the farm.

To tell the truth, she'd rather be in the shed dehusking the nuts instead of sitting out here waiting to see what Dad, and Rodney, were up to.

A nasty thought gave her a smile. With luck, someone might ask Dad how he'd improved the soil and increased the harvest.

Well, he wouldn't have a damn clue. Every time she'd tried to talk to him about it, he'd waved her off.

'I trust you, darling. Just keep doing whatever you've been doing. It's working well.'

Dee bit back the groan that rose to her throat as the door to the rest room squeaked open.

'What did you think of her red dress?' A conversation drifted across as the ladies' room door closed. 'She looks a bit brassy, I thought. All that dark hair, and dark skin, and long red talons. Way overdone for a little dinner like this.'

'Nice one,' Dee said under her breath. *I bet she's the one I saw in a pair of jeans.* She didn't recognise the voices.

'She mustn't know she doesn't have to try so hard to nab him. Rodney's determined to get his hands back on his family's property. If he marries Deanne Peters, he'll probably get it for a song too.'

A nasty chuckle came from out near the basins. 'Like a dowry, you mean.'

'Yeah.'

'And what about poor Yvonne?'

Yvonne? Dee screwed up her nose. *Who the hell was Yvonne?*

'He thinks he's being smart'—the louder of the two women continued over the sound of running water—'but I've seen him leave her place just before dawn *every* day this last week. Her hubby's on one of his fly-out weeks. Rodney walks over late at night and leaves her place before sun up. It's only because I'm up for Liam's early feed that I see him from our front bedroom. The first night I saw him creeping around I thought it was someone up to no good, and I almost called Daryl to go outside and check. That would have shown him.' She laughed and lowered her voice and even though she felt like an eavesdropper, Dee strained to hear. 'He always checks to make sure no one's around. He's such a well-respected pillar of the community too. I heard he's going to run for council in the next elections.'

'What a sleaze.'

'I reckon Yvonne'll give him hell once he marries that snooty Dee Peters. I was surprised when she married that Chad bloke; she's always had a thing for Rodney. But I guess she wasn't good enough for him. No money there.'

'Good enough to screw, though. Can I borrow your lipstick, love?'

Dee cringed. It was hard to reconcile her friend, Rodney, with the man they were talking about. She leaned forward and put her face in her hands. Could this week get any worse? Not that she cared two hoots about any night visits Rodney was making. More fool him, but it was his business, not hers. She was pleased she'd not fallen for him;

there'd always been something that had stopped any romance on her side. Maybe because it had always seemed as though he was in Dad's pocket was the reason she'd put a barrier up.

But going away to uni and working hard on the plantation had meant that Dee had few friends locally and Rodney's friendship had given her someone to go out with.

She stood and threw the wad of wet paper in the bin inside the cubicle, flushed the toilet and opened the door. Straightening her shoulders, she flicked a dismissive glance towards the two women whose mouths dropped open, and then had the grace to look embarrassed.

'It's fine, ladies. You let Yvonne know she is quite welcome to the lovely Rodney,' she said as she crossed to the basin.

Chapter 3
*Friday - 10 p.m.
Hilltop Nuts.*

Dee drummed her fingers on her leg as Rodney's car climbed to the lookout. The last thing she felt like was driving up there and watching the moon rise. She wanted to go home and talk to her parents. Before she did, she'd pull the letter out again and read it with a clearer, more logical head. Until she'd called the solicitor, she had doubted the contents, but on top of Dad's treatment of her tonight, a few past comments and events had come to mind, and she was starting to wonder if there was some truth in the strange direction her thoughts were taking her.

'I'd much rather go straight home, Rodney. I'm really tired. It's been a big week.'

But he'd been persistent. 'Do you know how hard it was to get the esky in the boot?'

She gave in. It would be a chance to pick his brains about Dad's intentions. Forewarned would be forearmed when she confronted her father.

The carpark at the lookout was deserted and Dee slipped her high heels off before she got out of the car. While Rodney took the esky out of the boot, she leaned forward and ran her fingers through her curls, ruffling them and combing out as much of the sticky gunk as she could. The grass was soft beneath her bare feet as she walked across to the picnic tables on the edge of the bluff. Hitching up the calf-length evening dress, she perched herself on one of the tables at the end of the grassed area while she waited. The sky was crystal clear and a mass of brilliant stars twinkled above. In the distance the lights of cars on the motorway flickered red and white against the backdrop of the town lights further down the coast. The air was sweet and cool, and Dee took a deep cleansing breath, calm stealing through her as she looked out over the countryside she loved.

'Come and sit with me,' Rodney called. The moon was already up and there was enough light to see where he'd spread a picnic rug on the grass. As she walked over, he opened a small cooler bag and took out a bottle and two glasses. There was a pop and foam ran down the sides of the dark bottle.

'You don't want to get breathalysed on the way back to town,' Dee said as she stood beside the rug.

'I'll be fine. I look after the Sarge's investments for him.'

'So, one rule for some and another for you?' Disgust curled in her stomach. It wasn't the first time Rodney had hinted he was above the law.

'Don't be naive, Dee.' He gestured for her to sit down as he filled the first glass. 'That's the way things are.'

She sat down and pulled her knees up to her chin, tucking the sides of her dress beneath her thighs.

'Here you are, sweetheart.'

Dee took it from him and put her head to one side as he filled the other and then sat close to her. 'What's with all the sweetheart stuff tonight, Rod?'

His eyes were large and dark in the shadows and he looked away briefly before he turned his gaze back to hers.

'You don't like being romanced? I should have started earlier.'

'Not particularly.'

'Wow, you sure know how to hurt a man's ego.'

Dee shrugged. 'I'm not in a very good mood tonight.'

'I did notice that.' Rodney hesitated for a moment before he put his glass down and awkwardly got on one knee in front of her. 'Dee, it's been a night of celebration, and I want to draw it to a satisfactory conclusion.'

'A satisfactory conclusion?' She couldn't help chuckling. 'You sound like you're in the middle of a deal, not on a mountain in the middle of the night.'

'Well, you ungrateful wench, at least you've noticed the beautiful setting I brought you to.'

'I have. I just can't understand why we're here. Can we go home now?' Dee drained her glass and handed it back to him. 'Thank you. That was a very dry champagne.'

'It's *Veuve Clicquot*,' he said shaking his head with a sigh as he refilled it and handed it back.

'Why?'

'To celebrate.'

'Get up, Rod. You look like you're about to topple over.' She narrowed her eyes. 'How much have you had to drink tonight, anyway?'

'Only a couple of beers before this.' He put one hand on the rug and steadied himself before digging into his pocket and removing a small box.

Horror filled Dee. 'Bloody hell, what are you doing? You're not joking around, are you?'

Rodney shook his head. 'You're making it very hard, but I'm about to propose to you.'

'What!'

'Dee, would you do me the honour of being my wife?'

She stared at him. 'No, of course I won't.'

'Just listen to what I have to say, please. Calm down.'

All the emotion that had been building since Dee had opened that letter yesterday afternoon came bursting out in one wave. 'No. You listen to me. I don't know what you're on about, but I've heard some very interesting things tonight. Tell me why you want to marry me.'

'Um, because I love you?' He made it sound more like a question than a declaration of love.

'How about more like it's got something to do with buying our property back into your family at a reduced rate, and you get me thrown into the deal. Am I on track there? Dad can't help manipulating lives, can he?' Tears welled up in Dee's eyes and threatened to spill over. 'It's never stopped. Do you know he even organised for one of his client's sons to take me to the year twelve formal? I didn't care about not going with anyone, but it meant him losing face because no one had asked Gerard Peters' daughter.'

'Dee, you're overreacting. This has nothing to do with Gerard.' His gaze moved away from hers briefly. *'I'm* asking *you* to marry me. I would like to spend the rest of my life with you.'

'And I asked why. How about *you* give me a truthful answer? Why the "sweethearts" and the solicitous behaviour all of a sudden? The first time you've *ever* picked me up in your car, and now champagne on a mountain top? And a marriage proposal! Give me a break, you must think I am so gullible. I thought we were friends, Rod, but if you're jumping through his hoops, you're as bad as he is.'

'Now you're being unfair. We've been good friends for a long time, and now I want to take it to the next level.'

'Do you?'

'We're not getting any younger, Dee.'

'This has come as a complete surprise, so can't you understand why I'm wondering why? For goodness sake, we've never even shared a kiss.' Dee stood up and her glass tipped over; she watched as the liquid soaked into the rug. Rodney was still propped up on one knee looking ridiculous. 'You've given me no good reason to think you could possibly mean this.' She shook her head, confused. 'I don't get it.'

'I'm serious, Dee. I thought this would be a romantic way to propose.'

Anger and disbelief overrode her confusion. 'Oh, just get up and take me home. Or I'll walk.'

Rodney stood, his eyes narrowed, and his lips set in a thin line. 'If you won't tell me what's put you in such a shitty mood, you *can* bloody walk.'

'Oh, that's true love, isn't it, *sweetheart*?' Dee strode over to the car and waited for Rodney to pack up the rug, glasses and bottle.

Her chest heaved as she took a deep breath, and fought back her rising temper, but Rodney didn't read her well.

He came across to the car, and after he'd put the cooler and rug in the boot, he turned and tried to put his arms around her. 'Come on, Dee. Chill, sweetheart. At least tell me what's wrong. We can do this another time.'

Her mouth dropped open in disbelief, but she'd heard the desperation in his voice. 'Do what another time? Accept your proposal? Let's cut to the chase. What's Dad promised you if you marry me?' Her stomach clenched as she listened to him.

'Sweetheart, calm down. I know you're upset because your dad collected the award, but it is his plantation.' Rodney stepped back and ran one hand through his immaculately styled hair.

'Cut the sweetheart.'

'I think you're overreacting and taking it out on me.'

'Do you? I have every right to be upset tonight. On top of your bizarre behaviour, what about the fact that I have a letter telling me I am about to inherit some property in the Northern Territory and that I have a family with secrets up there? Is that a good enough reason to be upset? That I'm adopted and I've never been told?'

'Sweetheart, ignore it.' Rodney grabbed her arms and held her tightly. 'That letter will be a scam. I've seen them before, and I've advised my clients to ignore them. Throw it away and don't let a scam upset you. It's just someone after money. Phew, I can understand why you're upset. Just know I love you and I want you to be my wife.'

'Okay, so you say you love me.' She stood stiff and unyielding in his hold. 'What about Yvonne?' The shock on his face confirmed everything she'd overheard earlier, and she was certain now that Rodney had an ulterior motive for his proposal. 'Just drive me home, please.'

The trip back to *Hilltop Nuts* was silent, but Rodney reached over and took her hand as they pulled up at the house.

'I'll come in and wait with you until your parents get home. You need to calm down.'

'There's no need for you to come in.' Dee tried to tug her hand away, but his grip was firm.

'Have you told them about this letter?' He stared at her.

'No, but I'll be talking to them as soon as they get home.'

'Perhaps I'd better come in and be with you.'

'Why?' She tugged again and he let go of her hand.

'In case they haven't heard about those scams. I can fill them in.'

'There's no need for you to come in. And I'm sure Dad will be well aware of any scams going.' Before Rodney could move, Dee opened the door and climbed out, reaching in for her shoes on the floor. 'Goodnight, Rodney.'

'I'll talk to you tomorrow then. When you've had time to settle down,' he said.

Settle down!

Dee stood and watched as he drove away, his phone already up to his ear.

Ringing Dad, no doubt.

Dee wanted to know exactly what was going on, and she was going to find out even if it took all night. She took a quick shower and washed the hairspray from her curls and then slipped on a pair of trackpants and a comfortable T-shirt. Before she left her bedroom, she reread the letter. The words *"to confirm your identity"* jumped out at her again.

Slipping the letter into the pillowcase on her bed, she waited for them to get home.

Sad when she didn't trust her father.

If Gerard was indeed her father.

Within half an hour, her parents had parked the Audi in the carport next to the house. When Mum came through the front door, followed closely by Dad, Dee was in the kitchen, the coffee machine hissing beside her.

'Would you like a—' she began, but her father spoke over her as Mum pulled out a chair and sat down. Her eyes were wary as she looked at Dee, and then at Gerard.

'Why did you treat Rodney so badly? He said you had your knickers in a twist because I didn't take you up to the stage. I'm sorry, but in the excitement of the moment I didn't think. The poor bloke is devastated; he'd organised a romantic proposal for you, and we'd agreed for him to ask you and you treated him like shit, just because you felt hard done by.'

'So he rang you, did he?' Dee waited for the milk to froth, turned the machine off, stirred in a teaspoon of sugar before she answered, trying to provoke him into telling the truth, but he said nothing. 'I'm confused. What's going on?' Dee lifted the coffee cup and pulled out the chair beside her mother. 'Sit down, please.' She couldn't bring herself to call him Dad.

The legs scraped on the tiles with a squeal as Gerard pulled the chair back, sat on it and glared at her.

'Dad, I was really hurt because you didn't mention me when you got the award. But I'm more upset because Rodney told me you're selling up. Are you?'

'Possibly,' Gerard huffed.

'He told me you were selling the farm to him. When were you planning on telling me that?'

'When I was good and ready.'

'You know what, *Gerard?*' Dee kept her voice calm and cold.

'What?' His was equally icy.

'You are a lying shit.'

Catherine gasped and put her hand over her mouth. Gerard stared at her.

'So tell me the truth. What have I got to do with you selling the farm to Rodney?'

'All right. Rodney is keen to buy it, so we were doing a bit of a deal to avoid all the stamp duty, and the paperwork, you know. There's some investment money that—forget that.' He waved his hand as his eyes narrowed. 'Look, when you're in business, there's ways around things. He can't afford what I want—yet—but I suggested if he married you, he could give me three quarters of the cash now, and the rest in a couple of years. The place would go into your name, with a codicil added that as your husband he had equal ownership.'

'You suggested? What am I? Something to barter? It doesn't make sense to me.' Dee shook her head slowly, absolutely shocked that she was being traded like a couple of goats and a camel. 'I can't understand why you have to go through all that. If you're so damned keen to sell our farm, you'd get a good price from anyone after winning the award. It's one of the best plantations in the hinterland, especially now we're moving to the new net technology. So why sell it to Rodney and why for cash? What's so special about him?'

Finally, Gerard spoke. 'Rodney is an excellent colleague, and a good man. He'll take over the company while we travel, and he'll make the perfect husband for you.' A wheedling note came into his voice. 'And I was thinking of you. I know how much you love the farm, and how well you manage it.'

Dee's snort held no mirth. 'It all sounds a bit suss to me.'

'Look if I sold it to anyone else, you'd have to leave too. It would be a long shot to expect a new owner to keep you on as manager,' Gerard said.

'And you'd have to move out of the house,' Catherine chimed in. 'Rodney will make an excellent husband.'

Dee looked at both of them thoughtfully. 'I totally disagree with your scheme. I'm not marrying Rodney, so I'm not helping you out with your "bit of a deal". I'm disgusted that you would try to manipulate me like that.'

'Look, Dee. I'm your father and I know what's best for you.'

'Do you? Do you really?' Her voice rose as her temper overtook the crushing disappointment. 'I'm thirty-two years old and I think I'm old enough to know what I'm capable of.'

'Listen to me, Deanne.' The level of his voice matched hers.

'No. You listen to me. You know what? I hope I am adopted.'

'Adopted! Why the hell would you think that?' Gerard spluttered, but Dee saw the alarm in the glance he threw at Catherine.

'I have good reason to believe I am.'

'That's rubbish. You are *not* adopted. Look how much you look like your mother.'

Dee hesitated. He was right, there was a definite resemblance there.

Gerard sat back and folded his arms. 'Where the hell did you get this stupid idea about being adopted?'

'Rodney didn't tell you about the letter?'

Gerard's expression changed immediately, and Catherine let out a little gasp and put a hand on his arm.

'Letter? What letter?' he said loudly, looking around as though it would materialise in front of him.

'A letter telling me that I am about to inherit something from my blood family and due to a reason they can't tell me in writing, I'm not to know why it's been kept a secret until I contact them personally.' Dee stopped and looked at each of the people she had called her parents for close on thirty-three years. Gerard frowned and Catherine looked stricken as tears welled in her eyes. 'So I put two and two together, if my *blood* family is mentioned, what does that make you two?'

'You are our daughter and anyone who tells you different, to use your ladylike phrase, is a lying sack of shit.' Gerard looked at Catherine and gestured with his head. 'Catherine. In the bedroom. Now. Your mother and I need to talk privately.'

Dee shook her head slowly from side to side and then put the coffee cup on the table with a loud thump. 'No. There will be no private talking and no more secrets. You tell me now. If you won't tell me, I'll find out next week.'

'Next week? I can sort it now. Show me this bloody letter,' Gerard demanded.

'No. Rodney said it was a scam, but I don't think it is.'

'Rodney? Yes, he's right. It's a scam, just ignore it.' Gerard's face was bright red and a vein pulsed at his temple. 'He should have told me.'

'I guess he didn't think it was important enough that the woman he claims to love was upset by the fact that she might be adopted.' Dee stood quickly and the chair tipped over onto the tiles with a clatter. 'He was more worried about ringing you and telling you your cash deal wouldn't be going ahead.'

'Dee, calm down. You are overreacting.' Gerard stood and came around to where she was standing. 'Show me this letter.'

'No. You'll just put your usual spin on it, and cover everything with lies. I'm over it. I'll go to Darwin, and if you want me to come back here, you can damn well tell me the truth now.'

'Darwin?' His eyes widened and he grabbed for her arm, but Dee stepped away from him. The panic in his voice told her she was on the right track. 'Don't be stupid, Dee. We can give them a call together on Monday. Who wrote to you?'

'No.' She shook her head mutinously as she moved away from his touch. '*You* tell me the truth or I'm leaving tomorrow and I won't be back. You can take over the bloody harvest on *your* award-winning farm.'

Chapter 4
Friday – Midnight.
Hilltop Nuts.

As soon as Dee's bedroom door closed, Catherine walked quickly to the master suite at the other end of the house. Gerard followed and closed the door behind them. She took a step back from him as he reached for her, but she was too slow. Grabbing her shoulder, he pressed his fingers hard into her collarbone.

'What have you told her?'

'Nothing.' Catherine's eyes were unfocused, but her gaze slid away from his. 'Never.'

'If you're lying to me . . .' His fingers pressed harder.

'Why would I risk everything? Why would I risk losing my daughter? I've told her nothing.' Her words were slurred. 'You're hurting me.'

'I'll hurt you a whole lot fucking more if this deal goes to shit.'

'What deal?'

'Go to bed. You're drunk.' Gerard shoved her away from him and his lip curled with disgust. 'If we lose everything, it's on your head.'

'I haven't told her anything.' Catherine picked up a crystal ornament and screamed as she threw it at Gerard. 'I promised you and I never have. She is *my* daughter. Someone else must know. Someone else told her.'

'No one else knows. You are the only one. I'll bloody kill you if you have, Catherine.'

Catherine began to sob. 'I have not told *anyone*. Not in my whole life. Not once in thirty-two years. No one knows.'

'Well, how the fuck do you explain that she's got a letter from Darwin? Someone's told her something and she's been digging.'

'Maybe Bridget's come back. I knew she would one day.' Catherine's stupid smile made his anger deepen. 'Maybe Bridget wrote to her and told her something.'

Gerard stared at her. 'Your slut of a sister won't be back.' He walked across to the window and looked across the hills as worry churned in his stomach. 'We can't afford for Dee to know anything. Not now.'

Catherine went into the ensuite and slammed the door shut. Gerard pulled out his phone and pressed speed dial.

'Gerard, I'm sorry,' Rodney said. 'Dee was more upset about that scam letter than anything else. I'll take her out to dinner in a few days when she calms down. The sale will go through, don't worry.'

'We don't have a few days. She insists she's leaving for Darwin tomorrow.'

'Bloody hell. Over some stupid scam letter. She's a fool.'

'She is a fool.' Gerard kept his voice low. 'Tell me exactly what she told you about the letter.'

'It was one of those letters that does the rounds. Apparently she's about to inherit some property in the Northern Territory and that she had a family up there. You know, the usual scam shit.'

There was no need for Rodney to know the truth.

'Listen to me, and listen carefully,' Gerard said. 'I don't care that she won't marry you, we'll just have to find a better way to work the deal. Follow up a couple of our backup avenues. Just get rid of that cash as quickly as you can.'

'Okay. Will do.'

There was no need for Rodney to know he had bigger problems than getting rid of a measly two million.

Chapter 5
Hilltop Nuts
Sunday

When Catherine saw the hallstand go on the ute, she burst into tears and ran into the house. Dee tied it on and when the ropes were tight she went inside to say goodbye.

'Mum?' she called hesitantly. 'Are you there?'

Catherine came out of the bedroom holding a sodden tissue. 'Please don't go, Dee. There's no need.'

'I need to find out who I am, Mum.' She walked over and put her arms around the woman she'd known as her mother for her whole life. 'Am I adopted?'

'No, you're not.' Catherine's face was streaked with tears and she held Dee tightly. 'Where are you going?'

'I'm going to Darwin to see that solicitor.'

'But why have you packed everything?'

'Because I might stay away for a while. It's time I stood on my own two feet, don't you think?'

Catherine shook her head. 'There are things you need to know, but your father—Gerard—won't let me tell you.'

'Why?'

Catherine shook her head. 'It's very complicated. If you stay, we can all sit down together and talk about it. Please? It's not too late to change your mind.'

'We've already tried that. And all he did was storm off. Where is he now?' Dee hadn't seen him around as she'd packed the ute.

HIDDEN VALLEY

'He went to play golf with Rodney.'

The sound that came from Dee's lips was not ladylike. Her confusion and worry had deepened overnight. Her stomach was churning and she hadn't even been able to face a coffee yet. All she wanted to do was flee. 'I'll call you when I get there, Mum.'

'Drive safely. I'm terrified at the thought of you on those deserted roads up there.'

'Do you know them? Have you been to the Northern Territory?'

'I have.' Catherine's hand was shaking as she lifted the tissue and dabbed at her eyes. 'I'll miss you, sweetheart.'

##

Northern Territory
Tuesday 10.00 a.m.

Crossing the Queensland border into the Northern Territory four days later was a strange moment for Dee. She parked her ute off to the side of the road next to the "Welcome to the Northern Territory" sign. The heat hit her like a brick wall when she got out. Holding her phone she walked back fifty metres and snapped a photo of the iconic sign.

Was she supposed to feel as though she was coming home? Apparently, she'd been born in the Territory and spent her first two years here. That was as much as she'd got out of Catherine after Gerard had left the farm early on Saturday morning. As much as Dee had begged Catherine, her mother had refused to tell her anything else.

The road stretched out long and straight in both directions and disappeared into the shimmering haze above the distant horizon. The colours were so different to home, but the landscape had a stark beauty she'd never seen before. The sky was bigger and a paler blue, and the dry grass that partially covered the red dirt at the side of the road was a faded straw colour. She'd left the familiar lush green landscape of nut farms and sugarcane behind before she'd crossed the border into Queensland on Sunday morning.

The only sound was the swish of her sandals on the dry grass, and when Dee stepped onto the road, there was total quiet around her. She stood there listening to the utter silence for a moment before walking back to her ute. Looking at the load on the back she realised she was on her own now. All her worldly possessions were packed in three small boxes and two suitcases. The one thing she hadn't been able to leave behind reared up over the back of the ute cab, secured with ropes.

The antique hallstand had been left to her when Mrs Crichton had passed away. Her former primary school teacher had become a good friend to Dee as she'd grown up, and it held sentimental value. She'd called up Jenny and asked her to get Dave to come over and help her load it onto the ute early on Sunday morning.

Last night was the first night Dee had slept well since Friday night. She had learned very little that night, and the possibilities wouldn't leave her thoughts.

She hadn't woken until after eight this morning, and by the time she'd showered in the amenities block and grabbed a takeaway breakfast at the service station café when she'd fuelled up, the mid-morning sun was beating down relentlessly.

There was not another vehicle to be seen. After she'd left Camooweal, where she'd slept in a basic cabin at the service station caravan park, she'd passed very little traffic After checking the load on the back of her ute, Dee climbed into the still cool car, took a swig of water and set out for Three Ways where she was planning to stay overnight.

The events of the past week had been a shock, but she was gradually getting used to the dramatic change the letter had had on her life. There was still a great deal she didn't know but was determined to discover, and her hopes were pinned on the meeting at Baker and Baker in Darwin at one o'clock on Friday afternoon.

Catherine had clung to her wrist through the ute window when Dee had started the engine. Tears streamed down her face as she'd begged her to stay home one last time.

'Please Dee, don't listen to anyone. It's a scam, darling. Really, it is.'

Dee let the motor idle as she leaned back and folded her arms 'Well, easy fix. Tell me the truth.'

'We have already. You are not adopted; this is a wild goose chase. I can't understand why you have to go. And your father only asked Rodney to buy the property and marry you because he's in a bit of a financial bind, and he knows how much you love the farm. He did it for you.'

Dee didn't believe a word of it. The more her parents—or rather Catherine and Gerard—protested, the more she knew they were lying and there *was* something for her to find out.

Talk of Gerard's financial bind hadn't surprised her. He'd always been a player, and it was only a matter of time before he got burnt. Dee had bigger problems of her own to worry about. Her identity, and the person she'd thought she was for her whole life, was a lie, and she was determined to find out the truth.

Had she been adopted by Gerard and Catherine, or was Catherine her real mother? Or had they chosen her because she looked like Catherine?

Catherine's final despairing scream had not moved Dee as she'd driven down the driveway. She was determined to break through the secrecy and lies, and then she would decide what she would do.

Chapter 6
Wilderness Station - Northern Territory.
Thursday 4 p.m.

As the crow flies it was less than one hundred kilometres from Darwin to *Wilderness Station*. Ryan Carey wasn't surprised that Ellie McLaren was late for her appointment. He'd been keeping an eye on the road for the past half hour.

Cy, his cousin, rode along beside him as they led the cattle to the yards where the road train was waiting. 'Dad reckons he's going to start a vegie stall out on the highway if cattle prices don't improve.'

'He might have to, if they go any lower,' Ryan replied keeping his attention on the road. 'We can't do with another season like the last one.' Last year had been a challenging year for the station, as it had for the entire cattle industry. As well as losing Dad to a massive heart attack, it had been the warmest and driest year on record, and then was compounded by bushfires just as they were moving the cattle to the sweeter grass for the wet season.

'They reckon the national cattle herd is about to drop to the lowest in more than twenty years,' Cy said. 'Dad might need to set up that stall if we don't get rain.'

'Yep, up until now, the local demand for beef has been enough to keep the prices up, but that bloody export situation to China is a worry,' Ryan said. 'If we don't get rain soon, we're in trouble.'

'Might be time to look at other resources on the place,' Cy said with a sideways glance at him.

'Like what?' Ryan shook his head. 'We're a cattle station, not a mine or a resort.'

Some large stations to the west had gone into adventure tours and opened up areas to mineral exploration. A few weeks after Mum's funeral a couple of geologists had turned up wanting to do a survey for some rare mineral they reckoned could be out near the main camp. Dad had gone off like a rocket, much to Ryan's surprise; he was usually calm and quiet. He'd been vocal and told them never to set foot on his property again. They'd still carried on about lithium-rich pegmatite deposits, but once Dad had put the skids under them, they'd never come back, and they'd heard no more about it.

'This is a cattle station and that's what it will stay,' Dad had yelled after them.

At the time Ryan had agreed with Dad, but if the situation kept deteriorating, maybe he would have to look at diversifying. These days Ryan had little free time; looking after the two hundred thousand acres kept him busy and away from the house most of the time. When he managed to get back to the house, his days and nights were taken up with bookwork; he'd fallen behind with the recordkeeping over the past few weeks.

As they cantered through the cloud of dust kicked up by the road train an unfamiliar ute headed towards the homestead. Ryan turned his horse towards the vehicle.

'There's my appointment, Cy,' he said. 'I'll leave you in charge.' He left the three stockmen riding beside him and headed to the road train parked near the gates.

Just as well Ellie hadn't met it coming out, he thought, marvelling at how the massive trucks always successfully negotiated the road in from the highway.

'Hi there.' he called across to the woman driving the ute 'Ellie?'

'Yes, I'm Ellie McLaren. Sorry I'm late. I didn't allow for the road conditions.'

'No problem at all. Make your way up to the house, and I'll be up in five. Wait on the veranda and Joe'll get you a cool drink or a cuppa.' He grinned at her. 'Sorry, I'm Ryan Carey, if you were wondering.'

'I know. I remember you from primary school.'

He frowned. 'Do you?'

'I was a couple of years below you. And don't hurry. I've got plenty of time.'

'Appreciate it. Time's a bit tight at this end this afternoon. See you soon.' He watched as she drove past the road train and headed towards the buildings ahead. Once the dust had cleared, Ryan waited until the truck was loaded and headed to the green oasis of the front garden that always reminded him of Mum.

He smacked his horse on the rump and sent it to the paddock behind the house and walked towards the front veranda. Joe walked out as he approached.

'Here you go, love. This'll cool you down.'

Ellie nodded as she took a glass of juice from him. 'Thank you, that looks wonderful.'

'I make our own juice from the orchards down the back.'

She took a sip and raised an eyebrow. 'That's really nice. Mango? And something else?'

'Mango and orange juice, with lemon balm and pineapple sage leaves.'

She chuckled. 'I'll have to remember that and tell my mother. I grew up on a mango farm not far up the highway, and I'm sure we sampled every mango recipe known to man when we were kids.'

'Which farm was that?' he asked. 'I'm Joe, Ryan's uncle.' He gestured to Ryan as he joined them. 'His mother was my sister.'

'The Porter farm. I was Ellie Porter, and my husband and I have taken it over now.'

Joe stared at her for so long without speaking, Ryan frowned. Before he could speak, his uncle continued. 'Peter Porter's farm?'

'Yes, it was my Dad's farm.'

'He was the one who got himself murdered trying to make a quick buck, wasn't he?'

'Joe.' Ryan glared at him, stunned by his uncle's words, but Ellie flew straight into him.

'My father was murdered by a criminal who wanted our land. He did nothing wrong.'

'I knew your parents a long time ago. Your mother was a good friend to my sister. I was sorry when she took up with Peter.' His lip curled in a sneer.

'Was it really any of your business?' Ellie's voice was as cold as ice.

Joe didn't even seem to notice that he was out of line, and Ryan moved to stand beside Ellie.

'I wasn't fast enough,' Joe said. 'Your dad worked on *Wilderness* for a while. How's your mum doing these days? I used to dance with Sandra at our social nights before she married your father.'

'She's well.' Ellie's voice was clipped, and she glanced at Ryan.

'We had fun back in those days. Friday night dances in the hall up at Marrakai. And regular tennis barbeques here at *Wilderness*. Your mum was a real looker in the day.' His grin had Ryan frowning, but Ellie stood and turned her back to him. Her shoulders were stiff and square.

Joe turned to go inside and paused in the wide doorway. 'Give Sandra my best.' He disappeared into the house.

'Ellie, I apologise for my uncle's comments.' Ryan was seething. How dare Joe be so rude. 'Give me five and I'll just have a quick wash. Are you happy if we talk out here or would you rather do the formal interview thing in the office?'

'Out here is fine with me.'

'Thanks. I won't be long.' He hurried down the hall and went via the kitchen, but there was no sign of Joe. He quickly sluiced his face and washed his hands and was back out of the house before Ellie had finished her drink. He poured a glass for himself and held the jug up. 'A top up?'

'Thank you, yes.'

The ice had melted but the liquid still frosted her glass as he filled it. 'I've placed you now. You're Kane McLaren's wife.'

'I am.'

'How are your mangoes going this year? I met Kane at a farm field day last year, but I haven't seen him since then.'

'The farm's going well. Our long hours are finally paying off, but he still doesn't get off the farm much.'

Ryan sat on the other side of the small table from her, tipped his head back and drained the glass. 'So, you're interested in part-time contract work?' he asked as he put the glass back on the table.

'I am.'

'Have you had much experience with mustering? Helicopter or horseback?'

'Yes, I've done both, but I'll be honest. It's been a few years since I mustered up near Borroloola when I first got my license, but in the past few years I've worked in the tourist trade out of Makowa Lodge. That being said, I have no doubt I can do it. And do it safely. I'm aware of the new regulations, and the improved focus on safety now.' Her words were very formal, and he knew she was still upset by Joe's bullying.

'You've been reading up obviously.' Ryan nodded. 'So many stations have moved to helicopter mustering, it's hard to get pilots now. We've got our own team on the station, but the supply of ringers and stockmen is tightening up too, and we all have cattle to get to market.'

'Yes, times are changing. I've printed out my resume listing my experience, and I've put some phone numbers on there for you to call for references.' Ellie pointed to the file she'd brought from the car.

'How much experience on horseback?'

She nodded. 'I started as a jillaroo up on a station at Borroloola before I decided to get my pilot's licence.'

'Plus, you don't live too far away.' Ryan looked thoughtful as he put his glass back on the table. 'Do you have any questions about the job?'

'I do. It said in the ad that you charter the helicopters. What sort of machines do you lease?'

'Robinson 22s. The smaller the better.'

'Excellent. I've had most of my experience in them.'

'Sounds good. I'll make some calls, and I'll be in touch in a week or so. Thanks for coming over, Ellie. Tell Kane we'll catch up for a beer one day too.'

Ryan stood as she made her way to her ute and watched until she had driven away. He appreciated the cool of the farmhouse when he headed inside once Ellie had driven off. By the sound of clanging pots and pans, Joe was still in the house kitchen. He'd lived in an old motorhome on the station for a couple of years; he'd come to stay when Mum had been diagnosed with breast cancer. Joe had taken over the rose garden when Suzanne became too ill to care for it.

Ryan and his father had been busy on the station, and most nights when they came home, Joe was sitting out in the rose garden with Suzanne. Ryan knew it had made Mum happy, and he was grateful to Joe for being there in her last months. After the funeral he'd stayed on and, as well as cooking for him and Dad, Joe cooked for the stockmen and ringers in the mess near the workers' accommodation.

Ryan had been happy for Joe to stay on after Dad died, and although he tried to help with the house, he was more interested in the vegetable and herb garden. He had green fingers and with what the vegetable garden produced, he could have had a stall if he wanted. Joe's son, Cy, was an excellent cattleman, and having family around had helped Ryan cope with the loss of both his parents in such a short time.

Joe's rudeness this afternoon had come as a shock.

Now Ryan looked around as he walked up the front hall and past the living room.

Shame trickled through him as he paused outside the living room. Mum would have been horrified if she'd been able to see the state of the house now; she'd been so house proud. Feeling guilty, he went in and collected the coffee cups from the top of the television cabinet and the three empty beer bottles on the floor beside the sofa. He was pleased that Ellie had agreed to sit out on the veranda; inside the house was a pigsty. He would have been ashamed to take her through to the study; they didn't have time to keep the house like Mum had. Maybe he'd hire a cleaning firm to come out and give the place a onceover a couple of times a year.

'You there, Joe?' he called as he walked down the hall.

'Yes.'

Joe was lifting the meat out of the oven when Ryan walked into the kitchen. 'Beef smells good.'

Joe didn't answer and pulled the pan holding two large joints of beef out of the oven and put them down on the sink with a clatter.

'I've lost the bloody stew pot. It's not down in the cookhouse and I thought it might have got up here somehow. I'll need it when the muster starts, but I'll be blowed if I can find it anywhere.'

Ryan knew exactly where it was. 'Ask Cy. I saw it in the back shed a few days back.'

'The back shed? What was he bloody doing with my saucepans down there?'

'Ah, I'd rather not say. I guess you should ask your son.'

Last Ryan had seen the pot, it had been full of engine oil when Cy had been working on the big tractor. 'I'm going to Darwin in the morning. I'll pick you one up in town. Is there anything else you need?'

'No, I'm pretty right. I got a big order delivered last week. I'll go down the back and see if I can save my pot.' Joe wiped his hands on the towel that was permanently on his shoulder. 'Why the trip to Darwin?'

Ryan shrugged. 'The lawyer bloke rang. He wants to talk to me about Dad's will.'

'Jeez, that's taking a long time to settle.' Joe lifted his head from the vegetables he was chopping.

'Yeah, I'm a bit over it. The last thing I need is a trip to Darwin when we've got the muster coming up.'

'What's the holdup?'

Ryan shook his head as he put the cups on the sink, and the beer bottles on the bench. 'I don't know. Baker is being a bit vague. He said he needs me in the office tomorrow. Wouldn't tell me what it was about on the phone.'

Joe narrowed his eyes. 'Jeez, I hope Colin didn't have some huge loan or something he didn't let on about. With him having that sudden heart attack, there was no time for him to get his stuff in order.'

Joe seemed to take every opportunity to have a go at his dead brother-in-law and it pissed Ryan off.

'What's your problem with Dad, Joe?' Ryan's temper spilled over. 'And why were you so bloody rude to Ellie McLaren?'

Joe put his hand on Ryan's shoulder. 'I've never criticised, but I know your dad could be hard to live with. I often caught poor Suzanne looking unhappy over the years. But she was loyal to your old man. She never once said a word against him, and he didn't deserve her loyalty. Not by a long shot.'

'Dad was old school. He thought it was his responsibility to provide for his family, so he spent a lot of time out on the station.'

Joe's laugh was strange, different to his normal, happy go lucky character. 'Yeah, that's one way you could put it.'

Ryan knew that his father hadn't thought much of Joe and his itinerant lifestyle, but he'd seemed to accept his presence on the property after Mum died.

'I was pleased I was here to support her. Your dad left her here by herself a lot.'

Ryan spoke stiffly. 'My parents were happy, and Dad was heartbroken when Mum died.'

'For more than one reason. Your dad was a secretive bugger.'

Ryan stared at him. 'Secretive? About what?'

Joe put the tea towel over his shoulder. 'Your mother never knew much about what was going on.'

'What are you getting at? Do you think it's got something to do with why probate is so slow?'

Joe patted his shoulder. 'I tell you what. Don't take any notice of me. Sorry I upset you with that McLaren piece, but I didn't like her father. While you're in town, pick up some salami and I'll make pizzas to go with that beer. We'll have a bit of a yarn.'

'I'll look forward to that.'

Ryan lay there for a long time before sleep came that night.

Chapter 7

The McLaren Mango Farm.
Thursday 6.00 p.m.

Ellie turned her car into the driveway and headed towards their house, pleased to see her mother's car was still parked under the carport. She and Kane had worked hard renovating the property over the past three years; the old shed where Dad had died had been demolished and now a modern four-car carport stood in its place.

The farm was nothing like it had been when she and Emma and Dru had grown up out here on the family farm on the Arnhem Highway. Years had passed, death and tragedy had impacted all of their lives, yet it was hard to believe now that this was the same property where they had spent their formative years. Ellie sometimes wondered how Mum coped with visiting here where she had spent many happy years with Dad. Looking after James, the grandchild he had never seen, in their old place must be hard. Tears pricked at her eyes. Ryan's uncle had upset her; his words had brought back that dreadful time of their lives.

Damn you, Russell Fairweather. Even though Fairweather was in jail, and had received a long sentence, the loss of Dad's life as a result of greed and corruption was something that would stay with Ellie—and her two sisters—for life.

Parking behind Mum's car, Ellie brushed at the tears that had welled as she thought back to past days. The half-dead mango trees at the edge of the dam that had once cast wavering shadows across the water were long gone. The blue plastic drums that had slapped against the rotten wood of the short piers at the end of the jetty where she and Emma and Dru had sun-baked were no longer there. It was hard to believe that she was here as a wife and mother, and that she and Kane had resurrected the family farm. The green, healthy trees were testament to their hard work.

Shaking her head as she climbed out of her car, Ellie tried to push away the sadness.

The waste.

The loss.

Feeling like this wouldn't achieve anything apart from making her miserable. Forcing a smile onto her face she looked across at the trees; it wouldn't be long before they would be heavy with flowers. She could move on. If she had to see that Joe again, she wouldn't get into a conversation with him

Life is good. Focus on that.

The sound of James' giggle as Mum pushed him in the swing at the back of the laundry lightened her heart.

'Look, James, here's your lovely mummy.'

A squeal came from her little boy's lips as he gripped the rope and climbed down off the swing without any help. 'Mumma!'

Ellie held her arms open, and her heart was full as James launched himself into them. She looked up and caught the smile on Mum's face.

Yes, they were all fine. Enough time had passed; the healing was good, and it was time to let go. Her only lingering worry was that episode with Mum at the shopping centre before Christmas, but she'd seemed fine since then. No more mention of mysterious men, and Emma hasn't seemed too concerned when Ellie had talked to her about it.

'How was your interview, love?' Mum asked.

'Good. I should hear back from Ryan in a few days.'

'It's a big station, isn't it? And the house is amazing.'

'I didn't get to go inside.' Ellie hadn't intended telling Mum about Joe, but her curiosity got the better of her. 'I sat out on the veranda and Ryan's uncle bought me a cold drink while I waited. He said he knew you.'

'Ryan's uncle?'

'He said he knew you through the Careys. His name was Joe.'

'Oh yes, I remember now. Joe? I can't remember his last name.' Her mother shook her head. 'I hadn't given him a thought since I married your father and you girls came along. Over thirty years ago, that was.'

'He's working there, and he said he was Ryan's mother's brother.'

'Oh, Ellie, yes! That brings it all back. Suzanne and Colin Carey. That's how I started going out with your father. He met me at the store where I was working, and he made sure I got invited to the tennis nights at their place.' She smiled and Ellie thought how good it was that Mum could talk so happily about Dad now. 'Although it was a good few months after that before he finally worked up the courage to ask me out. Those were such fun times. I don't think we enjoy life now like we did back then. I might sound like an oldie, but life was so much simpler in those days. You're all so busy now. None of us had much money, but we made do, and we used to look forward to the end of the week. Spending those early days there with your father makes the memories of those tennis nights all the sweeter.' Mum's eyes lit up, and her smile was easier than it had been for a long time. 'I was good friends with Suzanne back then. Joe was her young brother.'

'I think he works as the station cook now.'

'Suzanne passed away a couple of years ago, but I lost touch with her when you girls were little. She was a bit older than me. She taught me how to do macramé, and she had the most incredible rose garden. Unheard of in the tropics! She became a bit of a recluse after she had children. Plus we all moved on with our lives. Marriage, children and all that. Or maybe she only ever had the one? Yes, I think they had one son.'

'That must be Ryan, the guy who interviewed me.'

'Probably, and then not long after Suzanne passed away, her husband, Colin, died. He had a massive heart attack out on the station, and it was too late by the time they found him. Very sad.'

'You're still up with all the local events, Mum.'

'I'm back to reading the papers and chatting to friends on the phone.'

'I'm really pleased to hear that,' Ellie said with a smile.

'Even though I live in Darwin now, this will always be home to me. I'm interested in the people who live here.'

'You'll have to keep me up to date. I don't have time to scratch myself these days. With James, and the farm—'

'Not to mention thinking of going back to work. You will be careful if you get that job, won't you, darling?'

'No need to worry, Mum,' Ellie said briskly.

'Okay, I won't be a nag. It's time this young man had a bath. I've cooked the veggies for his dinner, you've just got to put them through the *mouli*. I'm going home tonight.'

'Oh Mum, why don't you stay? It's late to drive back to Darwin.'

'No, sweetie, it's not long until Easter, and Emma and Jeremy will be here before we know it. I'd like to get an early start on my cooking tomorrow. Now, you and Kane and James are still right to come to town on Easter Saturday for dinner, aren't you? Dru called today. They're organised. They'll both be home too.'

'We'll be there. I can't wait for us all to be together. Even though we saw everyone at Christmas, it seems like ages ago. Will you be okay driving home tonight?'

'Of course I will.' Mum leaned over and kissed James. 'I'll see you in a few days. If you need me before then, ring me. There's nothing I can't cancel if you need me to look after James.'

'I will.' Ellie held James on her hip as Sandra went up to the house to collect her bag and car keys. The western sky was shot with a spectacular palette of gold and orange as the lowering sun caught the smoke from the fires burning off the grasslands. She looked up to the sky as anticipation curled in her stomach; despite Joe upsetting her, she felt good about the interview today, and she had no doubt she could do the job.

Fingers crossed.

'Bye, love.' Mum leaned in for a kiss.

'Bye, Mum. Give me a call when you get home and then I won't worry.'

Ellie stood there as the rear lights of her mother's car disappeared down the hill before their road turned onto the main highway. It was so good to see Mum getting involved in things again. She smiled as the sound of the tractor approaching the house paddock filled the air.

'Daddy,' James squealed excitedly as the noise of the tractor got louder.

'Come on, we'll wait for Daddy in the shed.' Ellie settled James comfortably on her hip as she walked along the drive that had been filled with gravel last year. He chatted away in his own baby language as he pointed at the shed.

Ellie's happiness was complete, and her mood was calm as the tractor appeared over the slight rise near the back paddock. As she was about to turn away a light flashed in the trees over near the dam. Staring at the spot for a few seconds, a shiver ran down her back.

James jiggled in her arms. 'Mumma, go.'

She shook off the foreboding; those days were long gone.

Chapter 8
*Darwin - Baker and Baker, Lawyers and Solicitors.
Friday 2 p.m.*

Ryan sat in the waiting room of the lawyer's office trying to curb his impatience.

A whole bloody wasted day.

By the time he'd driven to Darwin he was in a filthy mood. After checking the cattle in the southern paddock with Cy, they'd found a massive break in the fence near the back dam, repaired that, and then it had taken him an hour and a half to drive to Darwin, plus another fifteen minutes to find a parking spot.

Jiggling his feet on the carpeted floor got him a sympathetic look from the secretary.

'Mr Baker shouldn't be too much longer, Mr Carey.'

Ryan took a deep breath as he waited, trying to calm down. This was an important meeting, and he had to focus. Glancing at his watch, he realised he'd been sitting there for forty-five minutes. He'd been running late, but his appointment had been for one-fifteen. And he still had to go over to Big W or somewhere to get the set of saucepans for Joe. And the salami. When Joe had gone down to the shed to find his stew pot yesterday afternoon, he'd discovered that Cy had helped himself to more than one of the expensive copper-based pots.

Joe had gone ballistic, and Ryan had taken himself to the back veranda while his uncle had torn strips off his son. It was the first time Ryan had ever seen Joe lose it with Cy.

The door to the office opened and Mr Baker ushered a woman out. Her head was down but when she looked up at the older man, her eyes were red-rimmed with traces of tears on her cheeks, but still, Ryan looked twice. Olive-skinned with dark curly hair and a trim figure, she was very easy on the eye. She looked over and when she caught him checking her out, heat rose into his cheeks. He looked down at his hands resting on his thighs.

'Thank you for being so patient, Ms Peters. I'll see you again at, let's say, three-fifteen?' He turned to the secretary. 'Elise, can you please let me know as soon as Ms Peters comes back.' He threw a glance at Ryan as he said that, and he guessed that his appointment wasn't going to go long, if the woman was coming back in just over an hour.

Good, he might have time to check the rest of that boundary fence before dark.

'Ryan, thank you for coming in.' Mr Baker held his hand out and Ryan shook it firmly.

##

'No fucking way.' Ryan stared at the lawyer as disbelief took hold, and his stomach heaved. He'd been listening to the old guy for over fifteen minutes. 'You have to be bloody joking. How the hell can my father leave half of what is rightfully mine to a woman I've never heard of?'

'Please calm down, Ryan. I know it's a shock to you but—'

'Too right it's a bloody shock. It's not going to happen. I'll challenge it in every court in the land. I'll take that will with me, please.'

Baker kept his voice low and even as Ryan stared at him. 'It's watertight, Ryan. Why do you think I've taken so long to tell you this? I've been over the document with a fine-tooth comb, and I've sought advice where I've doubted even the slightest phrase or point of law.'

Ryan shook his head from side to side. The same physical weakness that had consumed him the night that Mum had died threatened to overwhelm him.

He could not do one thing to change this. He felt absolutely fucking useless.

'Why? Just tell me why? And who is this woman? The only relatives I'm aware I have are my mother's brother, Joe, who lives on the station, and my cousin, Cy. I don't know of any other relatives. What's the connection? Or is there a connection?'

'I'm not at liberty to disclose that.'

'Well, I'll be asking who she is when I meet this woman.'

'Ryan, please. I know how difficult this is for you—'

'Do you? Do you really? How the hell could you know what I'm feeling right now? Things are hard enough without giving half the bloody station away. I might as well walk off now.' He lifted his head and stared at Baker. 'My father was damn proud of our station being in his family for over a hundred years.'

'I can empathise. If it is any consolation, the young woman is just as distraught as you are.'

'Sure she would be. She's just stripped me of my inheritance. Everything I've worked for, for the past thirty-two years, and you tell me she's distraught. Christ, she's just inherited about ten million dollars' worth of land and cattle. I'll give her bloody distraught. When and where can I meet her?'

'She's coming back here to meet you at three-fifteen.' Mr Baker looked at his expensive gold watch. 'She shouldn't be long now.'

Ryan stared at the lawyer as the penny dropped. 'That was her? That woman who was leaving when I arrived?'

Right on cue, the intercom buzzed followed by the receptionist's voice. 'Ms Peters is back, Mr Baker.'

'Give us five minutes please, Elise. I will come out when we're ready.'

Ryan raised his eyebrows and waited.

Baker turned to him. 'Do you have a current will in place?'

'I do have a will, but it was made before my parents died. Just a will leaving everything to a wife and children I may have when I die.'

Baker shook his head slowly. 'And do you have a wife or partner now?'

'No.'

'I suggest that is something you need to address as a matter of urgency.'

'What?' Ryan stared at him. 'Get married?'

Was the old boy mad?

Baker smiled for the first time. 'No, Ryan. Update your will. Despite the property being shared, you are still a very wealthy man.'

Ryan shook his head. What was it about lawyers that they had to have all the Ts crossed and the Is dotted?

'Yeah, okay, I'll get around to it.'

'I'll be back with you in a moment. Would you like a coffee?'

'No, thank you.'

Five minutes later, Ryan fought hard to keep his face expressionless and his arms by his side as the woman who had taken half of his property from him sat across the table, clutching a laptop. He knew her eyes hadn't left him since she'd come into the room and seen him sitting at the table, but he'd kept his eyes on Baker.

Half owner. Apparently at this stage he would keep his half share, but only on the proviso that he welcomed her to the station and let her be a part of it. There was a bloody list of what she was to see, and what she would be responsible for. And what she had to do before she would inherit. How could Dad have left a detailed will like this and never given one hint of what he'd planned? Who the hell was she? And he knew the tasks on the list would be likely be unachievable for an inexperienced person—and a woman to boot.

Ryan managed not to show his disgust as he looked at the long red nails. What would she know about cattle with a manicure like that, and holding tightly to a laptop as though it was important to her?

Mr Baker sat down between them, as though anticipating that he may have to act as referee if the situation got out of control. Once he was seated, he turned to the woman, and Ryan looked at her. Her expression was filled with wariness, but her face was pale and her eyes wide. 'Ryan, this is Deanne Peters. Deanne, this is Ryan Carey.'

It seemed to be the right thing to do to stand and hold his hand out.

You taught me manners, Mum, he thought. Slowly the woman with the dark curls and the huge eyes stood too and reached across the table and took his hand with a firm grip. He hid his surprise when he felt calluses on those manicured hands.

'Please call me Dee,' she said in a quiet voice. They sat down again once they had shaken hands and the introductions were out of the way.

To be honest, she looked as confused as he was feeling, but he'd be damned if he'd show a glimmer of sympathy. For the first time, Ryan allowed himself to look at her for longer than a quick glance. It was in both their interests to be civil and listen to each other. As she turned her eyes to meet his, the movement was familiar, and Ryan frowned. For an instant she had reminded him of someone, but he couldn't place who. He stared at her intently, willing the fragment of familiarity to come back, but it was gone.

'Excellent, thank you. Both of you.' Baker's words pulled him back. 'I know this is a very difficult situation we find ourselves in, but we can all be civilised about this. Before we discuss the logistics of the ownership, and management of *Wilderness Station*, I'd like you both to take a moment to think about what you've learned this afternoon.'

Ryan couldn't help himself. 'I've thought of nothing else.'

'And so have I.' Her voice was firm, with a hint of huskiness.

Baker pursed his lips. 'I want you both to remember that no matter what happens, you are both in the same situation. And I am sure that you find this very unexpected. Nevertheless, we need to come to a consensus of what is best, in terms of management of the station, for the next six months.'

There was silence and then they both started talking together.

'I will continue to manage—' Ryan stopped talking and let her finish.

'I have had considerable experience managing our— managing a property for the past two years, and I'm more than willing to have a crack at this.'

Ryan spluttered 'A crack? It'll take more than a crack, sweetheart.' He couldn't help himself.

She burred up immediately. 'Don't call me that.'

'It will take more than a "crack at it", Ms Peters,' he said firmly. He swallowed the apology that hovered on his lips. That had been a low blow and not the way his mother had brought him up.

'Dee,' she said. 'As Mr Baker says, there are requirements in the will, and one of those is joint managerial status. I was merely using a phrase. What I meant by that is that I will give the property the very best I can.'

Ryan couldn't help himself. 'It's not a property, *Dee*. It's a station.'

'That's only a label, I'm sure it's a business, and that's what I'm well experienced in running. A land-based agricultural business.'

Ryan huffed in a breath. 'Okay, let's look at the logistics of this. How big was the property you managed? How many head did you run? And what qualifications do you have?'

She sat back and stared at him coolly as he fired the questions. Leaning forward, she held up her fingers and ticked off the answers.

'One. I have a science degree, specialising in agriculture and business. Two, there were no cattle, and three, the farm is a three hundred acre macadamia nut plantation. It might not seem relevant to you, Mr Carey, but good management and business sense is transferable, no matter what land or type of farming is in place. Our farm was recently awarded the best business in our region. And that was under my sole management for the past two years. I have no doubt I can handle this.'

His voice was low and rough, but Ryan couldn't hold back the anger driving him. His gut was tight and his mouth dry as he thought of the years of hard work that could disappear in one season. 'There is no need to handle it. We are going along fine as things are. I'm happy to keep running things the way I have been for a long time now, and I'll send the financial reports to you at your little nut farm.'

'That may be so, but I am sure you have heard what Mr Baker has read out to both of us. Once you show me around, we will be jointly managing the station. That is *not* negotiable.'

He stared at her and she didn't look away. 'How long have you known about this? It sounds like you've got some grand ideas already.'

Her answer surprised him. 'About an hour longer than you have.'

'Where will you live? It's a long way to drive from Darwin every day.'

'I don't live in Darwin. I'll be living on the property that I believe I now own a portion of.'

'You haven't inherited yet, sweetheart.' Ryan was pleased to see her lips tighten when he said "sweetheart". 'You have a *share* until all these ridiculous conditions are followed and then—correct me if I'm wrong, after six months, we come back to see Mr Baker and find out what happens then.'

'We will,' she said sweetly. 'And you might find that your share is no longer there if *you* don't follow the requirements.'

Their gazes met and held and there was no way he was looking away first.

The deadlock was broken when Baker stood. 'I have an appointment in the other meeting room, and I think it would be better for the two of you to get to know each other without my presence hindering what you may want to say or ask each other. You can be frank and say what needs to be said, without being intimidated by me.'

They both nodded. Ryan suspected he was being sarcastic; they couldn't get much franker than they had been.

'Is it acceptable to you both if I leave you for say, half an hour?'

Ryan stared at her again and she held his gaze steadily, but she didn't speak. 'I am sure we can be civilised, Mr Baker. What do you say, Ms—I mean, Dee?'

She nodded too. 'Yes, I have quite a few questions to ask you.'

Mr Baker walked to the door slowly. 'Thank you.' The door closed quietly behind him, and then there was silence.

***

Dee sat up straight looking across a huge leather-topped desk at the man with whom she apparently co-owned a cattle station. Frustration gnawed at her stomach. She stared at him still unable to believe what Mr Baker had outlined in detail for over an hour. Despite the details of the inheritance, she was none the wiser as to why she had been left it, or if there was any relationship with the deceased owner, or the man sitting opposite her with a face like thunder.

When she'd travelled to the Territory it had been to find out the truth about her parentage, not to hear that she had inherited half a bloody cattle station. When she'd asked who'd bequeathed the property to her Mr Baker's reply had been vague.

'I can tell you it is a company. The Wilderness Cattle Company. However, before you ask, I cannot tell you who the members of that company are.'

'Surely that is public information that anyone can get from whoever it is that registers companies or whatever?'

'No, not in this particular circumstance.'

'Perhaps I need to seek some independent legal advice.' Her friend, Sally, was a solicitor.

'Of course, you are at liberty to do that. I am sorry, Ms Peters, but my hands are tied.'

When he left her in the office with Ryan Carey, Dee closed her eyes and tried to breathe evenly. When she opened them, his gaze was fixed firmly on her face.

She wasn't sure where to begin or what to ask him first. He was a very big man, and he had presence. The office was small, but he seemed to take command of the space he sat in, and she drew herself up straighter in the chair.

She had let Gerard bully her for years and he'd got away with it because she'd always been trying to please him. No matter what she did, she'd never had his respect. So, there was no way she was going to be intimidated by this rough hulk of a man, and she certainly had no desire to please him. What the lawyer had said was black and white, cut and dried, with nothing open for negotiation.

What she wanted to know was more about who'd left her the property, and hopefully a clue to her parentage. It had to be tied up with the place; she had inherited—what had he said—ten million dollars' worth of land and cattle. The sheer size of the inheritance overwhelmed her.

Dee swallowed and was first to speak. 'So,' she said softly. 'Where do we start?'

'How about we ask questions each, turn about?' He put his hands on the table and she couldn't help comparing them to Gerard's and Rodney's pale smooth hands. These were the hands of a man who knew hard work; tanned and calloused with dirt ingrained in the creases. His workpants and shirt were dusty, and his metal-capped work boots were scuffed and dirty.

He caught her looking at him and shrugged, lowering his eyes to her hands, she had folded on the table.

'I'm sorry. I didn't have time to clean up or get changed before I drove up here. We had a fence to fix and I took a shortcut to the highway from the back of the station.' For the first time there was a lighter tone to his voice, and she sensed he was being genuine, not smart.

'I didn't have time to remove this ridiculous stuff from my nails. My mother insisted on getting them done for the awards night last weekend. My hands usually look a little bit more like yours.'

'Fair enough.' The ice was broken, and he relaxed into the chair. 'Where's your nut plantation? On the Ord River?'

'No. In New South Wales in the hinterland of Byron Bay.'

'New South Wales! I didn't think you'd come from so far away.'

'I didn't plan to. A week ago, I was quite happily in the middle of the harvest when I received the letter from Mr Baker. I had no idea I would be in the Northern Territory today.' Dee was finding it easier to talk to him and he seemed to be thawing slightly. 'So who goes first?'

'My mother taught me to be a gentleman. Ladies first.'

'Okay.' She bit her lip and tried to think what she would ask first. Her mind was teeming with questions, but she didn't want to put him offside straight up. 'Before I ask you anything, I want you to know I feel strongly about what Mr Baker said.'

'About what?'

'Once you show me around, we will be joint managing the station. That is *not* negotiable.'

'We'll see what happens,' Ryan replied, but his gaze was steady on hers and reassured her a little. 'Okay, first question.'

'Do you know whose will this is?'

'Of course, I do. It's my father's.' He spoke slowly.

Dee frowned. 'If you can tell me that, why wouldn't Mr Baker?'

'I don't know. This whole thing is off kilter for me. After hearing some of the wherefores and whyfores that Mr Baker has spouted this afternoon, it doesn't make any sense. Dad simply wouldn't have done that. He would have known that the six month window of no ownership would have a great impact on the property.'

'Okay, your turn,' she said.

'Right.' He leaned forward and put his hands on his thighs. 'How did you know my father, or are you related to my mother's side?'

'I find that impossible to answer, because I don't even know their names. I didn't even know it was your father who named me in the will until you just told me.'

'Colin and Suzanne Carey.'

Dee concentrated, trying to remember if she'd ever heard those names. 'I've never heard of them. The only connection I can tell you is that apparently, I spent the first two years of my life in the Territory. My turn.' Now that he had raised his parents, she didn't feel so bad asking. 'Is there any chance that they were my parents?'

'Absolutely bloody not.'

'Don't you see, there has to be a connection to one or both of them. Or someone else who had a share in the station.

No one is going to leave that sort of inheritance to a total stranger.'

His face reddened and his lips tightened again. 'How old are you?' he asked.

'Why? I'll be thirty-three on the second of August.'

He raised his eyebrows. 'I'll be thirty-three on the twenty-ninth of July, so unless we are long-lost twins born three days apart, I guess that disproves your theory. You are not my parents' child.'

'It could rule out your mother. Are you sure she gave birth to you? And what about your father?'

He leaned further forward, and his voice was hard. 'I won't take that remark the wrong way. Yes, my mother gave birth to me, and my father was a hardworking, god-fearing man, and there was no way he would have cheated on my mother. But in the farfetched scenario that he was your father, he was the sort of man who would have taken responsibility for any child he'd fathered, and not kept it a secret.'

'You didn't know him back then. You were a baby. So, you can't say that for sure. Maybe he's taking belated responsibility. You can't ignore the fact he has left me half the property.'

Ryan's cheeks took on a dull red flush. 'I was close to Dad all my life. He died suddenly in the middle of last year. I knew him so well I would stake my entire share of the property on the fact that he was a faithful husband. He was a good man.'

'Good people make mistakes. And I'm sorry to tell you that we often don't know people as well as we think we do.' Dee held her hands out to him. 'Look, let's forget this question back and forth stuff and just talk. I need to tell you my story, and you might understand more about me and where I'm coming from.'

To her surprise he nodded straight away. 'That sounds fair to me. I want to know why you immediately jumped on the shared parentage theory. When do you fly back to New South Wales? Are you free tonight?'

'I'm not flying back. I drove over this week. I'm here to stay.'

'O . . . kay,' he said in a slow drawl. 'If you're free tonight, that would suit me best. Then I won't have to come back up to Darwin.'

'Is there anything else we need to ask Mr Baker?'

'No, I've heard enough of the legal mumbo jumbo and the bizarre conditions. I'm sure if we have any more questions, he can answer by phone. We've got the main gist of this situation.'

'Okay. That sounds fine by me. Where will I meet you? I'm staying in a motel near the esplanade. We both have to eat, perhaps a pub meal?' Dee assumed his clothes wouldn't let him get into most places on a Friday night, but then she wasn't familiar with Darwin yet.

'Which end of the esplanade?'

'Um, up near the big park where there's a cenotaph.'

'Okay, I know it. The Darwin Hotel is only a block from there.' He glanced at his watch. 'It's after four now. I've got a couple of stops to make. Say I meet you there at six?'

Before she could answer, the door opened and Mr Baker came back into the room.

For the first time, he looked less serious, and his face creased in a smile. 'I was a little concerned about leaving you two alone, but you both seem to have survived. Do you have any more questions for me?'

Ryan took charge before Dee could reply, and she bit back the protest that rose. She was being oversensitive.

'Dee and I have come to an arrangement. We're going to meet for dinner tonight to discuss the situation, and we'll call you tomorrow before I go back to *Wilderness Station* if we have any more questions after we talk. Oh, hang on, it's Saturday tomorrow, isn't it?'

'That won't be a problem. I'm happy for you to contact me on my mobile on the weekend.' He pulled two business cards from the holder on the desk and gave them one each. 'I'll be happy to advise on anything I can if you call. Now if you have no immediate questions, I have another client waiting.' He reached out and shook Ryan's hand, then Dee stood and shook his hand in turn.

'Thank you, Mr Baker. I'll be in touch,' she said. 'I'll make an appointment to discuss a will with you.'

'And I will too,' Ryan said.

'Excellent, now you take care of yourselves, and don't hesitate to call whenever you need to.'

Chapter 9

Darwin.
Friday 6 p.m.

The man stood outside the Tropical Palms Hotel on the esplanade just up from Parliament house. When Dee Peters had come out of the lawyer's office, he'd followed her at a distance and was pleased when she turned into the small motel opposite the harbour. She walked over to a blue ute and checked the load on the back before disappearing into a room on ground level.

Once she was inside, he pulled his phone out of his pocket and dialled the familiar number. 'I've found her, and I've followed her to where she's staying,' he said as soon as the phone picked up. He kept his eye on the door on the bottom floor in case she came out again. This was one of the best jobs he'd had for a while. She was a much better looker than the tails he'd done recently.

'Good job. How did you manage to find her so quickly?'

'Pure luck. I followed Ryan Carey into town, and when he came out of the lawyer's office, she was with him. I recognised her from that photo you texted. He took off in his truck and she walked to the motel, so I followed her. There's a blue ute with DP numberplates I'm assuming belongs to her.'

'Yes, it does. Keep an eye on her and if she heads out of town, follow her. I need to know where she goes. I need to know what that lawyer told her. Or told them.'

'Do you want me to rough her up a bit?'

'God, no. Not yet anyway.'

'Okay. And something else you need to know; Carey is organising a helicopter for a muster. I heard him on his phone when he was walking to his ute.'

'I know. It's under control this end.'

'Yeah, and another thing, boss. Carey had a meeting with that woman helicopter pilot today. The one who shot that bloke a couple of years back at the mango farm.'

'Jesus, I don't know, aren't there any other pilots around? That just complicates things.'

'I thought that too. At least she doesn't live far from the station. And don't worry, she'll be easy to control. She's got a young kid.'

'Fucking women, the world would be a better place without them,' his boss growled.

'Only good for one thing, hey?'

'Now that you've found her, keep Dee in your sights, and I'll make sure that woman doesn't take that chopper up over the station. We're too close to have all this go up shit creek now.'

'You know you can trust me.'

'One more thing. What was the name of the lawyer's office?'

'Bakers.'

'I thought so. Okay,. I'll do what's needed at this end, and if you get in there and get me a copy of that will, I'll give you a fat bonus this week. But if you get caught it's your problem. You're on your own.'

'On it, boss. Gotta go. She's coming out of the motel room already.' He disconnected, put his head down and pretended to be looking at his phone.

His eyes lit up as she headed for her ute. Holy shit, she was a looker, and if things turned out the way they were hoping, he'd have a little fun with her when the time was right.

Chapter 10
The Darwin Hotel.
Friday night.

After unlocking the ute, Dee took out the small bag on the floor and carried it into the hotel room with her laptop. There was a safe on the bench next to the luggage holder, and once she'd secured her laptop and valuables in there, she went back to the ute and unloaded the two suitcases and the three boxes. The hallstand would have to stay on the ute; it would be a keen thief who undid the knotted ropes around the piece of furniture.

The air pressed heavily on her damp skin as the heat rose up from the concrete surface of the carpark, and soon her dress and underwear were wet with perspiration. After switching the kettle on, Dee took a quick shower. Standing under the cool water, she tipped her head back and let the fine spray cool her face as she processed the day. The first session had been a huge shock to her, but by the time she'd met Ryan Carey, she'd been calmer. Before she'd gone back to the office, she'd found a café and forced herself to eat a salad sandwich and have another coffee. The news that she was possibly a shareholder of a cattle station up here had been such a shock she'd felt ill when she'd walked out the first time.

After slipping on fresh underwear Dee pulled back the cover on the bed and lay on top of the cool sheets. She would take advantage of some quiet time to process everything she'd discovered today. Apart from knowing what the inheritance was, and the convoluted conditions around it, she was no closer to discovering anything about her family. For a short time in the office she'd thought that Ryan may have been her brother, but when he'd told her his age, she knew that that could not be the case. Half-brother maybe? That was a possibility.

What was the connection to the Carey family? Was Colin Carey her father? Suzanne Carey couldn't be her mother because Ryan had been born a few days before she was. Unless she'd lied and someone else had given birth to him.

Maybe *he* was the adopted child.

Dee's head began to ache, and she crossed to the small kitchenette and found a peppermint teabag in the selection next to the kettle.

What was her next step? Should she insist on going to *Wilderness Station* and checking it out, or should she stay in Darwin and try to find out more about the family? First step was to get a full birth certificate; she'd checked that out at home but all she'd found was a registration notice with her name—Deanne Maree Peters and her date of birth. One thing it did have was her place of birth and she'd never thought much of the fact that she'd been born in Darwin. She'd always assumed that Gerard and Catherine had lived there at that time. The more she thought about it, the more she realised the scarcity of information she'd been given by them over her life, about her birth, their families, and where they'd lived before they moved to Byron Bay not long after she'd started primary school. Dee had a memory of going to school in a city and Catherine had told her they'd lived in Sydney and Brisbane for a while.

Maybe it had been Darwin.

Any question she'd asked Catherine had been met with vague answers, but that was typical Catherine. For as long as Dee could remember, Catherine had been on medication to calm her anxiety, and if she didn't want to engage with someone or face a problem, she would retreat into one of her moods. Dee had often wondered why she was the way she was. Had it been caused by a family secret, a hidden past, a lost love? Had Catherine had an affair with Ryan's father? That would explain a lot because she and Gerard had never had a loving relationship, nor had he taken an interest in Dee as a daughter.

Dee leaned back on the padded headboard and as she sipped at her tea the headache eased. Overthinking was doing her head in; hopefully sharing information with Ryan might give some clarity to the situation. At least he'd agreed to meet with her tonight. She needed to get her thoughts in order and think about exactly what she wanted to ask him. There had to be some clue, some pointer to what this secret was. And more to the point, who *she* was. No one would bequeath a cattle station to a stranger, that was a given. There was a family connection, and she had to figure out what it was.

Now that she knew Ryan's parents' names, maybe she'd call and ask Catherine if she'd known them. But there was no point at this time of day; she'd be at least halfway through a bottle of wine by now.

Dee quickly finished her tea and went to her suitcase. She needed to hurry because she wasn't exactly sure where this hotel was. Picking out a plain dark blue cotton dress, she slipped it over her head and then pulled her hair back into a top knot. She frowned as she looked in the mirror above the bench. Even though her hair was a very dark brown, and Ryan's was white-blonde, his was thick and curled around his collar. Their complexions were similar too—olive. But her eyes were brown, and his were a pale blue.

He was a very good-looking man who gave out an aura of someone very confident in himself. Once he'd got over the initial shock of meeting her and learning he'd lost half of the inheritance he'd expected, he'd been approachable and responsive to her questions. Suggesting that they meet tonight and try to make some sense of this situation had been generous when he obviously had work commitments. In any other circumstances Dee knew she would have been attracted to him. She chewed on her lip as she brushed on a light layer of mascara, wondering if he was married with kids.

A tiny tendril of excitement unfurled in her stomach. Maybe Ryan was her half-brother and she might have a sister-in-law and nieces or nephews. Readymade relatives. Family was something she'd never had.

Or many friends. As she'd driven out of the gate last Sunday, Dee had felt sorry for herself for a brief moment, knowing there was really no one she had to let know she was leaving town; she'd been too busy working on the plantation since she'd come home from uni to follow up with old friends. Most of her schoolfriends had moved away, and those still in the Bay were married with kids, and involved in school and kid things Dee had no interest in. No wonder she'd been so accepting of Rodney's overture of friendship.

An easy mark, Dee, that's what Rodney had seen, she told herself. So, take care with whatever Ryan Carey has to say.

Reaching for her phone she checked the time and then pulled up Google Maps and found her destination; the Darwin Hotel was only a three-minute walk away. She had fifteen minutes to spare. Picking up her bag, Dee slipped the room key into it, and closed the door behind her.

She had a new future to discover.

A smoky haze edged the horizon with a soft pink as the sun hovered above the sea to the west, but the water of the harbour across the esplanade was flat and brown. As Dee walked out of the motel, she looked curiously at the man leaning against the concrete post at the carpark entrance. He'd been there when she'd gone inside, and he was still there, staring at his phone.

The Darwin Hotel was a couple of hundred metres down the street from her hotel, on the corner of a busy intersection. The streets were filled with traffic and pedestrians and Dee absorbed the vibe of the tropical city as she set out for the hotel. Even though Byron Bay was crowded with tourists, Darwin had a totally different feel. It was a city, but smaller than the cities of the east coast, and with a more casual feel, like a holiday town rather than a capital city. Even though it was early evening, the cafés and small bars were full, and the streets were crowded.

The hotel was packed as she made her way inside; it wasn't quite six and they hadn't made an arrangement about where to meet. If she couldn't see Ryan inside, she'd come back and wait out the front. The place was buzzing with a mix of patrons filling the two bars. Men in suits obviously from the office buildings around the hotel, workmen in high vis shirts, and tourists mingled. She walked through to the garden bar, keeping an eye out for Ryan.

'Dee!'

She turned and stared as Ryan slid off a bar stool. 'Sorry, I must have walked straight past you. You look different.'

'I went to a mate's place and had a shower and got changed.'

Dee looked up at him. His hair was damp and the curls she'd noticed before were more evident, curling in damp tendrils around his forehead, just like hers did when her hair was wet.

Excitement curled in her gut. They would get this sorted tonight; she was sure of it. She just had to be careful not to offend him and get him offside; any questions about his mother and father would have to be carefully phrased.

'You do look different.' His collared T-shirt was navy blue—a similar blue to her dress, and it accentuated the pale blue of his eyes and his tanned face.

Ryan voiced Dee's thoughts. 'We have the same taste in colours,' he said slowly.

'And the same curly hair,' she said. 'And the same complexion.'

His forehead wrinkled in a frown. 'But we won't jump to any conclusions based on that. I bought these clothes this afternoon. I was a bit grotty even for the pub.'

'Do you know the label is still on the collar of your polo shirt?' She reached up and pulled off the circular white label. 'You needn't have worried about going to the shops. We could have sat in the park and had takeaway.'

'It wasn't a problem. I had to go to Casuarina and buy a set of saucepans for my uncle.'

'Your uncle?'

'Yes, he's the cook on the station. What would you like to drink? We'll go and sit down and get down to tin tacks and try to sort this mess out. I'm going to have a light beer.'

'That's sounds good to me.'

Ryan nodded. 'Come and we'll see if there's a table spare in the garden bar, and then I'll get our drinks.'

The garden bar was a welcoming space filled with potted palms; the tables were each in a private alcove with a small fernery set into the back walls.

'There's a spare table over there. You nab it and I'll get our drinks.' Ryan headed back to the bar.

As Dee walked into the garden section, someone bumped her from behind. She swung around and frowned.

'Sorry, love.'

'It's okay.' She went to step to the side, but he moved and blocked her.

'No rush. Can I buy you a drink?' His eyes were dark and intent on hers. She frowned as she realised it was the guy who'd been outside the motel. He was wearing the same baseball cap with the red logo she'd noticed.

'No, thank you. I'm with someone.' Dee put her head down and moved past him. When she reached the table and looked back, he was still standing there watching her.

Sleaze, she thought, hoping he wouldn't follow her.

Chapter 11

The Darwin Hotel.

Ryan sensed early on that Dee was being very careful not to push his buttons, and he appreciated it. After he'd left her this afternoon, he'd thought of nothing else but the bloody situation, and what they could do about it. He'd managed to let go of his anger; he was smart enough to know it wasn't her fault. He wondered how he would have reacted if he'd been in her shoes. Being hit with an unexpected inheritance and then not being able to get any clear information about why, would have done his head in. She seemed much calmer now than she had in the lawyer's office and seemed to be making an effort.

So he would too.

Ryan watched as she lifted the middy of beer and drank deeply. She was a fine-looking woman, and he'd noticed a few heads turn as she'd walked across to the table.

He'd seen the guy hit on her, and had been about to come over, but she'd handled it and the guy had slunk off.

'Good beer,' she said. He grinned as she wiped the back of her hand over her mouth.

'That's one thing we do well up here in the Territory. Got the climate for it.' He lifted his and looked around the bar while he drank, before switching his attention back to Dee. 'So, you were going to tell me about your background. You jumped straight on the idea that we might share a parent.'

'It couldn't be your mother unless one of us has the wrong year on our birth certificate.'

'I haven't seen mine,' he said. 'I've never needed it for anything, but I'm sure it'll be in the office somewhere. Have you got yours?'

'Just an extract. I've never needed the full one.'

'I know you're thinking it's a parental thing because you've been left half the station, but honestly there has to be another explanation. Maybe a different, more distant family connection. A long-lost brother or cousin?' Ryan intended grilling Joe as soon as he got home. All he knew was that the station had been in Dad's family for a long time, and his father was an only child. His mother had been in her thirties when he was born, and Dad had been twelve years older; both sets of grandparents had passed before then.

Joe and Cy were the only relatives he knew of, but now Ryan frowned thoughtfully. That didn't mean there weren't more. It made him think seriously about what Baker had said about a will.

'Okay,' he said. 'Tell me about your family. Why do you think we could share a parent?'

Dee put her glass down and Ryan noticed her hand was shaking. She wasn't as calm as he'd first thought.

'I've discovered in the past week that things—as in people—can be very different to what we perceive as the truth. Getting the letter from the lawyers, and then talking to who I had thought were my parents for over thirty years'— she pulled a face—'and an unexpected marriage proposal has given me a totally different perspective on truth and on my life. So, look carefully at your family, be prepared to discover there might be secrets and even lies underneath the surface. If everything was what you expected, we wouldn't be sitting here. You would have inherited your whole cattle station and I would have no idea that I am probably adopted. And I've been thinking too. There are obviously others who are affected by whatever this family secret is. Otherwise it would be all cut and dried . . . you'd inherit the station and I'd be happily managing my macadamia plantation. Why is there a need for all this secrecy and documents that are closed off to us? Why is it going to take six months of me being on the station before it's all final? So, I'm sorry, Ryan, but you're going to have to move out of your comfort zone and think deeper.'

'Fair enough.' Ryan nodded. 'I've already been thinking, but I'm at a loss to know where to look. My simple perception of family has been with me for almost thirty-three years.'

'As mine was, and that was blown out of the water with one letter, and one talk with who I thought were my parents. And then that perception turned into a massive explosion listening to Mr Baker and then meeting you.'

'So you think you were adopted, and they didn't tell you?'

'I don't know.' Dee shrugged. 'I don't know who to believe and what to think. The two people I thought were my parents are denying my suggestion that I'm adopted for all it's worth.'

'So that would make you think they *are* your parents—I mean at your age, they'd surely think you would cope with learning you were adopted—or there is some reason why they don't want you to know.'

'I know. I am totally confused.'

'It sure is a strange situation.' Ryan looked at her thoughtfully, but she looked uncomfortable.

Dee looked down before she spoke. 'Okay, let's dig a bit with what I know. Have you ever heard the name Peters before? I mean did you know anyone called Peters when you were growing up? I wondered if there might be some connection there. I've been thinking, Mum insists they didn't adopt me, but if I stretched it, maybe it could have been like a kinship fostering. That my real mother—or father—might be a Peters.'

'No, I don't, but that doesn't mean that there wasn't someone called that around before I was born.' Ryan frowned. 'Can't you ask them? Where are they now?' He hesitated. 'Sorry, you did say you had a talk to them though?'

He was surprised at the bitterness in her voice. 'Oh, yes, I talked to them. The plantation I manage—managed—belongs to Gerard Peters, who I've always thought was my father. Getting the letter from the lawyers was a double whammy for me. As well as having to deal with this inheritance situation, I've not only discovered that there is a family secret, but I found out the same day that he's selling the plantation. And then I found out that Gerard's business partner proposed to me on Gerard's instruction to sort out some business deal they've got going.'

'Sounds like a charmer. Sorry.'

'No, you're right. He is.'

'I guess we're really in the same boat. Thinking we knew our families and then this has happened. Sort of takes away everything you took for granted. You've obviously asked them, and they don't know who your parents are?'

'I have, and I'm sure they know something, but for some reason, they won't tell me anything. So, in a nutshell I took off, drove across Queensland and the Northern Territory to come and find out what I could myself. And'—she held his gaze—'here I am.'

'Yes, here you are.' His gaze held hers steadily. 'What about going to the Births, Deaths and Marriages place tomorrow and getting your birth certificate? You know, it could be as simple as that. Your parents should be on it.'

'Yes, I'd already planned to get it, but tomorrow's Saturday.'

'Damn, it is too. Okay, one day next week. We'll come back as soon as we can.'

***

Dee and Ryan talked for more than two hours, questioning each other, conjecturing, and coming up with all sorts of possibilities as they tried to make sense of why his father had left a share of *Wilderness Station* to Dee. They'd eaten dinner, and Dee now had a wine in her hand while Ryan had moved from beer to Coke.

Dee kept coming back to her original conviction. 'I have to be a blood relative. That's the only logical reason why your father would have split the property.'

'Despite my initial reluctance, I guess I'm beginning to accept that might be a possibility too,' Ryan finally conceded.

'Especially with the detailed legal addendums or whatever it was Mr Baker called them.'

They were no closer to solving the mystery of the inheritance, but they were much easier with each other. A couple of times their hands had brushed as they made notes and pored over Dee's phone and they both pulled back as though they'd been burnt.

God, he could be my brother, or cousin, or a relation, she thought as attraction tried to pull at her.

Dee was impressed with the way Ryan operated; his thought processes were logical, and his ideas were sensible. They had come up with a plan of action, and he suggested that a DNA test was the first thing they had to do. Dee's phone had got a workout as they Googled the possibilities. In the end it was a simple procedure of applying for a kit, doing a cheek swab and sending it off to the laboratory.

'I'll pay for it,' Ryan said as they filled in the form on her phone. He opened his wallet and put his credit card on the table. The DNA sibling test was available to order and pay for online, and the results would be back five days after they posted the swabs to the laboratory.

'No.' Dee shook her head. 'It's only fair that I pay half.'

'We'll sort it out later. I have an idea.'

'Oh? What would that be?' Dee tipped her head to the side and their eyes met and held. Her cheeks heated and she looked away. Maybe he was her half-brother, and that's why she felt this connection.

Ryan shook his head. 'It's really strange, Dee. I really feel at ease with you, and that's not a pickup line.'

'I know it's not. We're in a strange situation here. So what's this idea you've got?'

'You said you did accounting as part of your degree,' he looked at her thoughtfully. 'And that you enjoy the bookwork side of looking after the plantation?'

'I wouldn't call it bookwork. I do it all on my computer. I have a software package that handles the income and expenses and generates the BAS each month. But yes, I enjoy the accounting side of things.'

'You need to come out to the station to look around, and this might be the way to do it without needing to explain why you're there. Before we work out this six month thing.'

'How do you mean?'

'I'll hire you as a temporary bookkeeper to get the station records in order and relieve me while we're mustering. I'd rather do that than announce that it looks like the station will be split. I think we might find out more if we do it this way. I'm not going to tell anyone what's going on. Not even Joe. I've given it a bit more thought. I'm not even going to ask him anything yet. I don't want to stuff up. That legal stuff is so detailed, and Baker did say our actions might change the eventual outcome, even though he wouldn't say how or why.' His tone was weary, and Dee felt sorry for him, able to understand where the feeling came from. It had been bad enough for her finding out that Dad was going to sell their place, let alone for Ryan, hearing that half his station had been left to her. She was still surprised by his co-operation and kindness tonight, because he must be feeling so frustrated and angry. In his place she would have been feeling a lot of resentment.

'Dee? What do you think?'

'Oh, sorry. I was thinking. But yes, that sounds like a plan. When do you think?'

'I'd say sooner rather than later. That way we can get the swab kits delivered to the one address and send the swabs off together. Did you have any plans?'

Dee laughed for the first time since she'd listened to Mr Baker earlier today. 'Plans? After today, I can barely think an hour ahead.'

'How long did you book your accommodation for?'

'Just for tonight. I wanted to check out the motel before I booked for longer.'

'Okay. How about you come down to the station with me tomorrow? It's too late for me to go back now, so I'll crash in town, and you can follow me down in the morning.'

Things had started to go a bit faster than she'd intended, but Dee nodded. There was no reason to delay, and it might mean that she'd find out what this was all about sooner.

'There's only one thing I need to say.' Ryan looked a bit embarrassed.

'Oh?' Suspicion began to raise its ugly head. Had she been gullible again?

'Um, the house and the financial stuff.' He drummed his fingers on the table.

'What about it?'

'It's all a bit of a mess.'

Relief flooded through Dee; she wasn't sure what she'd been worried about, but a messy house and a mess of financial records weren't threatening. 'Nothing that can't be addressed,' she said confidently.

'Okay, so that's all started. I'll put you on the payroll.'

'There's no need to do that.'

'You will, because it's not fair to have you working on my stuff for nothing.'

Dee covered a yawn, and her limbs felt heavy. 'I'm supposed to be doing it for six months, and you won't be paying me for that.'

'I draw a wage from the station, so if the six months goes ahead, so will you.'

'We'll discuss it later.'

'We will.' He put his empty glass on the table. 'Are you ready to go?' he said.

Dee pushed her chair back before slipping her phone into her small bag.

'My ute's parked down the road a bit, I'll drive you back to the motel.'

'There's no need to do that. I can walk. It's only a couple of hundred metres at most.'

'If you don't feel comfortable coming with me, I'll put you in a taxi. It's not safe walking around the streets of the city after dark. And I don't want to scare you, but that loser who hit on you earlier has been sitting over near the bar watching you all night.'

Goose bumps rose on her arms and she looked across at the bar. The creep was sitting there staring down into a beer. 'Okay, in that case, I'll gladly accept a lift.'

'He's pretty harmless, I think he's three parts cut already. I don't think the barman will serve him again, but better to be safe.'

'Thank you. You are a gentleman, Ryan.'

His cheeks flushed, but he smiled. 'It was the way I was brought up.'

Ryan put his hand on her elbow as they walked past the bar, and the drunk guy leered at her as they walked past. 'Night, love,' he slurred.

When they reached the door, she turned to Ryan with a frown. 'What bothers me is that he was hanging around outside the motel before. He knows where I'm staying.'

'All the more reason to be careful.'

When they reached his car, Ryan unlocked the passenger door and held it open for her. Dee wrinkled her nose as a cloud of dust rose when she sat on the seat.

'Sorry, it's a work ute,' he said as he swung himself up into the driver's seat.

'Ryan?'

'Yes, what's up?'

'Do you have a family? I mean, a wife and kids.'

'No. It's just me. The cattle work's been full on the last few years. No time to think about settling down. No time for socialising.' He paused before he turned the key. 'What about you? Partner?'

'Nope, just a wannabe fiancé, but that's another story. I've been too busy too.'

They didn't speak again as the ute started with the typical rattle of a diesel engine, and Ryan threw it into a U-turn and headed towards the esplanade. When he reached the motel, he drove into the car park and nodded at the office.

'Looks like they're still open. I might grab a room here instead of driving out to Winnellie. Do you mind?'

Dee shrugged. 'That's fine with me. Makes sense.'

Ryan parked the ute and walked her to her room. His eyes widened and he let out a low whistle when he saw her blue ute parked outside the door. 'That's yours?'

She nodded. 'It is.'

'Is that an SSV Redline?'

'You know your cars.' Dee didn't like the way he was looking at her.

'There must be good money in macadamias.' He seemed to have withdrawn a bit.

'Not really. It took me a long time to save up for that. It didn't come from the plantation account. I have a quad bike for getting around the orchard.'

'Hmm. I don't know how you'll feel about taking it down to the station. Red dirt and dust.'

'It'll wash,' Dee said shortly.

'Okay, then. I'll go and check in. I'll see you in the morning. Are you happy to leave early?'

'Whatever.'

'Okay, about seven. It's just under two hours down to *Wilderness*.'

'I'll be ready.' Dee turned and had her key in the door, but before she could open it, Ryan was by her side.

'I'm sorry. I didn't mean to be rude about your ute.'

She shrugged again. 'It's okay. I've got thick skin. I'll see you at seven.' Opening the door, she went inside and closed it without turning around again.

Chapter 12

Darwin - The Tropical Palm Motel.

Saturday - 4 a.m.

Just after four a.m. a small dark sedan drove slowly into the guest's car park of the Tropical Palm motel. The driver had already been in her room earlier, while the woman and the Carey guy had been eating dinner, but there'd been nothing of interest there to report to his boss, although going through her underwear had given him a buzz.

After he watched them leave the hotel, he'd gone home for a while and slept off the four beers he'd had, setting the alarm on his phone for midnight.

He downed two mugs of strong coffee and popped an E-bomb before he made his way to the lawyer's office. There had been no alarm in the building, and it had been easy to pick the back door and get inside.

Then things had gone to shit. He searched each cabinet under Carey, and then looked under Peters, with no bloody luck. An hour later, he cursed as he slammed a filing cabinet shut and jammed his thumb. Three bloody offices, plus a central bank of filing cabinets. He drew a deep breath while the pain receded. He knew to leave no sign that he'd been there, so it really didn't matter how long it took.

He was paid very well.

She'd only been in here yesterday, maybe they were on a desk somewhere or waiting to be filed. He did another swoop through the three offices, anger gripping him when he had no success.

He yawned, the eccy pill was wearing off, and he was getting cranky. He knew what names he was looking for and it was almost four a.m. by the time he struck pay dirt in the third office. He pulled out the file and began to read. The legal mumbo jumbo was complicated, and some of the big word shit was hard to understand, it threw him, but he got the general gist of it. Pulling out his camera he took photos of the dozen pages before neatly putting the file back exactly where it had been and letting himself out of the office.

He couldn't help one last drive by where she was sleeping. If only she knew what he'd found. Driving past the hot blue ute to the turning bay at the back of the carpark, he slowed down and looked at her room. It was in darkness as he'd expected and for a moment, he considered opening the door, and watching her as she slept.

Nuh, too risky. He could wait; the boss would kill him if he stuffed this up. He always found it hard to concentrate when he was coming down, and he remembered he hadn't texted the photos. Revving the engine, he swung the car around, and his eyes narrowed as he spotted the dust-covered ute parked opposite her blue beauty.

Jesus, she'd only met Carey today, and he was fucking well in her room with her already. Anger rose in him and he turned the motor off. Getting out of his car, he kept the door open and took his key and ran it down both sides of her ute. Along the back of the tail gate he carefully scratched a message for her.

Jumping back into his car, he threw another glance at her door. 'See how you like that, slut,' he muttered.

Anger simmered as he drove across to the Bicentennial Park and turned into Doctors Gully Road. Parking the car, he pulled out another E-bomb and downed it before he opened his phone and pulled up the boss's number.

If he woke the boss up, it didn't matter; he'd be bloody stoked to get this file. Just like I'll be when I get the bonus, he thought. He could geek all night long then if he wanted to. His fingers moved slowly as his vision blurred.

Got it for you, boss.

He attached the photos he'd taken.

See Carey-Peters-Porter file photos attached.

Chapter 13

Darwin.
Saturday.

Dee had set her alarm for six a.m. but was awake before it went off. It was still dark outside, so she made herself a cup of coffee and lay on the bed checking her emails on her phone. There was nothing of interest; emails from the local Macadamia Association president back home didn't matter to her anymore; especially the one congratulating the winners at the awards dinner. She deleted them all, and then scrolled through the news as she drank her coffee.

Nothing much of interest, just the usual politics. She'd usually check the market price of the nuts, but she resisted.

As Dee put her phone down, it buzzed with an incoming text. Her eyebrows rose as **Mum** flashed up on the screen as the sender. A flash of guilt sparked in her, and she chewed on her lip as she read the message.

Ring me today, pls Dee. Missing you. I worry about you.

Before she could change her mind, Dee pressed the speed dial for Catherine, and it picked up straight away.

'Darling, you're awake already.' Catherine's voice was slurred.

'My usual getup time, M—' Dee cut off the "mum" before it came out. 'It's early for you to be up though.' Then she remembered the time difference. 'You don't usually surface before ten.'

'It's just gone eight here. I couldn't sleep. I was worried about you, and your father hasn't come home. You know how much I hate being here by myself.'

'Where is he?'

'Oh, he went to look at some property with Rodney up the coast yesterday. Where are you, Dee? Are you all right? I've barely slept since you left.'

'I'm fine. But I do have some things I want to ask you.'

'Oh not now, I'm sleepy tired. I'll probably go back to bed. I just wanted to know you were all right.'

Dee wondered if she was being evasive or drunk again.

'I'm fine, Mum.' The "mum" slipped out from habit before she thought. Dee put her head back and closed her eyes. To be fair, Catherine hadn't been a bad mother. If she was her real mother, that would make her happy. Catherine had encouraged her in everything she did, and it had only been in recent years she'd started drinking too much. 'I had a good trip and I'm staying in a motel near the gardens on the harbour. It's a pretty place.'

'Yes, I loved our time in the Territory. I loved Darwin too.'

'Did you grow up here?'

'I did. That's where I met Gerard.'

'I never knew that.'

'I know. There's a lot you don't know. I wish you did. It makes me sad.'

'Why, Mum?' Dee said quietly.

'Because it's life. *Sush* a waste.' Dee heard the clink of a glass and she held back a sigh. Eight a.m. and Catherine was already drinking. Or still? Dee wondered.

'Why? Because life sucks, you know. I never got what I wanted. But, Dee sweetie, when you arrived, it made up for everything. We couldn't stay there even though I wanted to.'

Arrived? Another word for born, or a different meaning?

'Why did we have to move? Where did we go?'

'You knew why we had to. We promised.' Catherine was staring to slur and ramble. 'Shydney, we went to Shydney and I bought you so many pretty dresses. Please come home, Dee. Do you still have your pretty red nails?'

'I'll come home when I sort all this out, Mum. But can I ask you a question?'

'All right. *Jush* one.' Another clink against the phone and then silence.

'Mum? Are you still there?'

'I'm here. What?'

'Mum. When I was little'—Dee thought carefully about the best way to get information from an obviously drunk Catherine— 'did we live on a farm up here?'

'You remember! You loved the cows and the chooks. You used to feed the chooks.'

'Did our farm have a name?'

'Don't you remember?'

'No, I was too little.'

'Silly little girl. It was Peters of course. Peters' Mango Farm.'

Dee's interest quickened. 'A mango farm? Was Gerard there too?'

'Yes, of course he was there. It was his farm. He loved me then. He was nice to me. Maybe we could go back there and he could be nice to me again. We had fun when we lived there. Better than here.' Her tone was that of a petulant child.

'Did we have friends called Colin and Suzanne?'

'No, Bridget was my bridesmaid. I'm gonna go bed now. Ni, ni, Dee.'

'Wait, Mum. What about the Careys? Did you know anyone called Carey?'

Dee waited for a couple of minutes, but there was no answer. Catherine had either passed out or gone to bed.

Dee put her phone down thoughtfully. At least she'd got some information. They'd lived on a mango farm, and Catherine had had a bridesmaid called Bridget. It was a better starting point than she'd had before.

##

Half an hour later, Dee was showered and dressed ready to go to the station. She'd deliberately dressed down to denim jeans and a plain white T-shirt. She packed the last of her toiletries into her bag and opened the door to go out and get her work boots from the front of the ute. Clicking the remote to unlock the door, she reached for the door handle and her breath caught.

A huge scratch down to the bare silver metal ran along the whole passenger side of the car from the front bumper to the tailgate.

'Shit!' Dee walked around the front of the car to check the driver's side. A matching scratch ran the length of the driver's side. Both sides of her car had been keyed deliberately.

As she stood here with her arms folded staring at the damage, a door closed behind her. She swung around to face Ryan.

'Morning, Dee,' he said.

'Look at this.' She pointed to the side of her ute. 'Some lowlife's keyed my car.'

'Jeez, they've done a good job on it. Front to back.' Ryan walked over and ran his fingers over the deep scratch.

'And they've done the other side too,' she said.

Ryan looked around. 'I wonder if they did all the others in the car park.'

'I don't know. I just came out to get my boots and saw it.' Dee shook her head. 'Bloody hell. My insurance policy is at home. I left so quickly I didn't think to bring it with me. I'll have to ring home again,' she muttered under her breath.

Ryan walked along the row of cars parked outside the rooms, and then crossed to the other side of the car park where his Land Cruiser ute was parked. He walked back across and stood behind Dee's ute and looked at the back shaking his head. 'I can't see any damage on any of the other cars. Just yours.'

'I'm going to have to get this sorted today. You go, and I'll come out to the station in a day or so. Just tell me how to get there.' Dee's voice wobbled and she shook her head. 'I can't believe it. What else can go wrong?'

'Have you upset anyone in town?'

'Give me a break. I've only been here a day and a bit.'

Ryan was still at the back of her ute staring at the tailgate.

'Don't tell me they've keyed the back too?' she asked.

'Sort of. Come and have a look.'

Dee walked around to the back of the ute and stopped dead, lifting one hand to cover the gasp she expelled. The blue paint was scored down to the bare metal, but this time the damage was a single word scratched onto the metal.

'Who the hell would do this?' she whispered as she stared down at the twenty centimetre high word covering the back of her tailgate.

SLUT.

She didn't know anyone in Darwin. She had no enemies and she hadn't upset anyone. Apart from Ryan.

Dee turned and looked at him, and immediately felt bad. Ryan looked as upset as she was.

Of course he wouldn't have done it.

Chapter 14
Saturday – Noon.

Dee sat in the passenger seat of Ryan's Land Cruiser as they headed south from Darwin. She stared at the scrubby bushland on each side of the Stuart Highway. Smoke curled around the blackened stumps and the pungent smell made her nose itch. Smoky clouds rose above the savannah, and the sky was a deep amber. Ryan had apologised twice for having to have the windows open, explaining his air conditioning needed fixing.

He pulled a face. 'To be honest, it's been broken for a couple of months. Just no time to get stuff like that done. A low priority.'

Despite having to get back to his station to organise the muster, he'd insisted on staying with Dee until she got her ute sorted. She'd been able to contact her insurer, and they'd found the policy without her having the policy number, and once she'd explained her situation, they'd organised for her to take it to their preferred panel beater in Darwin for an immediate assessment. Ryan knew where the panel beating firm was, and they'd moved the hallstand from the back of her ute and secured it on his, along with her boxes and suitcases.

Once her ute had been assessed, and booked in for repair, they'd headed off for *Wilderness Station*. Dee was quiet, her nerves were beginning to kick in. Ryan tried to start a conversation a few times, but she'd answered in monosyllables and he'd turned the radio on. It came on to an ABC country news program, but he immediately switched to a music station.

She flicked him an appreciative glance before settling down in the seat. That creepy bloke from the hotel had made her nervous, and it was taking her a while to settle. It was just her luck that some random had singled her out for a pickup and then trashed her car because he'd known where she was staying.

What bad luck that he'd seen her in the motel carpark before she'd gone to the pub to meet Ryan last night.

'Why is the scrub burning?' Dee opened her eyes as the smell of smoke increased.

'Early season burn off,' he said. 'Put your window up for a while if it's bothering you.'

'No, it's okay. I just wondered why no one seems to be worried about the fire spreading.'

'They're controlled burns. Up here we have a monsoonal climate, which means it rains pretty solidly for about half the year and is very dry for the other half. This time of year—the beginning of the dry—you'll see early dry season fires in the savannah. The fires are cooler than a wildfire and they reduce the fuel load. We also use fire on the station to improve cattle production. It alters the pasture and improves feed quality.' He glanced across at her. 'Sorry, I'm on my soapbox. Fire is a natural resource that we control and use. It's a big part of how we work up here.'

'No, I'm interested. It's very different to what we're used to. Hazard reduction control is a controversial issue in the east, but after the dreadful fires of 2019, I think governments are finally taking a more sensible approach. With climate change, I think we need to rethink a lot of our accepted practices.'

'Yep, we've had two record-breaking dry seasons back to back up here. Climate change is not something we can ignore.'

Dee nodded, and turned to look out at the burning grassland. The more she had to do with Ryan Carey, the more she liked him.

And was beginning to respect him.

The highway was busy, and the smell of the fires and the constant noise of cars and trucks passing them kept her attention on the road. After half an hour had passed, Ryan indicated to turn left, and they left the highway that she had travelled up on only two days ago.

'This is the Arnhem Highway,' he said. 'We turn off to *Wilderness* in about fifty ks but if you keep following this road, it takes you to Jabiru and Kakadu National Park. You should try and see Kakadu while you're here. It's one of the most beautiful places you'll ever see.'

'It's on my bucket list.' Dee sat up straight as they passed a road stall with mangoes for sale. A few minutes later, they passed another stall, and then around the next bend there was a farm with rows of mango trees as far as she could see. 'Are they mango farms?'

'They are. There's dozens along this highway; this is the main region for mango farming in the Territory.'

Dee peered at the gate of each farm as they drove past but realised that the chances of a farm having the same name almost thirty years after her parents had owned it were probably non-existent.

Finally she looked over at Ryan. 'I called my . . . I called home this morning. Early. Catherine told me that we lived up here on a mango farm when I was little. She said it was called Peters' Mango Farm. I wondered if it was along this highway. If it was, it wouldn't have been that far from your station, would it?'

'No, not far at all. Wow, that gives us a starting point, doesn't it? We can do some asking around. There's a small store at Marrakai in the middle of the farms, plus a tourist farm that's been there for years. Some of the growers have lived here all their lives.' His rugged face split in a grin. 'That's an excellent lead. Did she say anything else?'

'Not a lot, just one more thing. She said her bridesmaid's name was Bridget.'

'Well, that's a couple of things we can chase up. More than we had yesterday. Look, we can kill two birds with the one stone this afternoon. The helicopter pilot who's going to muster for me lives on the highway, and I was going to call her to tell her she's got the contract. If you're okay with it, we could call in and ask if Ellie knows anything about a Peters' farm. She grew up out here on a mango farm herself, and she and her husband have taken it over. If she doesn't remember—and I'd say she's probably too young—her mother might know something. She comes out here to babysit.'

'That would be awesome.' Suddenly, the thought of the damage to her car didn't seem so important. Maybe they'd get this solved much quicker than they'd anticipated. 'Thank you.'

'Hey, no need to thank me, finding out the truth is just as important to me. To be honest, I didn't get a lot of sleep last night. I was thinking about what you said about how we often don't know people as well as we think we do. I think sometimes we see what we want to see. I was thinking back to when I was a kid, and I remembered that my dad had his own room with a single bed. He used to sleep in there sometimes. I guess that's not really normal for a marriage, is it?'

Dee shook her head. 'I'm not a good one to ask about that. I don't think my parents—I mean my adoptive or foster parents—whatever they are, have what you'd call a normal marriage. Gerard is very selfish, and Catherine is—well, I guess the best word is—neurotic. There wasn't a lot of love in the house when I was growing up. Gerard moved into his own room years ago. He said it was so she could have a good night's sleep. I didn't grow up with "normal". He wasn't kind to Catherine.'

Dee was aware that her upbringing had impacted on the adult she had grown up to be. That's why she had trouble forming relationships and found it easier to immerse herself in her work and stay aloof. She knew Catherine had seen a psychologist, but she'd never felt the need. She could be strong without spilling her fears to a stranger.

But strangely, she was not being at all aloof with Ryan.

'So I'm most certainly not from what you'd call a normal family.' She turned her head and looked at Ryan wondering whether to tell him what she was thinking. 'I—'

She turned her head and looked at the green trees flashing by. Paddock after paddock filled with mango trees.

'You what?' he asked quietly.

She looked ahead as she answered. 'I've never been very good at relating to people. My age or older people. You're easy to talk to, and I feel comfortable with you. That's why I sense a connection between us.'

'The sooner we get this DNA test done and away, the better.' He turned his attention away from the road for a brief moment. 'I feel the same way, Dee. And that's unusual for me too. I'm a bit of a loner.'

She smiled and looked through the window again. The farms weren't that different to the nut plantations in the hinterland at home. Fancy houses set out the front of lush trees. You never knew what was inside a home by the exterior. To the world, the Peters of *Hilltop Nuts* had it all. Gerard, a successful businessman, Catherine, a good homemaker with lot of friends who she lunched with regularly, plus a loving daughter who managed the plantation. The award-winning plantation, she thought bitterly.

That's what the world had seen, whereas the reality was very different. And now Ryan was starting to see that about his family.

'So you're thinking there might have been trouble in your parents' marriage.'

'I feel disloyal thinking it.' He shrugged and his fingers beat a tattoo on the wheel. 'Maybe I will do some digging with my uncle. He might know; I just don't know whether he'd say anything, even if he knew. He was very close to my mother—his big sister. Mum's mother died when she was fourteen and she raised my Uncle Joe; he was a lot younger than she was.'

'Maybe leave it a while until we send the DNA back and get the results. There's no point creating trouble unnecessarily, is there?'

'You're right.' He smiled again. 'You've got a wise head on those shoulders, Dee Peters.'

She shook her head. 'It's called survival. I'm a master at it.'

And I didn't even know that's what I've been doing all those years, she thought.

Chapter 15
McLaren Mango Farm.
Saturday 1.00 p.m.

As they approached the entrance to the McLaren Mango Farm, Ryan slowed the Land Cruiser. Kane was in the front paddock moving the irrigation hoses and he waved to them as Ryan stopped the ute beside the fence.

'I'll be up in five, mate,' he called. 'Ellie's at the house.'

Ryan looked around appreciatively as they continued up the drive towards the house. The trees in the front paddock were strong and healthy, and long green grass carpeted the ground beneath them. He knew Kane had come to farming from the army, and had had little agricultural experience, but the place was a credit to them. Ellie had grown up on the farm, but it had been let go for several years, and coincidentally bought by Kane's stepfather. Panos Sordina had also been murdered, organised by the crooked industrialist who had been responsible for Ellie's father's death.

'Great looking place,' Dee said. 'So lush compared to what we've just come through from Darwin. It reminds me of northern New South Wales.'

'Kane and Ellie took it over about three or four years ago.' Ryan didn't see the need to go into the details of the murders. 'I think they've had their first harvest from the trees in the front paddock this season.'

'The trees look healthy.' Dee looked at the plantation as they drove up towards the house. When she turned to the front as they crested a small hill, she drew in a breath. 'Oh, what a beautiful house.'

Ryan's spirits sank. She certainly wouldn't say that as they drove into *Wilderness Station*, but he nodded. 'It is. They've done a great job. You should have seen it a few years ago; it was almost falling down.' He looked at the high Australiana homestead surrounded by verandas. Since he'd last been here, the house had been painted and the roof replaced.

One day he'd do the same for the homestead on *Wilderness*. Not paint or replace the roof, but make it look like it had in its prime.

Like a home.

As he parked the ute in the circular driveway in front of the house, Ellie walked onto the front veranda. Ryan jumped down from the ute and went around to open Dee's door. Holding out a hand, he helped her climb down.

'Thank you,' she said as he closed the door for her. 'I didn't realise how high up the Cruiser was.'

'Gets me through the creeks in the wet season,' he said.

'Maybe just as well I didn't bring mine.'

'Hey, Ryan, this is a nice surprise.' Ellie came down the steps and met them at the driveway. 'What are you doing here?'

'Hi, Ellie. I was heading back to the station, and I thought I'd save myself a phone call.'

She tipped her head to the side and held his gaze. 'A phone call?'

'Yep. I want to offer you the contract for the muster next week if you're still interested.'

'Woo hoo.' Her grin was wide, and she put up her hand for a high five. 'I sure am.'

'Great, I'll talk to you about the muster later, but first, Ellie, meet Dee. She's coming out to the station to help me get the bookwork in order and take over a bit of the office stuff while the muster is on.'

Ellie held out her hand to Dee. 'Welcome to the district, Dee. Where are you from?'

Dee took her hand and smiled; Ryan was pleased to see her relax. 'Darwin today, but I've not been there very long. I'm really pleased I've picked up a job so quickly. I used to live in the Territory a long time ago. When I was a child.'

Ryan shot a glance at Dee. 'Dee's family used to have a mango farm, but she was too young when they moved away to remember where it was.'

'Most of them are along the highway here, except for the ones down at Daly River.' Ellie nodded. 'We saw a lot of families come and go when we were kids. What's your last name?'

'Peters. My parents are Gerard and Catherine Peters.'

'How long ago?'

Dee chuckled and Ryan knew her well enough already to know it was forced. 'Um, would you believe almost thirty years ago? We moved to the east coast. I'd love to see the old farm where I was born.'

'You don't know where it was?' Ellie looked at her curiously. 'Have your parents passed away?'

'Ah, no,' Dee said. 'Long story.'

'It's too far back for me, but I'll ask Mum,' Ellie said. 'She'll know for sure. She'll be here tomorrow. I'm helping Kane fertilise the back blocks, and she's going to look after James.' She gestured to the house. 'James is our little boy. He's having a much needed sleep now.'

They turned at the sound of a motorbike and Kane appeared over the crest of the small rise at the top of the driveway. Climbing off the ag bike he held out his hand to Ryan. 'Hey, mate, I don't know whether to shake your hand or not.'

Ryan grinned at him. 'Because I've hired your wife for the muster?'

'That's why you're here, isn't it?' Kane's smile was wide. 'You're taking her on, are you?'

'I've offered her a job, and I guess by her reaction, she's on board. Kane, this is Dee Peters. She's working on the station for a while too. We're on our way back from Darwin.'

'Hi Dee. Welcome.'

'Thank you.' Dee spread her arms and gestured to the front paddock. 'You have a beautiful property and house.'

'Thank you. Our hard work has paid off, hasn't it, Ellie? It sure didn't look like this when we took over.' Kane slung an arm around his wife's shoulder and dropped a kiss on her cheek. 'Well done, babe. You'll be back in your sky.'

'I will. And you're the one who's worked hard, not me,' Ellie said leaning into her husband. 'I was pregnant and since then, babysitting. I haven't helped much.' Her grin widened. 'But now, I'm working I can help out. With a pay packet anyway.'

'We'll probably start on Wednesday,' Ryan said. 'I'll give you a call on Monday and let you know for sure, when I've got the chopper sorted. Can you pick it up at Jabiru for me and fly over?'

'I can.' Ellie's grin was wide, and her eyes were shining.

'Anyway, we'd better head off,' Ryan said. 'I've got a fair bit of work lined up for this afternoon once I get Dee settled in.'

'Good to meet you, Dee. What sort of work do you do? Jillaroo?' Kane asked, and Ryan smothered a grin when Ellie looked at Dee's long red nails.

'Oh, God, no. I'll be working in the office.'

'I'll look forward to catching up with you some more when I come over to *Wilderness*.' Ellie walked beside Dee as they headed over to Ryan's ute, and Ryan could hear their conversation. He knew Ellie would be friendly, and hoped Dee would relax knowing she'd be spending some time over on the station while she settled in

'That'll be good,' Dee said. 'I don't know anyone in the Territory other than Ryan yet. If you get a chance to ask your Mum if she knew my parents, that'd be great. And also, one of my Mum's friends was a Bridget. Did you know any Bridgets around here when you were growing up?'

Ellie frowned. 'There was a Bridget who made our school uniforms when we were in primary school. She was a cook on one of the stations, but she worked as a dressmaker too. I remember her because she used to come here to measure us, and she drove an old red VW that belched out black smoke. She moved away before we went to high school and we were ecstatic because Mum bought our uniforms in town after that.' Ellie giggled. 'I hope she was a better cook than she was a dressmaker.'

'Sounds like a bit of a character,' Dee said.

'Actually she was,' Ellie said with a grin. 'I have her name wrong. It was Birgit, not Bridget. I remember because she always used to laugh and say in her German accent, Birgit, not Bridget!'

As they drove out back out onto the highway, Dee's smile faded and her hands clenched in her lap.

'You okay?' Ryan asked.

'I am.' She nodded slowly. 'Sort of. It just hit me what I'm doing. I've left everything I know, and I have no idea what's ahead for me. If I find out who my real parents are, who knows what that's going to be like? If I don't find out, what do I do? I don't know a soul up here.'

Ryan reached over and squeezed her hand. 'You know me. And now you've met Ellie and Kane. They're good people.'

'That's true, but how much has me being here stuffed up your life? Losing your inheritance. It's such a balls-up, isn't it?'

'Maybe losing it. We don't know what's ahead, Dee. Let's keep positive.'

'You're a good man, Ryan Carey. You have every reason not to be nice to me.'

Ryan chuckled. 'My mum taught me good manners. And who knows? I may have gained a sister.' He glanced across at her and smiled as she looked back at him. 'And if not, I'm pretty sure I've gained a friend.'

Chapter 16
Wilderness Station
1978

Suzanne Carey smiled up at her husband of two weeks and three days as he opened the door of the Land Cruiser station wagon. She smoothed her hands down the legs of her new work trousers as Colin held out his hand and waited. His voice had been animated as he'd described Hidden Valley to her on the long drive out from the homestead, and she was looking forward to seeing this valley that was special to him.

It was a long way from the Lockyer Valley, not far west of Brisbane, to this remote valley in the Northern Territory wilderness. They had arrived at Wilderness Station three days ago and Colin had taken pride in showing Suzanne around the beautiful old homestead, and then driving her around to see to rest of the buildings that made up this sprawling cattle station. As he told her of the early settlement and history of his family, fascination gripped her, and Suzanne was proud and excited to know she was a part of the future of the Carey family.

She reached out and took Colin's hand—my *husband*, she thought with a smile—and stepped out of the car and he put his arms around her and kissed her thoroughly.

'Happy?' he asked when he finally lifted his head.

'Very.' Suzanne looked around and breathed in the fresh clean air, air that was free of the red dust of the station she was already becoming used to. 'Oh Colin. It's beautiful. Not at all what I was expecting.'

Colourful lilies carpeted the billabong next to the saltpan that glistened in the sunlight. The landscape was full of life and movement and teeming birdlife dotted the billabong. A light wind—Colin had told her it was called the *gunmaiyorrk*— blew from the south and ruffled the water.

'It's why my grandfather called it Hidden Valley. It was where they first settled, and he built a saltworks along the other side of the billabong. When we walk over you can still see the foundations of the old buildings.'

'The history of this place is amazing. I couldn't believe it when you showed me the old school and store yesterday.'

Colin cleared his throat. As much as he showed her affection, Suzanne had already noticed that he kept his responses low key. 'Not a bad place we live on, Suz.'

As they walked around the wide billabong Suzanne pointed to the high cliffs to the north. 'The colour of those cliffs is incredible.'

That did get a reaction from Colin. 'Actually, it's pretty ordinary this time of the year. I'll bring you out in the dry season when it's cold. The indigenous people here call it *Wurrgeng*—and that's when you'll see incredible colours. The whole sky picks up the red of the granite in the sandstone at sunset and turns to a pale orange. Above that you've got the high cliffs and the shining saltpans, and the green grass and trees. It's a pretty special place.'

She looked up at him. 'Your words are beautiful, and I can see why it's special.'

'It's different here in all the seasons. I'll teach you what the indigenous people call them. When we come back in the dry, the water will be off the flood plain and the salt pans dry and hard. We might even camp out here one night, because the morning mists are worth seeing too.'

'I'd love that. You love this place, don't you, darling?'

'This land is my heart and soul. I hope you're happy here, Suz, because I could never leave it.'

'Wherever you are, I'll be with you, and I'll be happy.'

'There'll be a lot of times you'll be at the homestead by yourself when we're out mustering.'

'Joe said he'd come and stay sometimes. He's spent a lot of time up in the Territory, and he's already said when our Dad goes, he doesn't want the farm at home. He prefers it up here. As long as that's okay with you. He would stay in the workers' accommodation and help on the station. I know you didn't get to see much of him at the wedding, but he is a good worker.'

'That's fine by me. I had a drink with Joe the night before the wedding and we hit it off.'

'I'm pleased, and listen, I've got plenty to do here. I'm looking forward to it, Colin. I have a house to turn into a home for us, and when the children come along, I'll have my days full.'

'I'd love to have a tribe of boys.' Colin grinned down at her.

'You only want cheap help on the station.' She tipped her head to the side and nudged him. 'Okay, I'll compromise. How about one daughter for every two sons we have?'

'That sounds like a good plan to me. God knows, we have plenty of spare bedrooms. Come and I'll show you the ruins and then it's time we were heading back. It'll be dark before we get home, and I don't want to hit a roo.'

'I have steak thawing in the fridge for dinner if you're happy with that.'

Colin dropped his arm over her shoulder as they walked around the billabong. 'I'm happy with anything you do, sweetheart. No doubts from you now that you've seen the place?'

Suzanne put her arm around his waist and leaned into the warmth of her tall, strong husband. 'No doubts at all, sweetheart. I'm going to love my life here with you.'

As they approached the four wheel drive, the quiet of the savannah woodlands in the early evening surrounded them, and the sky waited patiently for the smoke of the burning grasslands to fire the Kakadu sunset to molten gold.

Chapter 17
Wilderness Station.
Saturday 3.00 p.m.

As they'd driven to the station Ryan had outlined the accommodation arrangements on the station and suggested that Dee stay in a room in the main house, but she'd insisted she wouldn't feel comfortable doing that.

'You said you're not going tell anyone what's going on, so it makes sense that I'm treated like a worker,' she said when they arrived.

Reluctantly he agreed. 'Fair enough, but you can stay in the single donga closest to the house. There won't be enough room for your cupboard thing, but it can go on the verandah until we know what's happening. Most of the stockmen bunk down in the dorm on the other side of the mess building. You can come up to the house this afternoon and stay for dinner tonight, because I'll still be showing you the accounts.' He'd looked a bit sheepish. 'You may not be so keen to take the finances on, once you see the mess it's in.'

But what Ryan hadn't warned her about was the house. Being a station, she'd expected there would be a lot of land, but the house had been a shock.

'Which is the house?' she'd asked widening her eyes as they approached the buildings that comprised the main area of the station. As they'd driven through seemingly endless paddocks the monotonous red dirt was broken only by scrubby trees and termite mounds.

'Another five hundred metres on,' Ryan said. 'We came in a back gate. This is the working area of the station. In the old days, this is where the store and the schoolhouse were. Now we use those buildings for storage.'

'In the old days? How old is the station?'

Ryan changed back a gear as they crossed a cattle grill. 'My great-grandfather settled here after the First World War. About 1921 I think.'

'It must have been big to have its own store.' Dee couldn't get over the scale of the place. She hadn't imagined anything like this.

'It still is. These days the station is divided into eighty paddocks with an average size of twenty square kilometres. I spend most of my time out in the bush. We've got six permanent steel yards, and one lot of portable yards.'

'Where do you stay when you're out in the bush? It might be a silly question, but do you have more houses out there?'

Ryan chuckled. 'In a swag under the stars. We're lucky here. We've got a lot of natural watering points to camp beside, and that's where the cattle usually are. Springs, creeks, and swamps, although some can dry up before the wet season comes each year.'

Dee shook her head. 'It's a whole new world to me.'

'It's a great life. I couldn't live anywhere else,' Ryan said. 'I even get antsy when I'm in Darwin for more than a couple of days. Give me big open spaces over a city any day.'

'I know what you mean, although where I've lived is nothing like the size of your station.'

He pointed to the right as they passed a set of cattle yards. 'That's the bunkhouse, the mess and on the other side there are four single dongas.'

As they approached the homestead, Dee leaned forward. It was a massive building built with large sand-coloured bricks. The red iron roof rose to a peak high about a single-storey building fronted by a veranda held up by roughhewn posts. Although surrounded by lush green lawn, it was easy to see that where there had once been flower gardens was now neglected. Along the front of the house, the veranda was littered with crates and drums, and pieces of broken furniture.

Ryan parked the ute outside the middle of the verandah, and three small dogs came running through the open front door. He opened his door and climbed out and the small dogs clambered over him as he bent down to them.

Dee jumped down to the dry dusty ground, thankful for her work boots as she walked around to Ryan. The dogs ignored her as they licked his face and vied for his attention.

'Dee, meet Larry, Curly, and Mo.'

As she got closer, she could see that despite their energetic welcome, they were old dogs.

'They were my mother's, and they adopted me when Mum died.'

'Obviously not working dogs,' she said drily.

'No, they're spoodles. Mum loved her dogs. We always had a set of three with related names.' He grinned. 'Dad insisted on naming these three. Her first three spoodles before I was born were apparently named after the three musketeers; with this lot Dad loved his comedy so he chose the three stooges. But they're good boys, aren't you, fellas?' Ryan clapped his hands. 'Now, scoot back inside, you lot.'

Dee raised her eyebrows as they immediately obeyed him and disappeared into the dim interior of the house.

'Come inside, I'll show you the house. Please ignore the mess. Like I said, we've been busy.'

'Do you want me to take my boots off and leave them on the veranda?

'No, it's fine.'

Dee's eyebrows went up again as they walked through the house. It was huge with high ceilings and wide hallways going off in three directions from the main hall they'd entered at the front door. Their boots clicked on the flagstones that continued from the outside veranda through the house. A fine layer of red dust, broken only by little doggy footprints, covered the floor. On each side of the hall, various open boxes and crates of agricultural chemicals sat against the wall.

Ryan must have noticed her looking at them. 'We keep them in here during the wet. Or at least we have for the past couple of years.'

He might be a nice guy, kind and considerate, but the way Ryan didn't look after things surprised her.

His ute was old and grubby, the house was neglected, full of rubbish and in dire need of a good sort out and clean. She compared it to their immaculate house and sheds at *Hilltop Nuts*. She shook her head; there was absolutely no comparison.

'Once the muster's over, I'm going to hire a cleaning firm to come out and get the house back to what it was,' Ryan said as he opened a door at the end of the hall. 'I was thinking before I went up to Darwin that Mum'd be horrified if she could see it now. She was houseproud, and I'm a bit ashamed we've let it get to this state.' He sighed. 'But again, no time.'

Dee nodded. That comment had redeemed him fractionally. At least he was aware of the mess and intended doing something about it.

'We?' she asked.

'Just my uncle and cousin and me.' Ryan stopped in the doorway and gestured for her to step ahead of him. 'Cy and Joe spend a bit of time in the house with me some nights. Watching the footie and cricket.'

'It's obviously been a beautiful home in its day,' Dee commented. The room was dark and when he flicked the light switch on, she could see it was a study and a reading room. A large desk, two office chairs and shelves filled with novels and reference books lined the walls. Underneath the window two small floral sofas faced each other; a coffee table between them was covered with newspapers. Again, a layer of red dust covered everything, and she wondered how the dust got inside.

'It was. Apparently before I was born, the station was the social hub of the district. There used to be a couple of tennis courts out the back, but Mum and Dad put a pool in there.'

'So, pool parties?'

'No, having me must have cramped their style. I don't remember many visitors here when I was a kid even though we weren't that isolated. I went away to high school in Darwin, and when I was home, Dad was always out on the station. Mum looked after the house and sat in here reading. She loved this room.' He gestured to three boxes stacked on top of each other against the wall. 'She spent a lot of time here, especially in her last months before she went to hospital for the last time. She kept all the local newspapers from way back, and *Wilderness Station* was often in the social pages, she said.' His voice thickened. 'The last weeks she was here, she'd draw my attention to people in the photos as if I knew them. I think it made her happy to remember those times.'

Dee's ears pricked at the mention of social pages. It might be worth having a look and seeing if she could see her parents in any of the newspapers. If Catherine had been as social in those days as she was now, there was a good chance she'd be there. 'I'd love to have a look at them, if that's okay.'

'Of course.' His voice was back to normal. 'I hadn't thought of that. We might find something there.'

Ryan scooped up two coffee cups from the back of the desk as Dee stared at the piles of paper. He hadn't exaggerated. She tried not to react as he showed her the various boxes of invoices and accounts on the huge leather-topped desk. Not that you could see much of the desk under the stuff that covered it.

'Hmm. I see what you mean about a mess.'

'I warned you,' he said.

'Where's your computer?'

'It's not working. I keep meaning to take it into Darwin but it's not a priority.'

'Not a priority?' Disbelief began to take hold as Dee began to wonder what she had taken on. 'Who does your

BAS? Do you have an accountant? Are your records backed up anywhere?'

'No, I don't have them backed up. And I do it all, but I'm a fair bit behind. And no, I don't have an accountant. Dad always did it himself, and I will too. I just need to get myself organised and find more time to do it.' His voice was defensive. 'We have a big set up here, and the cattle have to take priority.'

'Get organised to do what exactly?' Dee stared at the desk and the boxes and the loose papers covering the desk.

'Like I said. Get it sorted.'

'Do you mean enter your income and expenditure once the computer is fixed?'

'Jeez, Dee. Yes. Of course that's what I mean.'

She shook her head and Ryan glared at her.

'It's very different running a cattle station to a what did you say? A three hundred acre nut plantation?' he said, his eyes narrowed.

'Perhaps it is, but it doesn't matter what type of business you're running or the scale of it. Good business practice and accounting procedures are essential, or you won't have a business.' She folded her arms and stared him down.

'Not all of us have the luxury of doing a degree with a business subject.' Ryan pushed his hand through his hair and glared back.

Dee bristled. She didn't have to take this from someone she barely knew. It had been one hell of a week and this was the straw that finally broke the camel's back.

'Hey, I'm offering to help you, but I can walk out that door right now if you keep that attitude up.'

Damn the inheritance, and damn Dad and Rodney and whatever they were up to. For a few seconds Dee did consider leaving. Forget about the possibility of an inheritance, forget about the mystery of her parentage and Rodney's strange behaviour. She wanted to run away, a long way from everything. And then she realised, she already had run away and look where it and got her.

'There's no need to be like that.' His voice was tight and held no apology.

'Take me down to my quarters please, and I'll consider my options.'

Chapter 18
Wilderness Station.
Saturday 6.00p.m.

Ryan drove Dee down to the small donga not far from the mess he'd pointed out earlier.

'I'll walk down and get you at dinner time.' He didn't look at her and his voice was cold. 'Dinner's at the house.'

'I'm fine. I'll find my way around,' Dee said.

'Suit yourself. Six-thirty.' He slammed the ute door and revved the engine as he drove away leaving her in a cloud of red dust, her bags beside her.

That put Dee in a worse temper, and she unlocked the door of the small building and shoved it open. Surprisingly, the accommodation was quite clean. A set of white single sheets and a towel were folded neatly on the end of the bed. There was a small bathroom with a concreted shower stall and a separate toilet off to the right, and a small kitchenette with a kettle and toaster along the back wall. Dee unpacked her bag and set up her laptop and hot-spotted it to her phone, but the service was too patchy to get internet or check her email. She made up the bed and lay back, wondering what the hell she was doing here. Her eyes were heavy and she snuggled into the soft pillow.

When she woke a while later, she blinked wondering where she was for a few seconds. It all came crashing back and she felt no better than she had two hours before. Glancing at her watch, she was surprised to see it was just before six.

A quick cool shower and clean clothes put her in a slightly better mood. Ryan had said to go up for dinner, so she would; she was starving because they hadn't had any lunch.

She strode back to the house from the workers' accommodation just before sunset. Her anger still simmered, but the time to think and the brisk walk eased her temper slightly. She'd needed to walk off her angst or have a stiff drink. But she wasn't going to go down that track; Catherine had used alcohol as a crutch and Dee had no intention of following in her footsteps.

She hesitated as she approached the house. There was no sign of Ryan's Land Cruiser. For a moment she considered going back to the donga, but she was hungry, and this was where Ryan said dinner would be. With a frustrated sigh, she realised she hadn't given this enough thought. Moving here to the station, she had given away her independence to some extent. Until she had her ute back anyway.

Looking around she spotted two garden benches with loose cushions at the far end of the veranda; she would sit and wait there until he came back. And consider her options.

If he came back. She'd been icy when he'd dropped her off, taking the key from him and refusing to let him show her around the accommodation.

He'd been equally as cold. For the first time, a reluctant grin tugged at her lips. They were very much alike; it seemed Ryan had a short fuse too. Dee's was quick to ignite, but she usually got over things quickly.

Walking along the lawn to the far end of the house, she looked at the garden and noted the remnants of a formal garden. Weeds grew in cracks between the bricks of a garden set out in a herringbone pattern. A few hardy flowers close to the lawn nodded in the lazy evening breeze; the lawns were obviously kept watered, and those plants fortunate enough to be close to the edge benefitted from it.

Ryan's mother had obviously been a gardener, and it was sad to see how a lifetime's work had been let go. At the same time, she wondered how her macadamias were faring at *Hilltop Nuts*. If they'd been harvested and dehusked and set out to dry as they should have been; the harvest of the first fall and the drying process should be done by now. A pang of regret lodged in her chest, but she ignored it. It didn't matter either way; the plantation was being sold.

To Rodney or whoever.

With a shrug, Dee crossed the lawn and stepped onto the veranda. She hadn't noticed when they'd arrived that it wrapped around both sides of the house, and now she assumed it went across the back. The cushions on the seat were too dusty to sit on, so she picked up each one of them in turn and beat them on the timber rail between the veranda and the garden.

As she turned to sit down a man came out of the house. He frowned and his tone was decidedly unfriendly as he called out to her.

'Who are you? What do you want?' He was short and thickset, and his chest and shoulders were bare beneath a navy blue barbeque apron.

'I'm waiting for Ryan to come back. He told me dinner was at six-thirty.'

'Why would he tell you that? Dinner's on down at the shed at seven-thirty after the boys have a beer.'

'Apparently I'm having dinner here at the house.' Even though she had taken an instant dislike to the guy, Dee assumed he was Ryan's uncle. She stood and held out her hand when he reached her. 'You're Ryan's Uncle Joe?'

'I am. Who wants to know?'

'I'm Dee Peters. I came down from Darwin with him today.'

'Peters?' Dee could have sworn his eyes narrowed and he looked at her closely. He kept staring at her for a while before he took her hand and shook it.

'First I've heard of it.' His tone was surly.

Thanks, Ryan.

'I'm quite happy to eat down with the workers if you tell me which way to go.'

Before he could answer, the rattle of a diesel engine preceded the rattle of the cattle grid, and Ryan drove into the yard.

Dee tensed waiting to see what his mood would be like, but he smiled as he got out of the ute and came on to the veranda. 'You two have met already, I see.'

'We have,' Dee said.

Joe's cranky grunt got a sharp look from Ryan. 'Cy said to tell you he's staying down at the shed for dinner. Did you make pizzas with that salami I brought back? I'm starving.' He grinned at Dee and she relaxed. 'I realised we didn't eat lunch when the guys tried to talk me into a beer.'

'Yes, pizza,' Joe said shortly. 'Did you get the muster sorted?'

'I did.'

'And what about the rest of the legal stuff? I was surprised when you didn't come home last night.' This time Joe's look at Dee was longer and held a hint of speculation.

No, we didn't spend the night together, she was tempted to say, but refrained.

'Not a lot to tell. It's just delayed a bit.'

'Again? That bloody lawyer's useless.'

Ryan shrugged. 'No rush. We have a guest tonight. I've hired Dee to help me get the office stuff up to date.'

Another grunt before his uncle walked back to the door. 'Pizza's on in fifteen minutes.'

Dee bit her tongue. She was tempted to say what a charmer Joe was but couldn't pick Ryan's mood. Maybe he'd been putting on a front for his uncle, but his next words surprised her.

'Sorry,' he said. 'Joe can be a bit rude sometimes. When he gets to know you, he'll be totally different. He's a lot of fun.' Ryan touched her arm. 'And I'm sorry. I can be bloody rude too. I'm really sorry about before, I was out of line. I know you don't have to be here yet, and I appreciate what you're doing while we wait for that test kit to turn up.'

'It's okay, I was just as rude to you. I was thinking before how alike we are.' It was a nice change to have a man apologise.

He looked at her thoughtfully. 'Do you think?'

She nodded. 'Short fuses.'

A frown creased his forehead. 'If you're right that means my dad played up. I don't know how I feel about that.'

'We'll wait and see.'

'I'm going to grab a quick shower. Do you want come in and talk to Joe?'

Dee pulled a face and shook her head. 'Uh uh.'

'Are you happy sitting out here? I'll get you a drink. What would you like?'

'Surprise me. And yes, I'm enjoying the sunset.'

'It'll be a beauty tonight with that smoke lingering.' He disappeared and a couple of minutes later reappeared with a glass of white wine. 'I thought wine was more conducive to watching a sunset than a stubby of beer. I'm showing you I can be civilised.'

Dee chuckled as she took the glass from him. 'Thank you. Did you read my mind when we had words this afternoon?'

'I didn't have to. Your thoughts were clear in your expression. You had me feeling like an abject failure.' He laughed as he headed back to the door. 'I won't be long, and I'll come and have a drink with you.'

Chapter 19

Saturday 6.30pm.

For a while Joe thought the call wasn't going to pick up. It rang out the first time and he threw the mobile down in disgust. Taking a deep breath, he picked it up and tried again. This time it picked up on the second ring.

'What the bloody hell are you playing at?' he demanded.

'What?' The voice was cold.

'Why is she here? Did you send her to check up on me?'

'I have no idea what you're fucking talking about. Who's where?'

'Your daughter's here. She obviously knows what's going on. We can't risk it. You can't let things get screwed up now. We've waited so bloody long for this. Why the hell has she turned up here when we're about to start? It's all in place. Unless you've sent her to check up on me?' Joe's voice was hostile now, and he was having trouble staying calm enough to get his message across.

'Don't be stupid. Are you sure it's her?'

'No doubt at all. Her name's Deanne and she looks just like her mother. Could be a bloody clone.'

The sigh was long, and he waited for instruction, and for a moment he thought the call had dropped out.

'She's already seen Baker.' The reply finally came as he was about to hang up and call again.

'So did Ryan and there's some hold up with the will.'

'Good, looks like Baker's done as he was told. I don't trust the weasel.'

'All right. As long as you know what's happening and you're calling the shots.'

'Don't you worry about that. What's she doing up here anyway?'

'That fool lawyer sent her a letter.'

'Fucking Colin. He's still causing shit from the other side of the grave.'

'Look. I'll sort it this end. I've got some things happening here. Just keep an eye on her, and if you think you need to do something, do it. And remember if it comes to a situation where you have to do something, she's not my daughter.'

'Do something? Would you like to be more specific?'

'Don't be a dumb arse. You know what I mean. You've done it before, and remember I know that, if you get any ideas about double crossing me.'

'You trust me to make that call if I think it's needed?'

'Yes. If she goes anywhere near the valley, or if it looks like she knows what's going on, deal with it. It would get rid of one of our problems.'

'It's getting a bit complicated up here.'

'Yeah, I don't trust Baker, he hasn't got the balls his brother had. I don't trust him. Fuck Reg for dying. I've got someone else watching them too, but the first sign that anyone talks about it or goes out there, you call me. Right?

'Right. And don't worry, I can deal with her. If you can cope with it, just give me the word.'

'Are you doubting my commitment?'

'Ah, no. No, I'm not.'
'Just watch her closely and wait for my call.'

Chapter 20
Wilderness Station.
Saturday 7.00pm

Ryan stood beneath the shower and let the warm water run over his face. His thoughts scared him; and he wondered if he would be better off taking a cold shower. He'd seen the look on Joe's face; his uncle had immediately assumed that there was something going on between him and Dee. He was caught; he didn't want to tell Joe what had happened at the lawyers. If it hadn't involved Dee, he would have been up front with him, but until they sorted out this bloody split inheritance—and the reason for it—as well as the rest of the conditions that Baker had to give the details of, he was going to be vague. As far as anyone knew, Dee was here to work in the office.

If Joe wanted to think Ryan was interested in her, so be it.

The problem was he *was* attracted to her, and it scared the living daylights out of him.

The more he thought about it, the only logical explanation was that Dad was Dee's father, and if that was the case, his father hadn't been the man Ryan thought he was. And worse, that would make Dee his half-sister.

He was going to have to keep his thoughts to himself, and keep his distance until the DNA test kit arrived. He was just grateful it was going to be a fast process.

When he got out of the shower, he decided he needed a quick shave, and then cursed himself for doing it. If Dee hadn't been there for dinner, he wouldn't have bothered. Her presence was a wake-up call. There was a lot of things around the house that he usually couldn't be arsed doing, and he'd let far too much go lately.

From next week, after the first muster, he'd clean out a room every week. It was time to get the homestead back to the way it should be. When he'd done that, he'd get a professional company to come down and spruce the place up.

It needed it. It had nothing to do with Dee being there, he told himself.

He headed out to the veranda with the bottle of wine to top up Dee's glass, and a beer for himself. The sun hovered above the flat western horizon as he joined her on the garden seat and Ryan took pleasure in her enjoyment as she stared wide-eyed at the sky.

'That's incredible, look at it.' Dee nudged him as he was about to lift the beer to his mouth. 'Look at those colours!'

He took a swig and grinned at her. 'It's the smoke that does it. If you hang around here long enough, you'll see hundreds of them. After the muster is over, I'll take you on a tour of the station, and we'll go out to Hidden Valley one afternoon. Even *I* think it's a spectacular sunset out there.'

'And here I was starting to worry you had no soul,' she said with a chuckle. 'Where's Hidden Valley?'

'It's right on the eastern border of the station, almost joins Kakadu National Park. Millions of years ago, there was a series of lakes out there, but now they never fill up, even in the wet. It's got something to do with the clay-floor basin.

Back in the nineteen twenties when my great-grandfather first settled here, he built a saltworks out there, and supplied salt for the curing of buffalo and crocodile hides. That's how he made his fortune and established the station. He used the money to build the house, the store and the schoolhouse, and stock the station with cattle. The saltworks was abandoned a long time ago.'

'So what's so spectacular about out there?'

'The colour of the dark sandstone cliffs that overlook the wetlands. If you're there at sunset at the right time of the year, the colours are incredible. The whole sky reflects the red of the granite in the sandstone and turns to a soft apricot. Above that you've got the high cliffs back lit by the sun, and as far as you can see is the glistening silver of the salt pans, surrounded by the soft green of the grasslands. It's a pretty special place.'

'Do you run cattle out there?'

'No, we rarely go out there. It's about eighty kilometres from the house. It was one of Mum's favourite places. She wanted to go back out there before she passed away, but she wasn't well enough for us to take her. It's a rough trip in a vehicle, but not a bad ride if you've got a few days to spare. I should ask. Do you ride?'

She nodded.

'Excellent. I promised myself I'd go out and say goodbye for her, and you know what? I never have. I'd say it's almost three years since I was last out there. I can't believe I left it for so long. I've let Mum down in a few ways since she died.'

'Don't feel like that. I'm sure you've done the best you could. Look at what you're looking after. I'm still getting my head around the size of this station.' Dee shook her head. 'Once all this is over, and before I leave, you can take me out there to say goodbye for her and show me one of those spectacular sunsets.'

Ryan lifted his beer bottle and clinked it against her glass. 'I'll hold you to that.'

'And I'll make sure you do.'

He settled back in the chair. 'Now tell me all about your plantation.'

***

As much as Dee had worried about having dinner at the house, it turned out to be a reasonable evening. Joe seemed to have got over his surliness. He kept up a constant stream of anecdotes about the station, and some of the characters who had worked there over the years. When the pizza was finished, he stood and excused himself.

'Cy's helping out in the mess tonight. He's happy to lend a hand anywhere. All he had to do was put the pizzas in the oven. I'm just going to go down and see if he managed that. Nice to meet you, Dee. If there's anything you need, give me a holler.'

'Thank you.'

When he left, Ryan seemed preoccupied again. Dee had to ask him the same question twice.

'Sorry. I was thinking about the muster next week,' he said apologetically when she repeated herself.

'Are you sure you want to show me the accounts tonight?' she asked.

'Yeah, sure. If you're still happy to.'

'I'd like to.' Dee justified to herself that she wanted to get it finished, but if she was honest, it was more to do with wanting to be in his company.

'Okay, let's go now. The sooner we start, the sooner it's done.'

And the sooner I'll be gone. Dee read between the lines.

She followed Ryan to the study, and he stood back to let her enter first when he opened the door. It was hard to deal with his moodiness; he'd been so friendly and warm when they'd sat together and watched the sunset.

'You sit in the big chair,' he said wheeling over the smaller desk chair. Before he sat beside her, he reached for an old-fashioned ledger.

'The current financial year's records that need to be written up are in here. The box at the back of the desk are ones I've entered. Once I've done them, I stamp the invoice or receipt with the station stamp.' Ryan reached in and pulled out an invoice. 'See. It's got the station name and address on it. It's an easy way to see what's been done at a glance.' He leaned over to show her, and she got a whiff of a fresh soap smell. Her physical reaction was over the top, and as Dee moved away, her tone was probably harder than it should have been.

'You don't have an "entered" stamp?'

He lifted his head and held her eyes. 'No. I'm a cattleman, not an accountant. My system has always worked for me.'

She shrugged and gestured to the ledger. 'You said that you did have a computer. Does that mean that you have entered it electronically at some point?'

'Dad did, and I did for a while, but as I said the computer needs fixing or replacing.'

'Okay,' she said slowly, trying not to ruffle him. 'Do you know what software program you used?'

'Just a spreadsheet.'

'Look, I'm going to be here for a while. Until that DNA test kit arrives and we send it off and wait. How do you feel about me entering what you've already added to the ledger, and the rest of these, to a program I use on my laptop? I can start you an account on the cloud, and then when your computer is fixed—or you get a new one—it's only a matter of logging in and adding to it.'

'If you don't mind, that'd be great. I'd really appreciate it.'

'The program I use calculates the GST and does the BAS for you. It's only a matter of emailing it in when it's due.'

'Sounds like heaven to me. I'll put you on the payroll from today.'

Dee shook her head. 'Do you think that's necessary? Doing this will fill in my time while we sort out the bigger issue. The inheritance.'

'Yep. I want everything to be above board.' Ryan reached across the desk and pulled out a smaller box. 'These are expenses that didn't have a column in the ledger book. New stuff that has come up since Dad set it up, and I haven't done a column for these.'

'Will you trust me to set it up?'

Their eyes met and held.

'Yes, I will.' After a pause, Ryan cleared his throat. 'Did you want to have a look at some of those old newspapers tonight? I can show you where they are, and we—or you—could make a start.'

'Oh yes, please. Anything to get out of this feeling of being stuck in limbo.'

He got up and walked across to the back of the large room where he'd pointed out the three boxes earlier. With a frown, he cleared off the coffee table that was between the two sofa chairs and then lifted the top box off the pile. 'There should be a pair of scissors in the top drawer. Can you pass them over, please?'

'Do you want a coffee before I call it a night?' Joe appeared in the doorway and looked curiously as Ryan stood there holding the box of newspapers. 'I hope he's paying you well, Dee. Ryan's not known for his recordkeeping.' His eyes stayed on the box Ryan was holding.

'Of course,' Dee replied. 'He knows the going rate. And no, to the offer of coffee, thanks. I'll be going to bed shortly too.'

'Me either.' Ryan put the box down and came back across to the desk. 'Do you have any more accounts in the kitchen, Joe? We might as well get them all entered while Dee is here. I thought you'd gone for the night.'

'I forgot to put the dishwasher on. So you're not staying long, Dee?' he asked turning to Dee.

'As long as it takes,' she said holding his gaze. 'I've got other jobs lined up after I finish out here. But no pressure.'

'A good way to see the country, I guess. A mobile bookkeeper.'

'It is.' Dee waited until he'd left the room, and the sound of his footsteps faded down the hall.

Chapter 21

Wilderness Station.
Saturday 10.30 p.m.

Dee leaned forward and tapped her fingers on the side of the coffee table as frustration took hold. It was getting late and her patience was wearing thin. 'I think I was too hopeful.'

They'd been through about a third of the newspapers in the first box, and it had been a slow process because various items of news—unrelated to what they were looking for—caught Ryan's attention. She'd managed to hold her impatience in.

He scratched the back of his neck. 'Don't give up hope. We've hardly looked at any yet.'

'It's a shame they don't seem to be in any order.' The local community newspapers had not only jumped from month to month, they'd covered a period spanning twenty years from the early eighties to 2001 when the newspaper had stopped production. 'How long were your parents married before you were born?'

'Um. I'm not sure exactly. About ten years, I think.'

'That makes sense. The earliest one we've seen was 1982. Your mum must have been the one who kept them.'

'She was. The only thing I remember Dad reading was *The Land*. Although look at this, the price that a breeder was getting in 1985 wasn't that much less than today's prices. Maybe he did read this paper too, and Mum kept them.'

Dee tilted her head back and looked at the ceiling. A huge crack ran from the dusty light fitting over to one corner.

'Sorry. Are you getting impatient with me?' Ryan folded the newspaper and put it on the floor on top of the small pile of papers they'd already looked through. It had been his idea to go through each one from the front page to the back. 'You never know,' he'd said. 'They might have been in the paper for something else, so it's silly just to look at the social pages. Maybe when they bought the mango farm or something.' Dee went through each paper first looking for Catherine and Gerard, and then Ryan would look at it, looking for his parents. The problem was he kept getting sidetracked, and it was doing Dee's head in. Cattle prices, unseasonal rainfall, and even the results of a footy game twenty-five years ago had him commenting.

'The honest answer? A bit.' Dee stood and stretched. 'I'm sorry, I'm not known for my patience.'

'Okay, I'll pick up the pace. Yell out when you've had enough. We don't have to read them all tonight.' Ryan passed her the next paper from the box. This one's April 1987. How about we call it a night when we're done with it?'

'When you looked at them with your mother, can you remember if there were photos of your parents as well as the friends she pointed out?' Dee reached out and took the paper and leaned back in the chair.

'I'm pretty sure there was.' His brow wrinkled in a frown. 'Yes, there must have been because I remember noticing how dark Mum's hair was and how Dad had a good head of hair back then. Mum went grey when I was at high school, and Dad was almost bald when he died. I didn't recognise him until Mum pointed him out.'

'Well, let's keep at it for a while longer, because those photos are in here somewhere.'

All was quiet as they both scanned the papers they were holding.

Dee's eyes narrowed as she read the results of the Marrakai Tennis Club Easter competition in 1987. She put the paper on the table and ran her finger down the report.

'What is it?' Ryan lifted his head and looked at the paper she was reading more closely.

'It mightn't be anything, but a couple of names jumped out at me. It's the list of the winners and runners-up for the ladies' doubles in the Easter tennis comp at Marrakai. The runners-up were Catherine and Bridget Sloane.' Dee tapped her finger on her lip. 'I asked Catherine if she had a friend called Suzanne and she said no, Bridget was her bridesmaid. Maybe the Bridget she mentioned was her sister, not a friend.'

'Do you know what Catherine's last name was before she was married?

'It was Sloane.' Dee widened her eyes and spoke softly. 'Catherine Sloane.'

'A coincidence?'

'I doubt it.'

Ryan got up and stood behind Dee's chair, reading over her shoulder. 'Hey, I think you're on the right track. Look at the winners of the men's doubles at the bottom.'

Dee looked to the bottom of the page and read the caption.

'Colin Carey and Peter Porter. That's your father! So if it is the same Catherine and Bridget, they did know each other before we were born.'

'And Peter Porter too.'

'Who's that?' She looked up at him with a frown.

'Ellie's dad. She was a Porter. Her father died when she and Dru were still at school. It was a pretty traumatic time for the family. He was murdered on their farm a few years ago.' He looked thoughtful. 'I remember how upset Mum and Dad were, because at first it was thought he'd committed suicide.'

'Oh, no. That's dreadful. Is Drew her brother?'

'No, Dru. With a U. A sister. There are three Porter girls. Emma was in my year at primary school. She's a doctor now.'

'Ellie said they had that dressmaker. And she worked as a cook on one of the stations.?'

Ryan looked thoughtful. 'I wonder if it was *Wilderness*. There's no other big stations close enough that have enough workers to need a cook. It's only us from here to Kakadu to the east and the Stuart Highway on the west. The rest are small holdings: mango and vegie farms and the like. If Ellie remembers her, I should too, if she was a cook on our station. But she said it wasn't Bridget, didn't she? So I'd say it was a different person.' He screwed up his face and tapped his fingers on the table until he finally shook his head. 'Anyway, I don't ever remember having a female cook here, and I used to go down there with Dad. There was always warm biscuits and cake in the ovens for the ringers and stockmen to take out to the camps. They were all blokes who cooked in the mess. I'm sure I'd remember if there had been a woman.'

Dee jumped up and crossed to the desk. 'We need to start taking notes. To try and link what we're finding.' She spotted an unopened ream of paper on the edge of the desk. 'Can I open this and use some?'

'Of course. This is your office now.'

She frowned and hunted around the desk. 'Where would I find a pen?'

'Hmm. That's a good question. Maybe in the third drawer down.'

It took four attempts before Dee found a pen that worked and started to write up what they'd found.

April, 1987. Mention of Colin Carey, Bridget Sloane, Catherine Sloane. (and Peter Porter)

Bridget. Was she a cook on Wilderness? (Ryan, too early no memory) Maybe Birgit? A dressmaker? A few years later (from Ellie).

'Now we need to be more methodical. I think we should open the other two boxes and sort the papers into date order before we read anymore. Then we can date our notes in sequence.'

Ryan yawned and Dee glanced at her watch.

'Don't you pike on me now. It's only eleven o'clock,' she said.

'Eleven o'clock! That's way past my bedtime.' But his words were accompanied by a grin.

'You go to bed if you need your beauty sleep. I'll work for a while yet. I'm too pumped to sleep.'

'I'll stay up with you. How about a coffee after all? I'll go and make us a cup. Then we get the papers sorted tonight and then go to bed? I've got a big day tomorrow.'

Dee nodded, preoccupied; she'd already started to sort the remainder of the box they'd been working through. 'We should have done this before we started. I didn't realise how mixed up the dates were.'

Ryan stood. 'Milk? Sugar? Black?'

'White with one please.' By the time Dee looked up, he'd gone. She turned her attention back to the box of newspapers and resisted opening them as she lifted them out one by one, but she did glance at the front page as she sorted them into piles by month and year.

'Holy hell.' Taking in a quick breath and holding it with shaking hands she read the front page of the paper dated May 2, 1987.

Aiken's Farm sold for record price, said the by-line of the article on the bottom half of the community paper. Dee didn't care about the farm or the record price; it was the picture of a very young and much slimmer Gerard Peters that caught her attention. She skimmed the article:

Recent research has shown that the northern half of our territory is in a prime geographical location to produce mangoes that harvest well before the harvest of existing main plantations of national mango production in North Queensland, particularly Bowen and the Atherton Tablelands. Gerard Peters, a recent arrival to our district, is enthusiastic about the potential for our small community to produce early crops. Mr Peters said: Leaf water potential studies indicate that mango trees have a degree of drought tolerance, and that the extended dry season in the Northern Territory won't impact on fruit quality. Recent international studies have investigated yield responses in mangoes to irrigation below potential evapotranspiration replacement, and results indicate that the reduced water inputs can still successfully maintain yields.

'Bullshit!' Dee exclaimed as Ryan came in with a tray holding two coffees and a packet of Tim Tams.

'What?' He stared at her.

'Absolute bullshit. I would bet everything I own on it. He wouldn't have had a clue about anything agricultural. He sounds like a bloody CSIRO scientist.'

'He?' Ryan squinted as he balanced the tray. 'He who?'

'I've found Gerard. My father. Or my adopted father. Or whatever father he reckons he is or not.' She drew in a deep shuddering breath knowing she wasn't making sense. Here was the link she needed for a starting point. She was pretty sure it was the right Catherine she'd found, and now Gerard had moved to the same district a year later. There was no mention of Catherine in the article. 'God, this makes me angry. How much easier would it be if they'd simply tell me the truth!'

'And my parents have passed, so unless they tell you, we have to figure this out ourselves.' Ryan said, passing her the coffee mug. 'Why so secretive, do you think?'

'Oh, it'll be something to do with money. I have no doubt of that. He's a schemer of the first order.'

'According to this, Gerard bought a mango farm here in May 1987. I think we need to sort these papers and work forward from here. That was eighteen months before we were born.'

'So he could be your father.'

'He could.'

Dee added Gerard's purchase, the date and the name of the farm to her notes and then she counted off the years on her fingers. 'We were born in July and August 1988, so they would have fallen pregnant around November 1987, six months after he bought the farm.

'Who would?'

'Our mothers, whoever they are.'

His lips formed into a tight line. 'I know who my mother is. It's yours we're looking for.'

Chapter 22

Wilderness Station.
Sunday breakfast.

'I can't believe that wind outside,' Dee said the next morning as Joe joined her in the kitchen of the big house. She'd been heading straight to the study, but Joe had heard her and offered her breakfast.

'The breakfast cereals are in the pantry and there's milk and yoghurt in the fridge.' He'd been friendly and cheery, and she'd relaxed a bit as he'd shown her around the kitchen. 'Just help yourself through the day,' he offered. 'How long did you say you'll be staying here?'

I didn't.

Dee shrugged. 'As long as it takes.' It was the second time he'd wanted to know that.

'And you're working on a Sunday?' he asked curiously.

'Might as well get a start.'

'Fair enough. I'm heading up to Darwin this morning, and I won't be back until late tonight. You're quite welcome to use the kitchen up here for meal, or if you can put up with a mob of noisy ringers and stockmen who'll smell like cattle, my son, Cy, helps out in the mess when I have to go away. Have you met him yet?'

'No, I haven't and thank you. I'll just grab a toasted sandwich or something when I take a break.'

'There won't be many of us around this week. Cy's going out to the muster. He's head stockman. Bloody brilliant on a horse.' Joe was being extra friendly. 'He's been riding since he could walk. Do you ride?'

'Yes.'

'Where did you say you were from?'

She held his gaze. 'All over.'

He nodded and gave her a wave as he walked out.

Dee had almost finished her coffee when Ryan surfaced. He poured a coffee for himself and joined her at the table. 'It's going to be a hot one today. That wind's up already.'

'I thought every day was hot up here,' she replied.

'Yeah, but depending on the season, it's different types of hot. It's better than the build up to the monsoon season,' he replied. 'At least the humidity's dropped by this time of the year. My mum hated it, she used to say it sent her troppo.'

'If it gets worse than this I can understand why.'

He looked at her intently. 'If things pan out the way Baker hinted, you could still be up here for the monsoon season.'

'Whoa, just slow down. I have no idea where I'll be in six months. And I'm sure that's not the way you want things to turn out anyway.'

'Okay, we'll be patient and take things one day at a time.'

Dee frowned as she sipped at her coffee. 'You're very cheery for someone who's had their expectations turned arse over head. Not to mention a very late night.'

'Arse over head?' Ryan chuckled. 'I guess that's one way to put it.'

'Well, you are. I'd be a screaming mess.' She looked past him through the window. 'I *was* a screaming mess when I found out our plantation was being sold.'

'Losing your cool and getting worked up about things doesn't change anything. I was upset for a short while when Baker told me, and I know the shock made me rude to you, but I've had time to process it. We just have to be patient and wait.'

'You'll have to teach me how to be patient.' Dee looked away as a strange feeling shimmied through her. Ryan was such a good person, he could teach me a lot of things, she thought.

'You'll have to teach yourself today.' He grinned at her. 'I'm heading out to the stock camp and I won't be back until sometime tomorrow. Will you be okay here? Joe's going to Darwin, but he'll be back before dark.'

'I'll be fine. I'm a big girl. Granted, I'm out of my comfort zone, but immersing myself in your accounts and the newspapers will stop me getting bored. What will you be doing? I know nothing about how a cattle station works.' Knowing that Ryan was worried about her was an unfamiliar feeling and filled her with warmth.

'You want the long or the short version?' Ryan asked.

'The long. If you have time. I guess I need to know a bit about how the place works. Just in case I'm here for a while.'

'I'll talk to you while I cook some bacon and eggs. Want some?'

'No, thanks. I've already had muesli.'

Ryan crossed to the fridge and took out three eggs and a handful of bacon.

Dee watched as he put the bacon in the cold pan, and then lit the gas. 'You know your way around a kitchen.'

'I do. And a campfire.' He stood at the gas stove and talked to her as the bacon started to sizzle. 'Okay, our main job is to breed and fatten cattle. On a station the size of *Wilderness*, the cattle work is divided up into different areas we call camps. I'm going out to the main stock camp today to get the guys ready for the muster. They're responsible for mustering the cattle into the yards, and then processing them. This means drafting off wet and dry cows, mothering up calves and pulling off the young ones that are old enough to be weaned. Once that's done, they either need to be walked back out to their paddock or taken to the abattoirs. We don't export anymore.'

'Wow, I had no idea it was complicated.' Dee laughed. 'I grew up in the hills where I watched the black and white cows eating grass looking after themselves. I was a country girl but had no idea about cattle.'

'I'm sure the black and white cows of your childhood didn't look after themselves.' Ryan removed the bacon and put it on a plate and the cracked the three eggs into the pan.

'So tell me about the muster. What happens there? And what will Ellie do?'

'Okay, so we've got ten breeder paddocks and they're mustered twice a year. The reason we muster twice is so that our cows can gain weight over the wet season and get back to calf quicker after having their weaner taken off them.'

'Okay, I think I'm following It's logical. And makes financial sense.'

'There's six guys at the camp at the moment—sometimes we have jillaroos too—plus our head stockman, so there'll be seven of us on horseback and one on the motorbike. Plus Ellie up in the helicopter in the air. She's the most important.'

'So what's Ellie's job?'

'She'll head out early and start to grid the paddock.'

'Grid the paddock?'

'She'll start in the furthest sections of the paddock to move the animals she spots towards the paddock where we have the yard trap. The chopper doesn't spook them because being creatures of habit they'll follow the well-worn tracks to the water point they know. When we get out there on horseback, she'll have them on the move. We'll keep the stragglers up, make sure none of them stop or decide to lie down, and keep the mob moving. She'll keep sweeping the paddock to bring more in and join the first mob.'

'Do you ride all the way out there?' The light caught Ryan's eyes, and Dee found it hard to look away.

'No, I'll drive out. The stock horses are kept at the camp.'

'I saw helicopter mustering deer in New Zealand on a documentary once. It looked dangerous.'

'Yep, it is. But at least we're relatively flat out here, A skilled pilot is worth their weight in gold, and they're hard to get. This is the first time we've used Ellie. Hopefully she'll deliver.'

'So what happens when you get them to the trap thing?'

Ryan flipped his eggs onto the plate and came over and sat beside Dee. 'There's a lot more to it. The key is a slow start and when the main mob comes to the paddock where the yard trap is, the helicopters and the bike bring them in and those of us on horseback will hold them and "break in" the weaners. Often they haven't ever seen a horse before so they're pretty nervous until they find their mums.'

He lifted a forkful of eggs and bacon to his mouth and then burst out laughing and put it back on his plate.

'What? What's wrong?'

'You should see the expression on your face. I've never had such a rapt audience.'

'Well, it sounds really interesting. I'd like to come out and see it one day. I guess it's on that list of instructions.'

'Probably.'

'I wonder when he's going to give it to us.'

***

When Ryan finished his breakfast and coffee, he stood and took his plate and mug to the dishwasher. It had been nice sharing the start of the day with Dee. He went to take her mug but she shook her head.

'I'll refill it and take it to the study with me.'

'It was good having company for breakfast,' he said as she topped it up from the kettle. 'Thanks for hanging around.'

'My pleasure. Now I'm an expert on mustering.' Her eyes were bright as she smiled up at him.

Ryan thought how much better she looked than she had in Baker's office. It was hard to believe it was only two days since they'd both been given the news of the inheritance. 'Are you sure you're going to be okay here today?'

'Yes, I have plenty to do. I hope I may even solve our mystery while you're away.'

'Did you hear back from Catherine?'

'No, total radio silence. I tried to call her earlier, but the call went straight to voicemail.'

'Why don't you focus on the newspapers today, and not worry about the accounts?'

Dee shook her head. 'I'll make a start setting up the spreadsheet with your categories, and when I've got that done I'll start reading the rest of the newspapers.'

Ryan came to a decision. 'Look, there's some personal files in the filing cabinet. I've never really been into them much. Only to look for a will after Dad passed, but it was held at Baker's.' He shook his head. 'Now I know why. If you finish the newspapers and need anything like dates and things, you might find them in there.'

'No, I wouldn't feel comfortable. I'll wait for you to come back and we can do that together. Between the newspapers, and your accounts, I'll have plenty to do for a few days.'

'Okay. Whatever you feel easiest with.'

Dee led the way out of the kitchen, and she paused in the hall. 'Ryan?'

'Yes?' He stood in the doorway.

'How does the mail come? I mean, when the test kit arrives. Do you have to collect the mail from town somewhere?'

'There's a mailbox out on the main road. Don't worry, it's locked, but Joe and I've both got keys. We check it whenever we come through. The kit won't go astray, but I'd say it won't arrive until at least Wednesday.' His smile was kind. 'Patience, Dee.'

'Yes, sir.' She pulled a face at him. 'Okay. I'll focus on the newspapers.'

'I'll see you late tomorrow. I'll be back for dinner and then I'll head out again on Wednesday really early.'

'I hope it all goes well. Say hello to Ellie from me.'

Ryan froze. For a moment, he'd moved instinctively to lean over and kiss Dee goodbye, and shock jolted through him.

For Christ's sake, what had got into him?

Chapter 23
Wilderness Station.
Saturday September 19, 1987.

The loud thwack of a tennis racket returning the ball was soon followed by a squeal and a cheer.

'That's out!' Colin yelled. 'Our point!'

Suzanne Carey looked across to the court where the mixed doubles match was being played. Surprisingly she'd enjoyed the evening and had spent most of it sitting on the lawn in conversation with Sandra Wardell.

Colin looped his arm around Bridget Sloane's shoulder. 'Winners are grinners,' he called across the net to Gerard Peters and Catherine—they'd been very chummy tonight, she'd noticed. Suzanne relaxed, pleased that they'd won; Colin was never a good loser; he'd been trying to talk her into playing tennis with him for years, but Suzanne hated playing. The four players headed across to the table at the edge of the lawn, walking through the middle of the cricket game the kids were playing.

'Not for me. I've got two left feet.' Suzanne had declined to play when Colin had asked her at the last minute who she'd like to pair up with for the doubles. She knew he was only making a show of being the considerate husband. 'I'm very happy to sit here and chat for the evening.'

Suzanne soon discovered she and Sandra had a lot in common, both having grown up in southeast Queensland, although Sandra was a fair bit younger than she was.

Suzanne and Sandra took a wine from the tray Joe offered. Her brother was looking after the beers and wine for everyone, and he'd put on a white shirt and bow tie to look the part.

Suzanne had watched to see if Bridget had reacted, but she'd been too busy playing tennis to pay Joe any attention. Suzanne beckoned to him. 'Go and sit with Colin and meet Gerard, the new guy,' she encouraged.

'I'll go and get the salads out soon, and start the barbie,' Joe said with a wistful look at the table where Bridget was now sitting.

'No, you won't. I'll sort out the salads and stuff when Colin lights the barbeque and starts to cook. Now go and relax.'

'I'll help too,' Sandra said.

'Thank you. Now tell me what you're doing up here in the NT?' she asked as Joe got a beer and made his way to Colin's table.

'My uncle owns the store down at Marrakai,' Sandra answered. 'My aunt is pregnant with twins, and I was between jobs, so I've come up to help for a year or so.'

'And you've made some friends already by the look of things.'

Sandra looked across to the other table where Peter Porter was had joined the tennis players. 'Yes, Peter drives the delivery truck for the store. He asked Colin to invite me and he drove me here.'

'Peter's a nice guy,' Suzanne replied. 'He often comes out here with deliveries, and he's helped out on the station too. He's a hard worker.'

'And a good looker,' Sandra said with a smile. 'Who knows, I might end up staying in the Territory.'

'Have a year here first and make sure you can cope with the monsoon season. It does my head in.'

'I will be, but it looks like my driver's interest lies elsewhere.'

Suzanne followed Sandra's gaze and raised her eyebrows. She'd never felt comfortable with the Sloane sisters.

Catherine was sitting on Peter's lap, and Bridget was cosying up to Colin. Joe and Gerard were in a conversation, and Suzanne pushed away the frustration that threatened to rise. She couldn't help Joe without it being too obvious, besides she really didn't want to because she didn't like Bridget anyway.

Yet another social occasion where the Sloane sisters made sure they were the centre of attention. And Colin had the hide to say *she'd* been rude to them.

With a smile, she turned her attention back to Sandra. 'Would you like to come and have a look at the house before we go to the kitchen? It was built in the 1920s and it's a beautiful old building. I'm gradually refurbishing all the rooms, new curtains, and new spreads and the like.'

'Oh, I'd love to. I noticed the macramé hangers on the veranda as we came in. Did you make them?'

'I did. It's a new hobby I've taught myself.'

'Would you teach me?' Sandra asked.

'I'd love to. Now come and I'll show you my rose garden on the way in. They've just started to bud.' Suzanne linked her arm though Sandra's and as they walked across the lawn, she didn't spare a glance at the table where her husband was sitting.

An hour later, Joe wandered into the kitchen where Sandra and Suzanne were still chatting at the kitchen table.

'What's this, ladies? A cup of tea! You're not old enough for the CWA yet.'

'I beg your pardon, I'm in the CWA,' Sandra retorted. 'And I'm only twenty-five.'

'Sorry, sorry.' Joe held his hands up and smiled at the young woman.

Suzanne looked at them thoughtfully. Now if only she could get Joe interested in Sandra; she'd make a lovely sister-in-law. 'We can have a wine with dinner. Speaking of which, has Colin got the barbie going yet?' She glanced up at the kitchen clock above the door and got a shock at how late it was.

'The kids are getting hungry and starting to ask about sausage sangers, so I came in to get some bags of chips and the bread rolls out of the pantry.' He looked away.

'And the barbeque?'

'I'll fire it up now. I was waiting for Colin to come back.'

Suzanne stood and pushed her chair in. 'Come back? From where?'

'He mentioned that he was looking for a cook down at the stockman's quarters and he took Bridget down to the see the kitchens.'

'Why would he do that?' Suzanne knew her voice was cold, but she didn't care.

Joe shrugged. 'Apparently she's looking for a job.'

'Well, we've made everyone wait long enough. If I'd known he hadn't started cooking yet I would have come out. I lost track of the time in here chatting to Sandra.'

Joe hurried out of the kitchen with the bread rolls and chips.

'Sandra, in the pantry you'll find some boxes of Jatz, and a couple of bottles of gherkins. Can you get them while I chop up some cheese?' Suzanne opened the fridge, mortification making her stomach roil.

'Sure.'

Suzanne tried to hold her temper in as they left the house carrying two large platters of Jatz, and chopped cheese and gherkins. Chaotic noise greeted them as they crossed the lawn. Two of the couples had five children between them and they screamed and whined and yelled. To Suzanne's distress, the older kids were playing some sort of chasing game and running through her raised rose gardens. Someone had turned the soaker hose on, and the ground was sodden, as well as some of the boys' shorts.

She dropped the tray she was carrying onto the barbeque table and hurried across the lawn. 'Get out of those gardens right now,' she yelled.

The kids ran sheepishly back to their mothers. The men had joined Joe at the barbeque, each with a beer in hand. And of course Catherine was there too, looking at her with a supercilious smile.

Those Sloane sisters were trouble; she'd thought Colin had more sense. What did it look like, him being gone with that Bridget for so long? Suzanne took a deep breath and attempted to look composed, but she doubted if she succeeded. They guys around the barbeque looked happy enough, but a couple of the women threw unimpressed glances her way.

'Everyone okay for a wine?' she asked with a fixed smile. 'I'll just pop in and bring out the salads and some more cordial for the kids.'

'Do you need a hand, Suzanne?' Sandra asked with a sympathetic smile.

'If you could top up the wine glasses and dig some cans of soft drink out of the esky for the kids that would be a help. Thanks, love. I really appreciate it.'

As Suzanne walked into the kitchen the smell of frying steak and onions followed her as Joe took charge. She blamed the onion for the tears stinging her eyes. Once inside, she leaned against the fridge and pressed her forehead against the cool metal.

It wasn't fair.

She wasn't the one who wanted to have tennis afternoons and supply dinner and drinks for half the region. She wasn't the one who wanted to impress the locals and brag about how well they were doing.

King of *Wilderness Station*, that's what bloody Colin wanted to be.

And she was the one left looking like a fool because she'd not been there to make sure dinner was on time, because she'd spent an hour talking to the first woman who'd shown her true friendship in ten years.

##

Suzanne lay in bed, her body rigid with tension and her eyes firmly closed when Colin stumbled in and turned the light on.

'You in bed already, love? I thought you were in the kitchen.'

She ignored him.

He came around to her side and the bed dipped as he sat near her pillow. She tried not to react when he belched, and the stale smell of beer drifted over her; beer with an undertone of musk perfume rising from his clothes as he reached out and shook her shoulder. She squeezed her eyes together tightly.

The bed moved and next she heard the thump of his boots one at a time as he took them off and threw them into the corner. The bed moved again as he got up and moved around to his side.

'Shit,' he mumbled. 'I forgot the bloody light.'

The light went out and again she was cocooned in blessed darkness. The bed dipped on the other side and within minutes Colin was snoring.

He didn't even have a shower to wash that woman off him.

Scalding hot tears slipped from Suzanne's eyes and trickled down her cheeks. She wondered if she was the only one who'd noticed the red dust on the back of Bridget's tennis shirt where she'd obviously been lying on the ground.

The worst part had been the satisfied glitter in her eyes as she'd smiled at Suzanne across the table.

Chapter 24
Wilderness Station.
March, 2020.

Dee booted up her laptop and opened the tax spreadsheet she kept for *Hilltop Nuts*. For a moment, her thoughts turned inward, and disappointment crept in as she scanned the figures that she had entered religiously every day until ten days ago. She wondered if Gerard would ask for a copy of the spreadsheet for the BAS return at the end of the quarter because all the farm records were in her cloud account.

If he did, he could go take a flying leap. It was his farm, and he could worry about the tax return. Maybe she was being bloody minded, but . . .

With a determined sigh she turned to the ledger on the desk and ran her finger across the headings at the top. Ryan was her opposite as far as keeping up-to-date records but listening to him talk about the scale of just one mustering job, she realised what a huge concern this station was and how much responsibility he held. Another personality trait they shared, they each liked to be in control; Dee sensed that like her, Ryan didn't trust easily, and she realised what a big step it must have been to allow a virtual stranger to enter the invoices. By the look of things, he'd taken on the management of the station singlehandedly when his father had died.

His father? Or her father too?

It didn't take long for Dee to become immersed in the work and the morning passed quickly. By the time her stomach grumbled and told her it was lunchtime, she'd created a spreadsheet for *Wilderness Station,* logged onto the cloud and created a backup copy for Ryan to access, and entered half of the first box of paid invoices. At least he'd made the time to keep them in date order, and that had made her task all the quicker. She stamped each one with the station stamp when done and clipped them together. On the side of the desk was a list of questions Dee added to each time she wasn't sure of the heading to put an expense under. Again, the outgoing expenditure made her realise the scale of the business. Her interest fired as she began to see a pattern in the expenditure. Not so different to the nut farm.

With a yawn and another stomach rumble, Dee leaned back and stretched her arms high.

Coffee and food were her next goal before she came back to the invoices. Her gaze settled on the boxes of newspapers they'd sorted last night, but she would leave them for later in the day. Wind whistled up the hall and a door banged somewhere in the house. She jumped as the roof iron above her creaked. Pushing her chair back, she stood and crossed to the window. A small dark blue sedan she hadn't heard arrive was parked halfway down to where her donga was located, but there was no sign of anyone around. It hadn't been there earlier. For the first time, a tingle of nervousness made itself known; she was on a cattle station, a long way from anywhere, and where she didn't really know anyone. The study door was shut, and she'd been so immersed in what she'd been doing she wouldn't have heard anyone come into the house. Despite the heat, Dee shivered and rubbed her arms as she quietly crossed the room.

As she put her hand on the doorknob to open the door, quiet measured footsteps came from the hall. Her breath caught and another shiver ran down her back, and she lifted her hand from the knob.

It was silly to be scared, she told herself, but the instinctive fight or flight reaction kicked in. She looked around for something to protect herself with but the heaviest object in sight was a small stapler. As she turned back to the door, she froze as the handle began to turn slowly. Moving quickly and silently she stepped to the left and pressed herself against the wall behind where the door would open.

Her heart thudded as the door opened slowly and soundlessly. Poised for flight or action, Dee held her breath and waited, but whoever it was must have been satisfied there was no one in there, and the door closed again. As she stood still, she could hear each door in the hall opening and closing as the intruder—or whoever it was—searched for something or someone.

The footsteps approached again, and a cold shiver raised the hairs on the back of her neck. She held her breath again waiting for the door to open, but the footsteps kept going past the study. A couple of minutes later, a car door slammed shut and an engine started up. She hurried across to the window and stood to one side as the car drove past the house. The small sedan had tinted windows, and she couldn't see the driver.

Biting her lip, Dee crossed to the door and slowly opened it and looked down the hall. There was no sign of anyone. Taking her courage in her hands, she moved quietly down the hall to the kitchen, but it was quiet and empty.

Hurrying back into the study, she quickly saved her work, shut down her laptop and put it in the leather case.

Leaving it at the front door, she went back in for a box of the newspapers and the notes she'd made last night. Her last quick trip was to the kitchen where she grabbed a couple of apples and some crackers from a box on the kitchen bench.

She was well and truly spooked—even if it was her wild imagination—and there was no way she was coming back to the house to work until Ryan or Joe came back. There was water in the small fridge in her room, and she could survive without coffee. If she got too hungry—or scared again—she'd make her way down to the mess and have dinner with the stockmen.

Hitching the box under her arm and slipping the laptop case over her shoulder, she stepped out of the door into the blowing red dust.

Chapter 25
Tuesday 8.00 a.m.
Ellie.

'You be careful up there tomorrow, won't you, Ells?' Kane stopped behind her and the smell of coffee tickled her nostrils. He placed a mug beside her, and Ellie reached for his hand before he could move away.

Ryan had called in to the McLaren Mango Farm before lunch on Sunday. He'd detoured on his way out to the stock camp and shown Ellie the map where Stock Camp 33 was, and then pointed out the massive paddock the cattle were scattered across, and then ran his finger along the marked track he wanted them to head along to the bore where the yard trap was.

'I'm heading out there now to see that nothing's changed, and to talk to Cy about the muster. He's gone on ahead.'

'Cy?' Ellie had asked.

'Cy's my head stockman; he'll be on the motorbike for the muster. If you can go out and start the cattle moving as soon as it's light enough, we should get done by the end of the day, if all goes well.'

'What could go wrong?'

Apart from me stuffing up, she thought to herself.

'There's a few wild bulls in the mob who've got a mind of their own, but we'll take control of them from the ground. We'll all wear portable UHF transceivers to talk to each other and to you in the air.'

'Okay.'

'Ellie, I know this is really short notice, but I'm staying out there tomorrow night and I was wondering if there was any chance of you flying out to the camp on Tuesday. We need to go over a few things. If you can't, that's fine, I'll come over here on my way back in tomorrow night to take you through it, once I see how far out the cattle are.'

'That's not a problem at all. Mum's coming down—not that you need to worry about my babysitting arrangements.'

'Great. I'll ring Jabiru now and confirm an R22 for tomorrow. I've already checked, and they've got two available.' He gestured to his ute. 'I brought all the WHS paperwork with me. You won't need to worry about that for tomorrow, but you'll need to have it all read and filled in before Wednesday.'

The paperwork for the muster pilot was rigorous, but Ellie read through it twice after James had gone down for the night and completed the appropriate sections that were the pilot's responsibility.

Now, she looked at her husband as he handed the coffee over. 'Thank you. And you should know you don't have to tell me that. You've seen me fly dozens of times.' She flicked a cheeky glance at her husband. 'You've even been up with me once.'

'Scariest experience of my life,' he said with a grin. 'Or maybe not. Maybe the time you drove me down to Jim Jim Falls in the Lodge truck was scarier.'

'You deserved it all, back then. You were a cranky bugger.'

'I did have a lot on my mind, but not enough to stop me noticing the hot helicopter pilot.' Kane leaned down and brushed a kiss across her lips as she looked up at him. 'But I mean it, you be careful tomorrow.'

'I will.' Ellie squeezed his fingers. 'We've been through a lot together since then, haven't we?'

'We have and I want at least another sixty years with you.'

'I'll be careful,' she promised. 'I'll even do two pre-flight checks like a certain hunky engineer taught me. Maybe even three.' She giggled as he pulled a face at her.

'Two will be enough. Nearly ready for bed?'

She held his hungry gaze, and a delicious tremor ran through her. Three years with this man and she loved him more every day. 'I am.'

Ellie's hands were slick with perspiration as she walked onto the tarmac from the office of the charter helicopter company in Jabiru on Tuesday morning. She'd been waiting outside the charter company's office at the small airport before they'd opened, and nerves had taken hold.

Don't be silly, she told herself as she looked over at the two choppers beside the hangar.

'Hey, Ellie, great to see you back in action.' Leonie, the girl manning the front desk smiled at her. The staff at the small airport knew Ellie from the years she'd worked at Makowa Lodge, the tourist complex on the South Alligator River.

'Great to be back, Leonie. I've sure missed flying.'

'But you've got a gorgeous little boy to make up for it.' Leonie laughed. 'Not to mention a pretty hot husband. Am I allowed to say that?'

Ellie had smiled. 'You are.'

Once she'd filled out the required paperwork, shown her license and lodged a flight plan, she headed out to the bright yellow bird.

She shook her head as she walked around doing the pre-flight check. Her one crash—a controlled crash—had been caused by sabotage to the fuel lines, and she always checked them first now.

Clutch check, blade, rotor, engine, tail rotor, fuel tanks, flex coupling, yoke flanges, fasteners—yep, all tight.

Twice she walked around the bird, to make Kane happy. And to ensure her safety. Ellie smiled—if anything spooked the cattle it would be the colour of the R22. Anticipation building, she buckled herself in and pushed the wiring light test switches. Slipping on her headset, she keyed the mike.

'Jabiru Tower, this is Robinson R22 helicopter'—she glanced down at the flight manifest— 'N223JK at the Jabiru top hangar ramp and ready for departure to the southwest today. Request close traffic.'

'Roger that, N223JK, traffic closed. Have a great day, Ellie.'

Taking a deep breath, she savoured the moment as she depressed the engine starter button until it fired, and then reached over to push the fuel cut-off.

Seconds later the chopper lifted off the short runway and tipped forward as it gathered speed. That wonderful rush of being in the air filled her and Ellie couldn't hold back the happy yell that burst from her lips. She looked down onto the small township below. Civilisation quickly receded; the houses got smaller and then disappeared as she flew over Bowali Visitor Centre and turned to the south west. This country was a part of her, and she didn't have to refer to the map that Ryan had given her to map a flight path.

To the west, verdant thick forest contrasted with patches of scrubby trees on red dirt interspersed with a network of narrow channels; the silver water on the floodplains glinted in the morning sunlight. Following the narrow ribbon of highway that edged the trees, Ellie continued southwest until the dramatic escarpment wall appeared near Nourlangie.

The tourist patter still rolled off her tongue even though it had been three years since she'd regularly taken tourists up for Makowa Lodge.

'Kakadu has many attractions,' she said, surprising herself at how quickly it came back. '140 million years ago, Kakadu was under a shallow sea. The sea cliffs forming the shoreline are now the dramatic escarpment wall that can be seen at Gunlom, Jim Jim, and Twin Falls and from the Gunwarde-warde Lookout at Nourlangie.'

She wouldn't go as far south as Jim Jim Falls, but Ellie grinned as she remembered the first time she'd driven down there with Kane. Their early relationship had been rocky, but it hadn't taken her long to fall in love with the dour ex-army helicopter pilot.

As soon as she'd fallen pregnant with James, she and Kane had made a mutual decision that she would not fly. It had been over two years, but oh, how wonderful it was to be up in the air again.

Up in the air, where the world was clear and true. And all hers.

Contentment filled Ellie as she changed direction for *Wilderness Station*, and she fought hard to keep that feeling. Sometimes her happiness frightened her, and she worried about how much she had to lose if something went wrong. She knew it had been the sudden death of her father, and the crap afterwards, that had damaged her ability to trust that happiness could last.

Talking a deep breath, Ellie convinced herself that nothing would change; she wouldn't let it. A wonderful husband who loved her, a farm that was getting more successful each year, two sisters she'd grown very close to, Mum, healed and happy and keen to help out as often as she was needed, and most of all, James, her gorgeous little bundle of joy. The love she had felt for her child as soon as he was born had shocked her, as much as her growing desire to have another baby.

It was time to talk that over with Kane.

Her happy anticipation grew as Ellie flew over the land she loved.

Chapter 26
Wilderness Station.
Tuesday 9.00 a.m.

Ryan looked up as the sound of a helicopter filled the air. He pulled on the reins and brought his horse to a stop as Ellie hovered the helicopter a hundred metres to the left. Digger stood quietly and Ryan leaned forward and rubbed the horse's neck. 'Good boy.'

A few minutes later all was quiet again when the rotors stopped, and Ellie climbed out of the chopper. Ryan dismounted and tethered the horse.

'Morning, Ryan. Glorious day.' Her grin was wide and he smiled back.

'That it is, Ellie. I'm pleased to see the wind has gone. It came through hard yesterday.'

'It did, but that little bit of rain last night cleared the air. Everything looked green and sparking from up there.'

'Good, you got it over your way too, did you? I'm hoping we got it at the station, I didn't end up getting back there last night.'

Ryan had radioed home camp and asked one of the more reliable stockmen to leave a message under Dee's door. He hoped she'd received it; he felt guilty leaving her there, but there'd been a lot of stray cattle in the outer paddocks and he'd been flat out helping Cy.

'Ready for a cuppa? The boys are on their way over for smoko.' Ryan pointed to an area near the boundary fence where two camp kettles on a butane stove were coming to the boil. A circle of cut-off stumps provided somewhere to sit.

'Love one.' Ellie followed him over as a group of stockmen approached on horseback and a cloud of red dust hovered over the paddock. 'That stove's a bit upmarket. What happened to the days of a billy over the fire?'

'We still do that at the main camp, but this is quicker when we're moving from paddock to paddock through the day. We're always conscious of fire when there's so much feed around.' Placing the two enamel mugs he'd taken from his saddlebag onto one of the stumps, Ryan waited until the stockmen dismounted and wandered over with their mugs. His cousin led the way.

'Ellie, this is Cy, our head stockman. He'll be the one doing most to the talking to you tomorrow.' He paused as Cy wiped his hands on his trousers and reached out and shook Ellie's hand.

'Pleased to meet you, Ellie. I'm Joe's son. Said he'd met you the other day.'

Ryan noticed Cy checking Ellie out as she walked over to one of the stumps. Rolling his eyes, he reminded himself to tell Cy that she was married. His cousin was an excellent stockman, but he was an out and out lady's man. Ryan had already had one irate father turn up at the property chasing Cy a couple of years back. His daughter had gone back to Darwin pregnant after working as a ringer on *Wilderness Station*.

Cy had denied it. 'Not me, mate. I wouldn't have touched her with a barge pole, because she spent every night in a different swag.' He'd disappeared for a few weeks, off droving with Joe, but Ryan had always wondered. It had never been mentioned again when they'd returned. It disappointed him that Cy criticised the woman for behaving the same way that was acceptable for him.

But he was a damn fine cattleman, and they'd always got on well.

Ellie was quiet as Ryan dropped tea bags in each of the mugs. He walked across to where she was sitting and nodded to the rest of his team. 'And here we have Pete, Steve, Alex, Ringo, Charlie and of course the inimitable Bluey.'

The stockmen nodded to Ellie, and Ryan added hot water to the teabags he'd put in the mugs. Her eyebrows rose as he held out a small Tupperware container.

'Carrot cake. Joe makes it for smoko,' Ryan said.

The men each took a slice and then wandered off to the stumps talking quietly among themselves.

'Luxury,' Ellie said. 'When I was up in the Gulf, we were lucky to get a stale Arnott's biscuit.'

'Joe looks after us well.'

Ellie looked around as she sipped the steaming tea. 'I saw a large mob of cattle to the south when the escarpment ended. Is that the mob we're moving on Wednesday?'

Ryan nodded. 'Yeah, there's about a thousand head, give or take the few dozen stragglers and escapees.'

'I noticed a small mob over in Hidden Valley. Looked like a couple of big wild bulls.'

'They could have been wild water buffalo, there were a few out there last time I was out there,' Ryan said, tipping the last of his tea onto the ground. 'It's about time I went out there and checked around.'

'As long as they leave your campers in peace. I've heard water buffalo can do some damage.'

'Campers? What campers?' Ryan frowned. Cy walked over and leaned on the fence next to them watching two steers head butting in the paddock.

'I thought you must have had a campsite set up out there for tourists. There were three off-road campers and half a dozen or so four wheel drives parked at the edge of the salt pans. I'm sure I spotted a portable loo too.'

Anger filled Ryan at the thought of their pristine valley being compromised. 'There shouldn't be. Where were they exactly? They have no right to be there.'

'They were directly below that waterhole on the top of the escarpment. I remember where, because it made me think of the plunge pool at Gunlom Falls. It's closed now.'

'That's our private property and as far as I know the gates are locked. I'd better get out there and take a look as soon as I can.' He gestured to Cy. 'How long since you've been out to the valley? Any cattle out that way?'

'Nuh. And I haven't been out that way for over a year.' Cy spat out the gum he'd been chewing. He walked across to the fence, picked up the whip that he'd left on the stump and cracked it.

'That's smoko done,' Ryan said glaring at Cy. His cousin was putting on a tough guy show because he had a female to impress.

'Righto, boss. Let's get this show on the road.' Cy stood and jerked his thumb at the stockmen. 'Back to work, boys.'

'Charming,' she said as Cy followed the others back to the horses. The motorbike roared and he did a wheelie as he took off.

'Sorry, he can be a bit of a pain at times,' Ryan apologised. 'He's twenty-one and still got a bit of growing up to do.'

'Don't worry about it, I've seen worse than that. Listen, I can take you up over the valley now if you like. Before I go back to Jabiru.'

'That'd be great, thanks. I can show you the paddock boundaries from the air and point out the track to the bore while we're up there. We've only found half the mob so far.' He stopped as Cy roared up beside them.

'Which paddock first, Ryan?' he asked.

'The eastern side,' he replied. 'Okay, Ellie. Thanks, let's go up now.' He turned to Cy. 'Put your UHF receiver on, and we'll get this knocked over quickly. When we're done, I'll get you to lead Digger back to the camp and Ellie can drop me back at my ute.'

##

Ryan decided to show Ellie the route first, but he found it hard to focus on the upcoming muster; he was worried about who'd been out at the valley. It was a long way out from the homestead and the yards, and about fifty kilometres from the highway. There was a road through from the south off the old Jim Jim road that came through Black Jungle Springs where Bill Jarragah lived. When Bill Jarragah had worked for them on the station, he'd often cursed the state of the back road. Ryan knew it was impassable for most of the year, and that was one of the reasons they didn't go out there much. They didn't run cattle in Hidden Valley; it remained the paradise it had always been. The valley was untouched and had been since his great grandfather had worked the saltworks out there a hundred years ago; there'd never been cattle—or humans—out there as far as he knew.

A few years back his father had been approached to sell the land to a development company that had been planning an eco-resort in the Territory, and Dad had put the skids under them. Apparently, the location was far enough away from the South Alligator River that it would be accessible to fly tourists in all year, even in the wet.

'Stupid fools,' his father had said. 'Who the hell would want to have a holiday in the middle of nowhere? And they are not getting their hands on our valley. And that's my last word on it.'

The developers left and didn't try again.

Ellie had the R22 over the bore before Cy reached it on horseback, and Ryan pointed out the track the cattle would hopefully move along to seek the water.

'It's a pretty easy route by the look of things.' Ellie's voice came through his headphones and he gave her a thumbs up. The cattle were about twenty kilometres out, and all going well, they should reach the bore paddock by dark on Wednesday.

'Yep, good and flat and the track is well marked. Follow it out to the back paddock where you saw them on the way in, and I'll show you the couple of hazards where you might have trouble.'

He pointed to the east and Ellie turned the helicopter and headed in the direction he pointed. She took them in low and they had a clear view of the ground all the way out to the paddock. Ellie flew over the mob, and some beasts looked up curiously, but didn't move.

'They'll have more energy in the cool of the morning,' he said, and this time she gave him the thumps up. 'Take us back to the bore now, Cy'll be back, and we'll test the UHF transceivers.'

Ellie used the anti-torque pedals and the cyclic between the seats and Ryan was impressed with her flying. Her references were excellent, and this morning she'd proved that she was a skilled pilot.

Cy came through loud and clear as they tested the radios.

'Okay, Cy, we're heading off now. I'll see you later.'

'Right, boss, make sure the beer's cold, over and out.'

Ryan turned the transceiver off and slipped it over his head. 'Okay, Ellie, let's go to Hidden Valley.'

The valley was forty or so kilometres to the east of their camp. Ryan looked down as they headed out, checking out the feed in some of the paddocks they hadn't used for a couple of years. He mapped out a plan in his head. If it they had a good wet season this year, he should be able to increase the herd by a few thousand head.

And then the current situation came crashing back to him. Next season was uncertain. Until he and Dee could get to the bottom of the family mystery, get the truth of the will from Baker and sort out the inheritance, his planning would be in limbo. He wouldn't be in a position to make long-term plans. And he still hadn't sorted out what he was feeling for Dee.

It was an utter bloody mess.

'Shit.' Ryan couldn't help the expletive that broke from his lips and his headphones crackled to life immediately.

'What's wrong?' Ellie glanced over at him.

'Sorry, just thinking aloud. All good.'

'We're almost to where I saw the campers.'

'Okay, go as low as you can, and I'll take a good look and then decide what to do. Maybe if there's somewhere suitable to land, I can see what they've been up to.'

On the third pass along the edge of the escarpment, with no sign of campers and vehicles, it was Ellie who swore. 'Honestly, Ryan, this is where they were. I know it was; there's the pool at the top of the cliff. I thought they were tourists. I know fly-drive four wheel drive packages to Gunlom were starting up when I left Makowa Lodge, but they shut it down last year. I thought this might have been the same sort of set-up.'

'Nope, nothing like that here. I wouldn't have the time, and besides that, the valley is untouchable as far as I'm concerned. It's our land, and like my dad before me, I'd hate to see it get ruined by four wheel drives carrying loads of tourists.'

'I agree. It's rare to see places like this left alone these days.'

'You might have spooked them flying over, Ellie. They obviously know they have no right to be here, because they had to break through a locked gate to get here. Hang on. Look, I can see wheel tracks down there. Can you find somewhere to land? Maybe over on the edge of the salt pan and we can walk back.'

'Yep, that'd be firm enough.' Ellie turned the helicopter and it wasn't long before the skids were on the hard salt pan. She shut the engine down and when the rotors had stopped, she took her headphones off, and Ryan did the same before unclipping his seatbelt.

The heat hit them in a solid wave once they were standing on the hard salt. A moment later, the sticky black flies arrived in a huge black swarm.

'Gah,' Ellie said, waving her arms. 'I don't know what's the worst. The heat or the flies.'

'Come on, let's get off the salt, and it'll be a bit cooler, but I can't guarantee the flies will go.' Ryan took off in a light jog and Ellie wasn't far behind him. When he came to a sudden stop, Ellie almost ran into him. He stared in disbelief at the edge of the salt pan.

'What the hell is that?'

Chapter 27
Wilderness Station.
Tuesday 7.00 p.m.

By the end of the second full day working in the study—with the front and back door of the house locked—Dee was well and truly sick of spreadsheets, invoices, and her own company. Ryan hadn't come back last night, and someone had slipped a note under the door of her accommodation when she'd been reading the newspapers. She'd almost jumped when she'd heard them outside, but by the time she'd opened the door, there was no one there, just a note saying that Ryan had been delayed and would be home later in the week. So there was someone around, even though she hadn't seen anyone.

Dee's neck ached, her eyes were gritty from the constant computer work and the red dust that blew in late each afternoon when the wind picked up. But at least she'd finished entering Ryan's data. All that was left were the invoices and payments where she wasn't sure of the category.

There'd been no sign of Joe, and Dee had made herself some light meals from the contents of the fridge and the walk-in pantry. Her single conversation had been with Catherine, a short while ago and surprisingly she'd been receptive to questions, although there had been no answers that had satisfied Dee's curiosity.

'Where did you live when you were up in the Territory?' Dee had asked.

Catherine sounded sober, but her answers were vague. 'Not far from Darwin. In the bush.'

Dee didn't want to let on that she'd been exploring the past through the newspapers. She'd finished going through the second box and was planning to go through the final box tonight after she'd eaten.

'On a farm?'

'Sort of. We had some mango trees, but Gerard spent most of his time at his office in the city. That's when his business really took off.'

'Where did you meet him? Did you grow up in Darwin?'

'Yes.'

'So why did we move?'

'Oh, more chance of deals in the east, you know.'

Dee could imagine Catherine waving a vague hand.

'Have you heard of a place called *Wilderness Station?*'

'No.' The reply came too quickly. 'Where are you, Dee? Are you in Darwin? I miss you, sweetheart. I think you should come home and get over this silly tiff with your father.'

Dee persisted. 'Did you play tennis when you lived in the "bush"? Is that where you met Gerard?'

'Dee, just get over this silliness. Why are you calling your father, "Gerard"?'

'If you'd give me some answers . . . Mum . . . I might be able to come home.'

'I don't know why you want to know all these things.'

'I want to know the truth. I want to know who my parents are, and I want to know why there is so much secrecy about this whole situation.'

'I don't know what you're talking about.' Dee knew Catherine well enough to know she was getting distressed, and sensed she was going to end the call any moment. 'We are your parents!'

'I'm going to find out whether you tell me or not.'

'Dee. Please. You can't.' The pitch of her voice rose. 'You mustn't. Please come home, and I'll tell you what you want to know.'

'I mustn't? Why not?' Dee couldn't help her mocking reply. How dare Catherine put conditions on the truth.

'You just can't. It's not safe.'

'Okay, I'll think about it, but one more question. Where's your sister, Bridget—or is it Birgit—these days?'

A stifled gasp, and then the only sound were the beeps of a call disconnected. Maybe it would have been easy to get the names mixed up. Maybe it was the woman Ellie remembered.

Dee went to the kitchen, and made a toasted sandwich and a coffee, even more certain that Catherine knew a lot more than she would tell.

Of course, she'd know.

There had been a definite reaction when Dee had mentioned *Wilderness Station,* and that sudden hang-up when she'd asked about Bridget or Birgit. Walking back to the study with a plate of sandwiches in one hand and coffee in the other, she used her hip to push open the study door.

Dee stood by the window sipping her coffee. The sun hovered above the horizon in a massive golden ball. The few clouds were long and narrow and tinged with the lingering remnants of smoke that had been in the air all day. Molten gold edged the pink clouds and rays of soft light shot up into the apricot sky.

Even with the red dirt and the flat land, the Territory held a beauty that was different to anything she'd seen before. She vowed to herself that whatever happened she would make sure she spent some time travelling around.

Whatever happened.

The bitterness of the coffee stuck in her throat and she wondered what she was going to find out and where she'd end up. Maybe tonight she'd find something in the newspapers. It looked like she and Ryan were going to have to find out for themselves. Catherine obviously wasn't going to tell her anything, and Mr Baker had been equally as vague when it came to specific information.

Dee's temper rose. How hard was it? Why did everything have to be a big secret? And a secret that was embedded in legal mumbo jumbo.

Finishing her coffee she placed the mug on the desk and then turned to the last box. It was bigger than the first two and would be too heavy to carry unless she divided it. When she'd sorted the newspapers in her room after she'd got jittery last night there hadn't been enough room to spread them out properly, and it had been hot even with the evaporative air conditioner going in the window. It had blown the piles of paper around and eventually she'd given up.

Now that Dee had locked up the doors, and got used to the quiet, she decided it was easier to stay up at the house and work for the evening. Logic had kicked in and she'd realised the person she'd heard had been someone coming into the house to feed the dogs; the three dogs hadn't bothered her, staying out on the back veranda since they'd greeted Ryan when they'd arrived. Dee had checked their water this morning, and their bowls had been full of kibble, so there was a logical explanation. She'd worked herself up over nothing. It was stupid to lock herself in that small, hot donga when she could use the large air-conditioned study, and the kitchen in the homestead.

There was a flashlight on the table at the front door, and she could use that to light the couple of hundred metres back to her room when she finished tonight. There'd been no other cars or visitors, and her nerves had settled. Her reaction to thinking there had been an intruder had been over the top. Being unfamiliar with the workings of the station had made her nervous. She had no idea who came and went, or who lived in the accommodation further down from the donga she was sleeping in, but she would be learning over the next few months if she stayed here. Once they had the results back from the DNA test, she would make a definite decision whether to stay or go. If she wasn't Colin's daughter, she had some decisions to make. If she wasn't entitled, why had she been left half the station?

Last night had been totally unproductive; she'd found no photographs or text about any of the people they'd found mention of on Saturday night. With a determined deep breath, she set to work, but Dee knew would have felt more settled if Ryan was here going through the papers with her.

Chapter 28
Wilderness Station.
Wednesday 10.00 a.m.

Dee pushed the crisp cotton sheet back and sat on the edge of the bed rubbing her eyes. She'd had a restless night, waking up several times, and dreaming of missing cattle that she and Ryan were trying to find. They'd been searching at *Hilltop Farm,* not *Wilderness Station,* but no matter how many times she tried to tell Ryan they were in the wrong place, he wouldn't listen to her. Her head had been full of facts and figures from the thirty newspapers she'd gone through last night, line by line, only to find no mention of anything remotely related to her search. But she had learned a lot about the variations of the local rainfall and temperature, and the mango harvest in the days when the plantations were starting up, but there'd been no further mention of *Wilderness Station,* or the Careys, Peter Porter, Gerard and Catherine or a Bridget. She glanced at her watch as she headed for the shower, surprised to see it was almost ten a.m.

There was no point hurrying, she knew the muster was happening today so Ryan wouldn't be back before dark. The accounts were done as far as she could without talking to him, but there was still a large pile of newspapers to get through. Being alone in a strange place was beginning to get to her, and she was looking forward to his return. If she had her ute, she would have gone for a drive.

Dee walked up to the house carrying the box of newspapers with her laptop balanced on the top. Over the past three days she'd noticed that the garden sprinklers came on each morning and afternoon. As a result the neglected garden and the weeds were lush and healthy, and she decided if she was bored after spending time with the newspapers today, she'd come out and do some weeding. It was a shame to neglect a potentially beautiful garden, but at least the shrubs and some of the roses seemed to have survived.

She frowned as she walked along the path beside the lawn and approached the house. The front door—that she'd closed when she'd left last night—was wide open and two of the dogs were curled up on the front veranda. There was no vehicle parked near the house. Slipping her shoes off at the door, she walked inside listening for the sound of anyone there.

As she walked silently down the hall, all was quiet. The tiles were cold beneath her bare feet and the house was cool. Her heart began to beat a little faster, and she swallowed to dispel the dryness of her mouth. The study door was open, and she knew she'd closed that last night.

Don't be such a wuss, she told herself firmly.

A sudden flash of movement to her right had her swinging around, eyes wide, and she almost dropped the box.

'Why are you creeping around the house like a mouse?' Joe said loudly as his large bulk loomed over her. 'Jesus, woman, you gave me a bloody fright.'

'I wondered why the door was open.' Dee's heart was thudding.

'And I wondered why it was shut. We never shut the front door.'

'Well, I'm sorry. I assumed if there was no one here, you'd want it shut for the night. Don't you worry about snakes?'

Joe didn't answer as he stared at her. 'What are you doing with those newspapers?' His lips were set in a straight line, and her skin crawled as she sensed malevolence in his look. She really didn't like him.

'I was reading up about the district. Is that a problem?'

'All right, no need to get your knickers in a twist.'

Dee stared at him. 'I beg your pardon?'

Joe waved a beefy hand as he walked away. 'You know what I mean. An expression only. It means there's no need to be touchy. If you can't take it, you've got no place working in the bush.'

She turned on her heel and headed down the hall to the study, hoping Ryan would come back tonight.

It was probably unlikely, because it would be a big day, and then it was apparently a long way back to the station house. But then chastising herself mentally, she wondered why she was putting her trust in Ryan. She didn't know him any better than she knew his uncle. Dee had always been slow to trust and it was a time to be even more wary.

Going into the study and closing the door behind her, she vowed she wouldn't be going to the kitchen until Joe left.

Chapter 29
Wilderness Station.
Saturday, October 31 1987.

Suzanne stood at the sink staring through the kitchen window. Red dust swirled in the paddocks as a gust of strong wind blew in. A storm was building in the east and dark grey clouds, fat with rain that never seemed to arrive, hung over the cliffs in the far distance. Closing her eyes, Suzanne imagined the lush green grass that would cover Hidden Valley, her favourite place on the station. She knew the six seasons from what Bill Jarragah had taught her and this was *Gunumeleng*, the pre-monsoon season, when the temperatures began to climb, and the sapping humidity wore her out. Most afternoons, a thunderstorm would build, and her anxiety built with it.

Bill told her that in this season the indigenous people had traditionally moved camp from the floodplains to the stone country to shelter from the coming monsoon. It would have been so much better if Colin's grandfather had built the homestead near the stone cliffs in the lush valley.

No point wishing for something that would never be. The one time she'd broached building a new homestead in the beautiful valley, Colin hadn't even bothered to answer. Shaking her head, Suzanne turned her attention back to the sink where boiled eggs were cooling in a bowl ready to peel for the tennis barbeque tonight.

With a sigh, she peeled the eggs and put them in the fridge. Colin's tastes were simple; he loved curried egg salad.

The few times she'd made anything a bit fancier for the barbeques, he turned his nose up.

No matter how hard she fought it each year, her anxiety increased with the humidity. She'd tried hard this year to be a good wife, and Colin seemed to appreciate it, but he'd also seemed preoccupied a lot of the time. His mood improved when the dry had arrived; cattle prices were up, and Joe had gone away droving as the camp cook. When Colin was happy, Suzanne's life was easier. She'd realised how much her brother's presence irritated Colin. Plus she'd thrown away the ovulation thermometer; she didn't hold out much hope, but if they were meant to have a child she would. At least their sex life seemed to have improved. She bit back a rare giggle. In frequency anyway—like the curried eggs, the act was always a no frills experience.

As usual, Suzanne wasn't looking forward to having a crowd here. It had only been two weeks since the last tennis night barbeque, but she'd made an effort. The incident with Bridget and Colin at the barbeque a couple of months ago had rattled her.

Since then, every time Colin wanted to host a tennis afternoon, or a barbeque at *Wilderness Station*, Suzanne had been the perfect hostess. Catherine was now engaged to Gerard Peters, the new arrival to the district, with an April wedding planned. Bridget was always aloof. Suzanne and Sandra stayed outside to chat as the tennis game filled the air with ball thwacks, curses and laughter. Her friendship with Sandra—despite her new friend being younger—had developed, and between social occasions on the station, they'd had a couple of shopping trips to Darwin. Sandra was going out with one of the Stuart boys. Why couldn't Bridget Sloane take an interest in some of the single men who sometimes came to the barbeques? Suzanne still worried about Bridget's fascination with Colin. She hung off his every word, and always insisted on being his partner in the mixed doubles. The few times that Colin declined—but he hadn't for ages—Peter Porter had stepped in.

Suzanne did her best to ignore her building jealousy. The one time she'd raised his friendship with Bridget with Colin, he'd laughed and ruffled her hair.

'Jealous, darling? Now that makes me feel very loved.'

In in his own way, she knew Colin did love her, and it was his disappointment that she hadn't fallen pregnant causing the ongoing tension between them. He would be fifty in three years, and Suzanne was thirty-five. Most of the time he was kind and considerate, but his refusal to see a fertility specialist had hurt her.

The afternoon passed quickly as she chopped salad, and set the thawing meat out under a cloth, ready to go out to the barbeque.

Suzanne glanced at the parking area as the first car drove in behind the house. Bridget Sloane's, of course. Rolling her eyes, she stayed inside.

The usual crew soon arrived, and Suzanne slipped into the bedroom to get changed. She'd bought a new dress in Darwin and as she stood in front of the mirror brushing her hair, she noticed the pallor of her face. Pinching her cheeks to get some colour into them, she reached for the lip gloss and mascara. It wouldn't hurt to make an effort.

Picking up a tray of nibbles on her way outside, she was soon perspiring. After putting the tray down on the Lazy Susan in the middle of the wooden table, she reached back and lifted the thick red curls off her neck, amazed that the four already running around the tennis court looked as fresh as daisies.

'You look lovely today, Suze,' Sandra said walking over with a cob loaf full of French Onion dip.

'Thanks, Sandy. I love your dress too. Canary yellow!'

'I thought I'd give Bridget a run for her money and get dressed up.' Sandra ran her hands down the slim-fitting halter necked dress and pulled a face. Suzanne tried not to smile but failed. 'If this dress doesn't get Peter Porter interested, I'll give up.'

'He still hasn't asked you out?' Suzanne looked over to the tennis court where Peter had partnered Catherine in the mixed doubles. A shaft of anger shot through her as Bridget walked over to Colin, and playfully patted his behind with her tennis racket. She turned back to Sandra who hadn't noticed.

'No, but I've been out with Kurt Stuart a few times since I last talked to you.'

'And?'

Sandra shook her head. 'No spark.'

'It'll happen. I know Peter's busy. He works for us too, and I know he's got at least three other jobs. He told me he's saving up for his own place.'

Sandra's face fell. 'I really don't think he likes me; he talks to you more than me.'

Bridget's high-pitched laugh reached them, but Suzanne turned her back to the court.

'How are you going?' Sandra asked quietly. One morning over a cup of coffee in a café in Darwin, Suzanne had spilled her fears about Bridget and Colin to Sandra.

Suzanne smiled. 'Really, really good. It's easy to ignore Bridget. I know that night I was worried about, back in September, she did that deliberately to make me doubt Colin.'

'Did what?'

'Smudged red dirt on the back of her clothes.'

'Oh. How did you know that?'

'Colin told me. She wanted to see the kitchen down in the mess and decided to make their walk alone look suspicious. He was so embarrassed. She's got a problem.'

'God, she's a cow,' Sandra said, but Suzanne could sense that Sandra found the explanation to be a little too convenient, as Suzanne had done at the time, but she wouldn't admit that even to herself.

It was a successful night; the food was excellent, the tennis was fun, the beer and wine flowed, and everyone was reluctant to leave when midnight rolled around.

Suzanne carried the last of the used dishes back to the kitchen, and on her way back decided to put the sprinklers on the rose gardens. As she entered the square garden, a couple in a close embrace sprang apart.

By the time her eyes had adjusted to the dark, the man had disappeared, and Bridget Sloane's dry voice chastised her. 'You're a spoilsport, Suzanne. I thought this was a private part of your garden.'

'You've got it in one, Bridget. *My* garden. I suggest you follow your man and get him to take you home. It's late.'

Bridget sighed, but her reply was enigmatic. 'He can't.'

Suzanne felt sick as Bridget's cat-shaped eyes glinted in the dim light of the garden lights. She smiled at Suzanne and made her way back to the veranda.

Suzanne's chest ached as suspicion rolled in, and she felt physically ill. When she hurried around the side of the house, the relief—and guilt—was overwhelming. Colin was sitting at a table, deep in conversation with Vic Romano. Bridget was pressed up against Peter Porter at the edge of the makeshift bar.

Thank goodness.

She felt sorry for Sandy and her chances with Peter, but if Bridget had transferred her affection to Peter, Suzanne knew she would feel a lot happier. Her smile grew and she was determined to be a good wife from now on, and not think the worst of her husband.

She thought Peter Porter had better taste, but if he chose Bridget over Sandy, that was his loss.

An hour later, when everyone had left and the tables were cleared, the dishwasher was loaded, and the leftovers placed in the fridge, Colin came up behind her. His lips brushed the side of her neck.

'Coming to bed with me, my gorgeous sexy wife?'

She turned and looped her arms around his neck. 'I think that's an excellent idea. Let's go and try to make a baby.'

'Let's try really hard.' Colin's lips descended on hers, and he kissed for much longer than he usually did.

Despite her pleasure in him seeking her out, the fleeting thought that she couldn't ask questions while her husband was kissing her did enter her mind.

Chapter 30
Wilderness Station.
Wednesday 4.30 p.m.

Dee opened the next newspaper, dated April 25th, 1988 as she sat near the window in the study. The late afternoon sun was streaming through and she reached up and pulled the blind down slightly before she turned the page. The wedding photograph on page two jumped straight out at her. Her heart almost stopped as she stared into the young faces of Catherine and Gerard. She looked at the date and then back at the photograph and her suspicions were confirmed. Over and over she looked at it, looked away and then her attention was drawn back to it until her eyes were burning from staring at the picture for such a long time.

God, she needed Ryan. Even a phone call to tell him what she'd found would have satisfied her impatience to share the news that they were on the right track.

She'd tried to call Catherine several times today, but she hadn't been able to get her to answer. Obviously, she'd hit a tender spot before Catherine had disconnected last night. Or she was still sleeping off too much wine.

Dee lifted her head as a faint rumble came from outside. As she listened, the familiar wop wop of a helicopter got louder. Jumping up, she opened the study door and hurried down the hall and out onto the front veranda. Joe had gone down to the mess about three hours ago and she hadn't seen him come back yet. She'd scooted down to the kitchen and quickly made a coffee and grabbed a muesli bar as soon as she'd seen him leave.

Excited anticipation eased her churning stomach and brought a smile to her face as she watched the helicopter land in the paddock on the other side of the fence. Red dust whirled as the rotors slowed, but before they stopped completely, Ryan climbed down, bent almost double and ran towards the fence. He waved as the helicopter lifted off the dirt and tipped forward as it gathered speed. By the time he reached where Dee waited at the fence, the helicopter was a small dark speck in the eastern sky.

'Hi there. Welcome back,' she said as a strange shyness took over. 'Did the muster go well?'

Opening the gate, Ryan came through to the house side. Pushing his stained Akubra back, he smiled at her, his teeth white in a red dust-covered face. 'Best muster for years. Ellie did so well, we had the whole mob at the bore just after lunch. We got them separated, and the truck comes tomorrow.' He kept his eyes on her as they walked towards the house. 'Sorry I didn't get back before the muster. Did you get my message? How's it been here?'

'I did, and it's been quiet, but productive. I've got most of your invoices entered. Just a few questions for you and you can send the BAS off.'

'Thank you. I didn't expect you to get it done so quickly.'

Dee couldn't help reaching out and touching Ryan's arm as she shared the rest of the news. 'You have to see what I've found.' She was surprised when tears filled her eyes, and turned away before Ryan could see them.

'Great. I can't wait to see it, but before I look at anything, I need a shower and a feed. Where's Joe? Has he looked after you? Kept you fed, and been decent company?'

Dee hesitated. She didn't like to say that she'd been alone most of the time. Maybe Joe was supposed to have looked after the place. As far as she knew he'd been in Darwin until today.

With a quick nod, she changed the subject. 'I'm pleased the muster went well and Ellie worked out for you.'

Ryan's voice was full of enthusiasm. 'She's a gun pilot. And boy, she knows cattle. I'm happy to give her more work.'

'I'd like to see a muster one day,' Dee said.

'I'll take you out next time.' He paused and his expression was hard to read. 'If you're still here, that is.'

'I'm staying until we get all this sorted.'

'When I've had a shower we'll sit and have a drink and you can show me what you've found.'

'And after that you can answer the questions I've got about the invoices and you can get your BAS sent off.'

'Do we have to do that tonight?'

'Yep. That's one thing you don't let get away from you.'

'Yes, ma'am.'

They reached the house and Ryan held the screen door open for Dee to go inside before him.

'Thank you.' She nodded and stepped into the cool dim hall. All was quiet from the kitchen end and there was no sign Joe had come back. He probably hadn't been expecting Ryan back, and was cooking dinner down at the stockmen's quarters.

Ryan followed her in and paused at the hall table inside the door, picking up some envelopes. 'Joe must have picked up the mail.' He lifted his head and looked over the letters he'd picked up. 'Unless you went out there?'

'Nope, wasn't me. I've not left the house yard.'

He let out a low whistle. 'That was quick!'

Dee looked down at the small flat parcel he held. 'Quick?'

'It's from that lab. The one we filled out the online form for.'

'Really?'

He turned the parcel over. 'Yes, and it's not obvious what it is. I suppose they try to be a bit discreet with the packaging. Joe would have thought it was something for the cattle.'

'So we can do the test and send it back sooner than later?'

'I think we should do it tonight and—oh, sorry, I forgot to tell you, I had a call from the panel beater. Your ute's ready. They were able to get the paint from the local Holden dealer, and did it straight away.'

'That's good. I did feel a bit isolated here without a vehicle.'

Ryan frowned. 'I'm sorry. That was my fault. I should have organised one of the farm utes for you, but I thought I'd be back before the muster. I struck a bit of a problem. I'll tell you about it later.'

'I was fine.' Dee wasn't used to the level of consideration Ryan was showing. She was a little flustered from the embarrassment of causing a fuss. 'It gave me the chance to get the finances done and most of the newspapers out of the way. There's not many left.'

'Well, this is what I suggest.' Ryan looked down at her, and that same tug quivered in her belly.

Inappropriate, Dee. She looked over his shoulder.

'I suggest that we do this'—he held up the package—'tonight, and then take it to Darwin tomorrow. We can pick up your ute if you're happy with what they've done, and if we have any questions after you show me what you've discovered, we'll call in to see Baker and nudge him a bit. What do you think?'

Dee agreed. 'Yes, I think we'll need to. If we have some definite questions, he might be able to answer them. I also want to get a copy of the will to send to my friend who's a solicitor.'

'Good idea. Okay, after I've had my shower and we've eaten, we need to decide what questions we have for him. Specifics that he can't be vague about.'

***

Ryan left Dee in the study and headed to his room at the far end of the house. He stood beneath the strong jets of the shower in his full-sized bathroom and enjoyed the hot water as it soaked away the red dust and relaxed his tight shoulder muscles.

Dee was stuck in his head, as she had been when he'd been on horseback and in the helicopter with Ellie. There was a new vulnerability to Dee; she'd agreed with everything he'd said, and the snarky attitude had gone. Her reply when he'd asked about Joe had been evasive, and he suspected that Joe had been rude to her; he could be a gruff old bugger, but he'd been a great support to Ryan over the past few years.

Ryan pulled on a clean pair of jeans and a fresh T-shirt and flicked the comb through his wet curls. He was past due for a haircut, and if there was time, he'd have one in Darwin tomorrow. When he walked back through the house, he could hear Joe in the kitchen, and he detoured that way.

Joe put down the plastic container he'd been holding as Ryan stood in the kitchen doorway.

'What's for dinner?' he said.

Joe shook his head. 'Only what's on down in the mess. Spag bol. I just came up for some more pasta.'

'Has Dee been eating down there?'

Joe shook his head. 'I don't think so, said she was happy to look after herself. I had to go to Darwin. How come you're back so early? Couldn't stay away?' There was curiosity in his tone, but it also held a note of criticism.

Ryan was non-committal. 'No, we finished early and Ellie dropped me back when she was flying back to Jabiru. Cy's bringing my ute in tomorrow.'

'Fair enough. I've got to go down to feed the boys now.' Joe jerked his head towards the hall. 'If you want to eat, come down and bring her with you.'

Ryan raised his eyebrows but didn't comment about Joe's rudeness. He was thoughtful as he walked back to the study. Dee was sitting in the corner with a newspaper on her lap. 'You were quick.'

He shrugged. 'I didn't want to be rude. You've had most of the time here by yourself. Joe said he went away. I'm sorry, I was under the impression he was only going for the day.'

'No need to apologise. I was fine.'

'Dinner's down at the mess tonight. Do you want to come down?'

'No, I'll stay up here. You go.'

'I'll go down and bring us some dinner back. I want to see what you've found. Give me five.'

As Ryan walked down to the mess, he was surprised by how angry he was at Joe. It was unfair of him, because as far as Joe knew, Dee was simply an employee of the station. Joe's attitude confused him; he was usually easy going. He'd been rude to Ellie, and now he was treating Dee the same way. He'd sit down with him later tonight if he got a chance and have a talk. Maybe he had itchy feet again and wanted to head off on a drove; it had been a while since he'd last been away.

The boys hadn't come into the mess yet, and there was no sign of Joe, but a big pot of spaghetti sauce bubbled on the gas stove filling the space with a garlic aroma. A pot of pasta boiled beside it. Ryan's stomach rumbled as he inhaled. He crossed to the shelf beneath the window where the bowls were kept. As he bent to get them, he saw Joe outside; his phone to his ear and his left arm pointing and waving. His body was stiff with tension and when he turned around, his face was red and angry.

As soon as he saw Ryan, he turned his back and walked away from the kitchen. Something had upset Joe big time.

Bugger waiting to talk to him later; he'd talk to Joe as soon as he came in.

As Ryan waited, he spotted some garlic bread in the oven; he took it out and pulled off a couple of slices each for Dee and himself

'Hey, put that back! It's not dinnertime yet.' Joe's face was still red, and he looked pissed off.

'What's got up your nose?' Ryan's intention of being supportive flew out the window.

'I told you, it's not dinnertime.'

'We're eating up in the house. I'm about to serve out two bowls of spag bol.' Sarcasm laced his voice. 'If that's acceptable to you.'

'I suppose,' Joe said gruffly.

'Dee and I are going to Darwin tomorrow.'

'Whatever.' Joe turned his back.

Ryan put the bread down. 'Who was on the phone? Why have you got the shits?'

'No one you know.' Joe walked away from him and tipped the spaghetti into a colander in the sink at the end of the stainless steel workbench.

'So what's wrong with you?'

Joe turned on his heel and faced Ryan. 'You really want to know?'

'Yes, I do.' Ryan tucked his thumbs into his jeans pocket and waited. He'd never seen Joe angry like this before.

'Bloody Miss High and Mighty up there taking over the house. Making herself right at home. Now you're taking her dinner up, waiting on her hand and foot. Too good to come down to the mess. You said she's an employee, but she's mighty evasive when you ask her a question. And she turned up out of the blue. I'd heard nothing about someone coming in to do the accounts.'

'Since when have you had to know everything I'm planning to do?' Ryan knew his voice was sharp, but Joe's words had got right up his nose.

He hesitated; Joe had always been a moody bugger and if he got a bee in his bonnet about something he was likely to take off for a few months. He'd done that a few times before Dad had died. Ryan knew he couldn't afford to lose a cook now with more musters ahead, so he took a deep breath and forced himself to stay calm. 'It's not like you to be so rude. What have you got against Dee?'

'How do you know she's honest?'

Ryan pulled his hands from his pockets and reached for the bowls. 'Trust me. I know she is, and she's already done a great job on the accounts.'

'Thinking with your dick, boy.' Joe's eyes narrowed. 'Must run in the family.'

Ryan froze. 'What the fuck is that supposed to mean?'

'You'll find out one day life isn't the bed of roses you think it is.' Ryan stared as Joe picked up a large knife and waved it around. He stopped and pointed it at Ryan's throat. 'Just like your mother did. If it hadn't been for me, she would have had a nervous breakdown. I reckon it was the stress of living with your old man that gave my sister breast cancer. She was always too good for him and he treated her like shit. You don't know the half of it, mate. Do me a favour and don't turn into him.'

Ryan stood there, rooted to the spot. He'd never seen this side of Joe before, the violence and the vitriol, nor had he ever heard such antagonistic criticism of his father. 'We'll talk about this later when you've calmed down.'

'We might and we might not. Now serve your dinner out and piss off.'

'I've lost my appetite.' Ryan served out one bowl of spaghetti and sauce, and slammed the door as he left the mess.

***

11.00 p.m.

Dee stared at the newspaper in front of her. No matter how many times she'd looked at this since she'd first come across it this afternoon, the strange feeling wouldn't go away. The more she thought about what it meant, the sadder she became.

'Are you okay?'

She jumped as Ryan slid a cup of coffee beside her. There was a crackle as he ripped open a packet of Tim Tams.

'Sort of.'

'How sort of?' He held out the packet and she shook her head. She hadn't even been able to face the bowl of spaghetti and sauce he'd brought up for her dinner. Ryan had put it in the fridge in the kitchen.

'Come on, Dee, you have to eat.'

Reluctantly she took a biscuit. 'I guess it's because this photo proves that Catherine and Gerard really aren't my parents. It's made it very real, and even though I was expecting it, it's sort of hit me for six.'

Ryan was watching her, and Dee was embarrassed when she had to blink tears away again. Before she'd put the tissue back in her pocket, Ryan was on the small sofa beside her and his arm was around her shoulder.

She turned her head into his shirt and her voice was muffled. 'Now I have to find out who my real parents are.'

'I'm sorry.' Ryan's hand caressed the back of her head and she closed her eyes. After a moment, she pulled back.

'I'm squashing my Tim Tam. But thank you, I appreciate your kindness.'

'Nothing worse than a squashed Tim Tam,' he said, and Dee knew he was trying to cheer her up.

When she'd finished her coffee, and a second biscuit—Ryan was on his fourth—Dee pulled the paper back onto her lap. 'Do you think it was someone they knew? Or did they just decided they wanted to adopt a baby?' She traced her finger over the people in the photograph and read the caption aloud.

'Mr and Mrs Gerard Peters of Peters' Mango Farm after their wedding at the Darwin Registry Office on Saturday. They are accompanied by bridesmaid, Bridget Sloane, Mr and Mrs Colin Carey of Wilderness Station, and Mr and Mrs Peter Porter. The bride was stunning in a slim fitting silk sheath, and the bridesmaid wore a scarlet V-necked princess style dress with shoulder pads. The reception was held at Neptune's on the waterfront. Mr and Mrs Peters will honeymoon in Bali.

'Your parents were there, and your mother is obviously pregnant with you.' Dee's voice shook. 'Look how proud your dad looks. Maybe Gerard and Catherine couldn't have children and when all their friends were having babies they decided to adopt me.'

'What do you mean all their friends?' Ryan leaned over her shoulder. 'Yeah, Dad does look happy in that photo.' Joe's words still rankled.

'Look. Your parents. Obviously having you.'

Ryan frowned as he stared at the photo. 'Are you sure the bride couldn't be pregnant? You really look like her.'

'I do, don't I. But she couldn't be. Look, Catherine's stomach is as flat as a pancake, and I was born four months after the wedding. If she'd had a loose dress on, I could believe it, but she's tiny. There's no way she's pregnant.'

Ryan sat up straight. 'Mum and Dad are gone, and your parents won't tell you anything. But there are a couple of things we can do.'

Dee sat still and looked at him. 'What?'

'We can call in and see Sandra Porter, and ask her what she remembers while we're in Darwin tomorrow. She was obviously friends with them if she and Peter were at the wedding. And we can go to the Births, Deaths and Marriages place and get your birth certificate.'

'Do you know where it is?'

'Nope, but I can soon find out.' Ryan pulled out his phone and started Googling. 'Darwin Ground Floor, Nichols Place, corner of Cavenagh and Bennett Streets. I know exactly where that is. It's only two blocks from the Darwin Hotel where we ate the other night.' His fingers flew over the letters and he kept reading.

Dee craned forward to see what he was looking at. 'Maybe it'll take a while to arrive?

'Do you have any ID with you?'

She nodded. 'My driver's licence, my Medicare card and a few bank cards. And I've still got my uni photo ID in my wallet.'

'Well, if they're happy with that, look what it says here. If you apply in person, you will receive your certificate immediately. You'll be able to collect it tomorrow when we're there.'

Dee jumped to her feet and let out a small squeal. 'That's fantastic. Can we leave really early so we get there as soon as it opens?'

'Of course we can. And we'll drop that DNA kit back in as soon as we have your birth certificate. I checked the other day; they do the testing in the private hospital in Tiwi. We can detour there on our way in.'

'I just had a thought.' Dee crossed to the desk where her laptop was set up. 'If we're delivering the kit and then we go in to pick up the results, it should be quicker than five days. Maybe?' She pulled up the lab website and opened the menu before going to DNA testing. Turning slowly to face Ryan, her voice shook a little as she told him what she'd read. 'If we get there at eight-thirty and drop the kit in, we can collect the results tomorrow afternoon after four.'

Ryan grinned at her and that familiar quiver fluttered in Dee's belly.

Please don't be my brother, she thought. *But then, if he's not, I'm even further from the answers I'm looking for.*

'Well, we have a very busy day tomorrow. Go to the lab, into town and then pick up your ute, and try to get an appointment with Baker. So we'd better get to bed, you know it's almost midnight? Come on, I'll walk you back down to your room.'

'There's no need,' Dee said, but she was pleased when he insisted.

The three small dogs met them at the front door and followed them outside. The night was still and clear, and Dee looked up at the sky.

'It's like black velvet with diamonds,' she said softly. 'I thought we had clear night skies at the farm, but this is so big. Oh look, a shooting star. Isn't that supposed to be good luck?'

Ryan took her hand and tucked it in the crook of his elbow. 'When I was a little tacker I used to sit out in the rose garden with Mum after dinner. She loved the night sky. She used to say a shooting star was a positive sign, a little bit of magic. And good luck for anyone who happened to see one.'

'So let's take that as a positive sign for tomorrow. We'll find out if we're related, and I'll find out who my parents are on my birth certificate.' Dee forced a laugh to cover up the emotion in her voice. 'And I'll get my ute back.'

'And we'll go and see Baker and drill him a bit more. And if you don't find out from the birth certificate, we'll find out where Sandra lives and ask her what she knows.'

'Sounds like a good plan.' Dee had control of herself again.

Before they reached the donga, Ryan stopped walking and Dee stood beside him.

'What's wrong?'

Ryan's eyes glinted in the moonlight as she looked up at him.

Her heartbeat picked up a notch as he lifted his hands and cupped her cheeks. It was hard to see the expression on his face.

'I just want to say one thing before tomorrow. No matter what we find out, and no matter what happens with the station, I want you to know now that I hope with all my heart we're not related.' His voice was gruff.

'Me too,' Dee replied softly.

Before he let go, Ryan leaned forward and brushed a light kiss on her forehead. 'Good night, Dee. Try to sleep. I'll pick you up at six, and we'll grab a coffee on the highway.'

He stepped back and whistled the dogs. Dee stood at the door and watched until he disappeared into the darkness.

Chapter 31
Wilderness Station.
Friday October 16, 1987.

Suzanne Carey squeezed the rag mop in the metal wringers and breathed in a sigh of relief as she held the bucket steady. It had taken her over an hour to work her way around the four verandas, but now the flagstones were gleaming. Last month, Colin had hired an itinerant worker from Jabiru to seal them with high gloss sealer, and when they were clean, they looked fantastic. When they were covered in red dust, Suzanne rolled her eyes, went inside and did her best not to let it bother her.

Life on a cattle station in the middle of the Northern Territory was very different to where she'd grown up on a small hobby farm in the Lockyer Valley, just west of Brisbane. The dust and the smoke on the cattle station bothered her asthma, but worst of all, the weather played havoc with her moods. Each year as the monsoon season built and her anxiety grew, Suzanne found it hard to sleep. She suffered from constant headaches and her energy was almost non-existent. Some days she felt as though the air was so thick and heavy it impeded her movement.

As the monsoon season built Colin was short-tempered with her, and she tried to ignore it, knowing that it was the build-up of the heat and the humidity that made him cranky. Maybe it was just as well they had no kids; she wouldn't have made a very good mother.

Each year when the rains finally came, her energy returned with the electrifying thunderstorms. The heavy rain turned the station into a vivid green landscape, and she would be content again for a few months. Her garden flourished and she took most of her pleasure from the roses and tropical blooms.

Bill Jarragah, one of the aboriginal stockmen on *Wilderness* explained it to her one day last year. He helped Suzanne look after the garden between his work at their cattle camps.

'We call it *Gunumeleng*,' he said as he helped mulch the rose garden one afternoon and the thunderheads built on the horizon. 'There'll be no rain from those clouds today, but we know as sure as the sun rises and sets each day, that the rains will come.' He stood and moved the wheelbarrow along to the next raised section of the garden. 'The humidity tells us there will be a new season of growth, and the land and the animals are thankful.' He'd shot a sidelong glance at her. 'We should be too.'

Suzanne sighed; she didn't have time to stand around now. She would have preferred to be inside at her sewing machine making the new curtains for the study, but Colin had insisted on inviting the crowd for tennis tomorrow. That would mean drinks and dips, and salads to go with the inevitable barbeque. Her brother, Joe, was here between camp contracts, and he'd offered to get started in the kitchen while she mopped the verandas. She looked up as Colin's ute rumbled across the cattle grid and before she could get his attention, he'd opened the ute door, and his cattle dog shot across the lawn, and onto the wet flagstones.

'Banjo, get off the bloody veranda.' Suzanne pulled the mop out and swung it at the dog, and he was off like a shot. It would be nice if Colin was a bit more considerate occasionally.

Her husband was grinning as he walked over and stood on the edge of the lawn. 'Garden looks good, Suze. And the veranda. Came up good, didn't it?'

'It did. All we need now is a decent barbeque area.'

Colin shook his head. 'What's wrong with cooking over the drums like we always have?'

'We've got a good-sized back veranda near the tennis courts and lawn to put some decent tables on. If you want to keep entertaining, it would be a much nicer area for tennis parties.'

'Okay. We'll see.' Her husband lifted his head up and sniffed. 'Something smells good. Is it all for tomorrow or can I have some for smoko?'

Suzanne shrugged; she knew Colin didn't like her brother. 'Joe's cooking. You'll have to ask him.'

Colin's expression closed off. 'Don't tell me he's going to freeload at our party tomorrow.'

'I'm not going to fight with you, Colin.' Suzanne sighed. That's all they seemed to do lately. 'Joe's pulling his weight and having him in the kitchen has freed me up to clean the house and the verandas. You're the one who wanted this big do, and I'm the one who gets stuck with all the cooking and cleaning.'

Colin's eyes narrowed. 'That's your job, love.'

Suzanne turned around and picked up the bucket and mop. Ignoring her husband, she walked across to the rose garden and slowly tipped the dirty water out at the base of her rose bushes. By the time she turned around, he'd disappeared, but his dusty footprints had turned to muddy streaks on the flagstones.

##

Saturday October 17, 1987

Late the following afternoon Suzanne stood in their bedroom looking at the three dresses hanging in her side of the wardrobe. She knew Colin preferred to see her in a dress. He was so old fashioned it drove her crazy. His attitude to women could have come straight from the 1950s.

Pulling a face, Suzanne opened the top drawer of the chest of drawers. A pair of capri pants and a light blouse would be more comfortable for running the food and plates out from the kitchen than a dress and heels. She quickly changed and put on a dash of lipstick and pulled a comb through her hair. It wouldn't be long before a convoy of utes and family sedans would make their way in from the highway. She wasn't looking forward to tonight; they were Colin's friends and he'd expected her to slot into his social scene when she'd come here as a bride ten years ago. The group had grown over the years with new arrivals in the district. Most of them had kids now and she got sick of the thinly-veiled curiosity about their lack of a family.

It wasn't for want of trying. Suzanne stared at herself in the mirror and forced her lips into a smile. It was time to get out of this mood; she was unhappy far too often lately.

With a bit of luck they'd all play tennis after the sun set—Colin was proud of the tennis courts that now had night lights—and she could get organised in the kitchen with Joe. He'd cheer her up.

'Not ready yet, love? That's good.' Colin poked his head around the door, and then closed it behind him as he came in. He winked at her and walked across and put his arms around her. 'I'm going to have a shower. Why don't you have one with me?' His hands crept down her back and slipped down the back of her capri pants, as his lips nuzzled the back of her neck.

'We don't have time. Everyone'll be here in a minute.' Suzanne wasn't in the mood, and she was still angry with Colin.

'It won't take long.' She froze when Colin grabbed her hand and put it on the front of his work trousers. 'I'll be quick, love, I'm primed and ready to go.'

Suzanne brought back the forced smile. 'Well, I'm dressed and ready to go and meet our visitors, so you'll have to take a shower by yourself.' She stepped away and picked up the comb. 'Besides it's the wrong time of the month. My temperature hasn't dipped yet.'

Colin scowled. 'Maybe if we forgot about the damn temperature and were a bit spontaneous for once, you'd get bloody pregnant. I'm going to have my shower.' Before the ensuite door had completely closed, he yelled out. 'And put a dress on. You look like you're going to feed the chooks.'

Suzanne stared into the mirror and smoothed her hands down the sides of her capri pants. They were a pretty pale blue, and the blue and white floral blouse was one of her favourites. She lifted her chin and headed to the kitchen.

Joe, God love him, had four platters of green salad sitting on the bench and was chopping the onions for the barbeque.

'Spuds are almost ready, Suzie. All I have to do is make the dressing.'

'Thank you. I honestly don't know what I would have done without you today.' She ran the tap and damped down four tea towels to cover the salads.

'You would have managed. You okay?'

'I'm fine. Why?'

'You didn't look too happy when you walked in.'

Suzanne forced her third smile of the afternoon as she twisted the water from the tea towels; she knew there would be many more forced smiles before the night was over. 'I'm good.'

'Who's coming tonight? The usual mob?'

'Ah, let me think. The Romanos, the Stuarts and the Johnsons are coming, plus Peter Porter. And Sandra. I know the two Sloane girls are coming too.' She glanced at her brother. 'You like Bridget, don't you?' Suzanne knew Joe was still keen to take Bridget out. She couldn't stand the woman and didn't want her as a sister-in-law, but Joe had laughed at her when she'd said that after he last barbeque.

'God, you women can be bitchy,' he'd said with a grin.

'So that makes thirteen adults including us and how many kids?'

'It feels like two hundred when they all start running around on my lawn. I'll keep an eye on my rose bushes.' Suzanne put her head down as she heard Colin walking up the tiled hallway. The outside fridge door creaked, and then he walked in holding two beers.

'Shout ya one, Joe?'

'Thanks, mate. I'll just go and have a quick shower.' He took the stubby from Colin, popped the twist top off, and drank half of it before heading down the hall.

Suzanne looked up as an arm snaked around her waist, and a light kiss brushed her cheek. 'Sorry, love. You look lovely. I can be a pig sometimes.'

She held herself stiff and nodded. 'You can.'

'I mean it. I was out of line. Still love me?'

'You know I do.' With a sigh, Suzanne turned and looped her arms around Colin's neck. As much as Colin could be difficult, she did love him. She'd agreed to marry him, and he did make an effort most of the time. 'Maybe we can take a raincheck on that shower later tonight.'

'Sounds good to me.' He nuzzled his lips into her neck. 'I love you too. Now promise me you'll try to enjoy yourself tonight.'

'I will.

'And make sure you talk to Catherine and Bridget. I thought you were a bit rude again last time they were here.'

Suzanne looked over her husband's shoulder and rolled her eyes.

Chapter 32
Darwin.
Thursday 10 a.m.

Ryan stood beside Dee at the counter of the Births, Deaths and Marriages office in Darwin as she handed over her credit card. Her identification documents had been accepted, and the clerk on the counter had sent the request upstairs. The payment was processed, and the woman gestured to the row of black padded benches along the wall behind them.

'Take a seat. I'll call you when it's printed.'

They walked over and Dee sat on the bench seat closest to the door.

'That seemed fairly easy.' Ryan sat beside Dee, moving slightly to the left to make sure his leg wasn't touching hers. 'Like the lab at the hospital. Being able to get the DNA results at two-thirty was a bonus.'

'Technology.' Dee jiggled her feet on the floor and folded her arms. Every twenty seconds she looked over at the counter. 'Soon we'll be able to do it all from home. Wherever that may be,' she muttered.

'Do you want a drink of water?' Ryan gestured to the water station in the corner next to a huge pot plant.

'No, thanks. I'd throw up. I feel sick enough as it is. Oh my God, I can't sit here and wait. I need some air.' She jumped to her feet and headed towards the door.

'I'll come out with you.' Ryan stood and went to follow her.

'No. You stay here and wait for them to call me. Then come and get me.'

Before he could agree, Dee was out the door in a flash of tanned legs half covered by knee-length shorts. Her slim fitting T-shirt showed off well-toned arms, and he dragged his gaze away. Ryan wouldn't admit it to her, but his gut was churning too. If Dee turned out to be his half-sister, this constant awareness of her had to disappear instantly. He leaned his head back against the wall and closed his eyes as the hum of conversations at the counter drifted across to him.

Family had been on his mind all night. He'd tossed and turned and had very little sleep. Knowing he was going back to the hospital where Mum had passed away before he'd had a chance to say goodbye had been hard, but the quick visit had been okay. The only familiar place was where he'd parked the ute and he'd looked away from the building where her ward had been; the laboratory where they handed in the test kit was in a building well away from that section of the hospital.

He'd coped. The news that the results would be ready earlier had dispelled some of his strange mood earlier, but the feeling that something bad was about to happen had grown as they'd got closer to the hospital this morning.

It had made him think about Dee; he'd had time to grieve for Mum and he had all his memories. For Dee, the arrival of one letter, a meeting with the lawyer and an old newspaper had turned her life upside down. She didn't know who her parents were, and he couldn't imagine what that would be like.

Life was so uncertain; like Baker said, he needed to make a will. Dee's arrival, and then hearing the stipulations of Dad's will had got him thinking about the future.

And that was problematic. Who the hell would he leave the property to? He'd been very slack not to do it before this, but at his age, it was the last thing a man thought of.

Ryan tried to think logically about his will discussion with Baker. He'd been angry with Joe last night, and he didn't like the way Cy behaved a lot of the time, but they were the only family he had. Like Mum had wanted, he knew he'd find a partner one day and hopefully they'd have some kids who inherited his love for the land and *Wilderness Station*.

He had known Dee for less than a week, but a connection had already been forged. No matter what the birth certificate and the DNA results revealed, he would look out for her.

Half-sister, friend or—

'Deanne Peters.'

Ryan jumped up as Dee's name was called. The woman was gesturing to him and he hurried over to the counter.

'Where did she go?' she asked.

Ryan lowered his voice. 'She's a bit nervous about seeing her birth certificate so she went to wait outside.'

'I'm not supposed to give it to you, but I did notice how stressed she was.' The woman slid a white envelope across the counter. 'Here, you take it out to her. Don't you open it.'

'Thank you. Much appreciated, and I'll give it to her immediately.' Before the woman could change her mind, Ryan took the envelope and hurried outside.

He stood on the footpath looking around and glanced across to the car park, but there was no sign of Dee. He was about to walk back to the car and wait for her to come back when he spotted her in Civic Park on the opposite corner. She was sitting on the grass under a tree, knees drawn up to her chest and face hidden by the fall of her dark curls. Ryan checked both ways for traffic and sprinted across the road, the envelope clutched in his hand.

Shit, he felt like spewing too.

When he reached the park, he slowed his pace until he reached her.

'Dee?'

She looked up and he held the envelope out to her.

'The lady gave it to me for you. Do you want to go back to my ute to open it?'

'No. Here is fine.' Her hand shook as she reached for the white envelope.

'I'll go back to the ute and give you some privacy.'

'No.' She gestured for him to stay. 'Please. Sit here with me.'

Ryan sat on the grass beside her but leaned back and looked over the park. He heard the envelope open and then there was silence. After a full minute he found the courage to turn his gaze back to Dee.

The birth certificate was on her lap and she was staring down at it.

'So?' His voice was husky.

Dee looked at him and it was hard to read the expression on her face; there was certainly no joyful excitement. Without speaking she picked up the birth certificate and their fingers brushed as she passed it to him. He ignored the tingle that ran up his arm. Holding the certificate up, Ryan skimmed over the words.

Deanne Maree Sloane.
Date of birth: August 3rd, 1988.
Place of birth: Darwin Public Hospital.
Mother: Bridget Lorraine Sloane.
Mother's occupation: Waitress.
Father: Unknown.
Father's Occupation: Unknown.

He looked up and Dee stared back at him.

'Well, that solves half the problem.' Ryan was almost as devastated as Dee looked. If her father is noted as "unknown" on the birth certificate about the only person who could tell them who he was, was Bridget. Or the DNA test results, if Dad was her father.

'Bridget must have been pregnant with me in that photo at Catherine and Gerard's wedding. That loose dress hid it and I didn't notice. Although I wasn't looking at her.'

'I wonder where she is now? At least you know who you're looking for. She's the one who can fill you in on the missing pieces.'

'As soon as we're home—I mean back at the station—I'm going to have a very long conversation with Catherine. No wonder I look like her. She's my aunt. And if she won't talk to me, I'll talk to Gerard until he tells me the truth.' Her voice was like steel. 'Someone will tell me the truth. Now that I have this proof, they have no reason not to.'

Ryan hesitated before he said what was on his mind, because he didn't want to put it into words. Finally he spat it out. 'And it doesn't help sort our relationship either. And if in the extremely unlikely event that my father had an affair with Bridget—your mother—we share one parent.' Ryan passed the certificate back to Dee and watched as she put her birth certificate back in the envelope.

Her eyes were sad as she looked up at him. 'I guess we'll find that out this afternoon.'

Ryan pushed himself to his feet and went to hold out his hand to help her up, and then thought better of it. He brushed down the sides of his jeans instead. 'Come on, we'll go and collect your ute and then we'll find somewhere to have lunch.'

Dee didn't speak as she followed him to the car park.

As Ryan looked for traffic, he noticed a man in a dark baseball cap sitting in a small sedan parked in a No Standing zone. He was staring at Dee, and when he saw Ryan looking he turned away and the car pulled out immediately.

He narrowed his eyes and stared at the car as it took off up the street.

Chapter 33
Darwin.
Thursday 2.00p.m.

Dee and Ryan didn't call in to see Sandra Porter; when Ryan called Ellie for her address, Sandra was already on her way down to the farm.

'Ellie said she'll be there tomorrow, so we'll call in then,' he said. 'She said she forgot to ask her mother if she remembered Gerard and Catherine.'

Going to the panel beater—Dee was really pleased with the paint job on her ute—was one positive outcome of the day. They'd left it in the car park there planning to pick it up after they'd been to the lab.

'Stupid to drive around in two vehicles,' Ryan had said and smiled as Dee looked longingly at her ute. 'Don't worry, you'll have your baby to drive later today. Are you sure you want to take it on the dirt roads at the station?'

She nodded. 'I need my independence.'

By the time they'd left the panel shop and had lunch, it was almost two.

'Ready to go to the lab?'

Dee nodded. Ever since she'd read the birth certificate details, she'd felt numb. Trying to cope with a whole new existence and make sense of what had happened was hard. She was impatient to ring home and decided to ring from her car before they headed back to the station. 'I might go to a shopping centre when we split up. I need to pick up a few things.'

'You'll be able to find your way home okay if I go ahead?'

Dee smiled for the first time in a while and held up her phone. 'I'm a big girl and I've got Google maps.'

'The service is patchy once you get on the Arnhem Highway,' Ryan said with a frown.

'I'll be fine,' she insisted.

Ryan nodded and turned onto Bagot Road.

It was an easy city to get around, and it was quickly becoming familiar to Dee.

Childhood memories? she wondered.

'I guess it's the sort of thing you have to take time to process,' she said half to herself.

'Process the test results, you mean?' Ryan asked with a frown.

'Yeah, that too. Sorry, just thinking aloud.'

'Ah, yes I get you. And true, it's going to take a while for you to adjust, I guess.'

'And once we get the test results, there'll be even more to process.'

An hour later as they sat in a coffee shop back in the city reading the test results, Dee thought later how close she'd been to the mark with that comment.

'Bloody hell,' Ryan said. 'You need a physics degree to read this.'

'Biology,' Dee said absently as she ran her finger down the columns. They each had a copy of the results and she was going through her copy line by line.

'All this percentage stuff doesn't make sense to me. What's wrong with a simple yes or no,' Ryan said putting his copy of the results on the table.

'Read the disclaimer at the bottom.' Dee kept her voice patient. She'd almost worked this out. 'The results can't be conclusive unless at least one parent is tested. That is, you and me and the parent we think we might share, but unfortunately that's impossible.'

'I'm getting another coffee,' Ryan said crossly. 'We've still got half an hour before we see Baker. Do you want one?'

'Yes please, half-strength this time, or I'll be like the Eveready Bunny when we're in his office.'

Dee was pleased to hear Ryan chuckle. 'Okay, I'll look after the coffee and cake. You look after the science.'

She ran her finger down the columns and read the disclaimer at the bottom again. It was taking a while to get her head around the meaning.

She read the words quietly beneath her breath. *"'The DNA of two individuals with different biological mothers is compared to determine the likelihood that they have the same biological father. For full accuracy it is recommended, that samples from one—and preferably both—biological mothers be tested if possible. This enables us to determine exactly which genes the two children inherited from their biological father(s) and thereby greatly increases the conclusiveness of the test.'"*

'Fuck,' she said loudly, getting a disapproving look from the elderly lady at the table across from her. 'Sorry,' she muttered, turning back to the letter. This time Dee turned it over and her eyes widened; she hadn't realised the summary of results was printed on both sides of the paper. Her smile grew as she read the conclusion.

DNA testing was carried out to determine the existence of a relationship between the two participants. Based on testing results obtained from the analyses of the DNA loci listed, the possibility that they share a common biological parent is one hundred percent negative. The extra genetic markers tested are enough to conclusively deny a relationship between the two participants.

Dee's smile was wide when Ryan came back to the table. 'Excellent. Cake,' she said. 'Did you get me a piece?'

'I got this for you. I don't want any. I'm too grumpy.' He stared down at her as her grin widened.

'Good, you can share mine, grumpy. We're celebrating.'

He frowned as Dee waved her copy of the result at him. 'Maybe I shouldn't feel so relieved because it creates another problem for me, but read the back of the page. It was printed on both sides. Your father is not my father. There is no relationship between us. However that does leave the problem of who my father is.'

'That's fantastic.' Ryan's face lit up after he'd read the back of his results page. 'So the next question is, if we're not related, why are we sharing an inheritance of my father's cattle station?'

Dee ignored the spike of hurt that his words caused and pulled the cake over. 'If you don't want to celebrate, I'll eat it all.'

'No, we'll share, thank you.' He reached over and broke off a piece of cake. 'Dee, we have to sort this out. I didn't mean that how it sounded. We haven't talked about what we'd do once we find out who your parents are.'

'Do?'

'About the station and the will.'

'I don't want to talk about it now, Ryan. I just want to process what we found out today.'

'Come on, share your cake and be happy with me.' He reached for her hand. 'You're not my sister, and I'm very happy about that.'

Chapter 34
Tuesday November 3rd, 1987.

On Melbourne Cup day, Suzanne came in from the garden, her arms full of roses. She'd stripped the bushes clean of all blooms because a severe thunderstorm had been forecast for later in the afternoon. Maybe this storm would reach them, and the heavy air would finally disperse. Perspiration had soaked her dress and a headache was building.

The light on the answering machine was blinking, and she carefully laid the roses on the dining room table. The sweet perfume of the Mr Lincoln rose, her favourite, filled the room and made her smile. As soon as she'd put the roses in water, she'd go and stand under a cool shower and get changed before Colin came in for lunch.

Pressing the button on the machine, she froze as she listened to the message. Bridget's voice was unmistakable, Suzanne put her hand over her mouth as she gagged and held back that nausea that threatened.

'Remember, room two thirty-three, Diamond Beach Hotel my sweet Coli-flower. See you soon.' A giggle, followed by, 'Don't forget to press delete.'

Suzanne forced herself to be calm and regain self-control. Her hands were still shaking when she heard the bathroom door open and close. It was only eleven-thirty, too early for lunch.

'Where are you, love?'

Suzanne swallowed. 'I'm in the dining room. I'll have a wash and set the table. I've made a salad, it's too hot to have a cooked meal.'

'Leave it in the fridge. I've got a major breakdown in the cool room next to the mess. I'm going to have to go to Darwin. I have to go to the engineer's workshop out at Pinelands. They think they can fix it today, but if they can't, I'll stay overnight.'

Suzanne amazed herself with her calm controlled reply. 'It's Melbourne Cup afternoon. Why don't you leave it until tomorrow?' She waited.

'I've got a few other chores to do. Not everyone stops for a blasted horse race.'

'Probably not,' she replied, turning back to the roses. Colin came over and pecked her absently on the cheek. 'I'll see you sooner or later,' he said.

She froze as she noticed he'd shaved this morning. Did he think she was such a fool that she wouldn't notice the cleanshaven face, the aftershave and the clean clothes?

'My ute's a bit grubby. I might take your car. You don't need it today, do you, love?'

Suzanne nodded and held her breath as Colin left the room. A few minutes later, she heard the purr of her Holden Commodore cruising off the station.

The roses lay abandoned on the table as she raced down the hall and out on to the side veranda that faced the gate. As she dragged in deep ragged breaths. the rear of her car disappeared over the hill to the north.

Not only was Colin going to meet that bitch, she'll be in my car.

Putting her hands to her face, Suzanne slid down the concrete wall, until she landed with a jolt on the flagstones. Not knowing what to do. Not knowing what to think. Not knowing where to go.

I should take his ute and go to the hotel and confront them. But she wouldn't give Bridget Sloane that satisfaction. Suzanne had no doubt that Bridget had left that message deliberately. She wanted them to be found out—she wanted Suzanne to leave Colin, and she obviously wanted to be here on *Wilderness Station* with him.

Well, the bitch could wait. Suzanne had no intention of going anywhere. But there was no way that woman was ever setting foot on their station again. It was time to put her foot down.

She raised a shaking hand to her face, surprised to see it come away wet with tears; she'd been unaware she was crying. In the far distance the first low rumble of thunder shook the sky.

What was the correct protocol when your husband left the house to go and meet his mistress? She had no one to talk to, and no one to ask. Even though she was friends with Sandra, she couldn't bear the thought of anyone else knowing. And it wouldn't be fair to burden Sandra with her awful problem.

The first guttural sob came from low in her chest and forced its way up into her throat; Suzanne gave in and let the pain consume her.

There was no one to hear her. She cried, she screamed, and she cursed. In that moment, she realised she could quite happily kill Bridget Sloane. If she'd walked in now, she would have got the shotgun from the laundry, loaded it, and pointed it at the scheming bitch.

She'd been so naïve. Colin and Bridget had played her for a fool all year. No wonder he'd been happier; she couldn't make him happy, but his mistress obviously had.

And he'd been sleeping with her every opportunity he got. Suzanne thought of all the times lately when Colin had been "held up" or had to go to Darwin for a part at short notice. He'd been at that woman's beck and call.

Suzanne turned her head and vomited on the flagstones. The tears rolled in a constant stream down her cheeks, and she pressed her palms onto her eyes so hard she saw stars.

Ugly and unloved. And infertile. That's where she'd failed Colin. That's why he'd gone looking elsewhere.

The afternoon passed, and Suzanne didn't move. Even when the storm hit with a roar of thunder and wind, she sat there with her eyes closed. The three dogs came running out and sat beside her, but she couldn't even summon the will to pat them. Sensing that she was upset, Athos climbed into her lap and the other two snuggled down on each side of her legs. The storm passed quickly and then a waft of sweet air, blessedly cool, touched her face. The back of her head was pressed hard against the sandstone bricks and Suzanne dragged in deep breaths of the fresh air.

Opening her eyes, she was surprised to see that the sun was already low in the sky. The sky to the north was a brilliant blue and the air was crystal clear. She would go to the end of the veranda and look at the valley. The sun would be on the distant cliffs, and that would calm her. Suzanne tried to straighten her legs and cried out in pain as the blood began to flow to her feet.

'Hello? Is anyone home?' A deep voice came from around the front of the house and Suzanne put her head back again and closed her eyes, hoping that whoever it was would just go away.

The three dogs jumped up and ran to the corner of the veranda, each of them yapping. Athos stayed where he could see her, but Aramis and Porthos ran around to the front.

Peter Porter appeared around the corner and hurried along the veranda until he reached her. 'Suzanne? What's wrong? Are you ill?'

'Does anyone ever call you just Peter?' she said stupidly. 'Or are you always Peter Porter?'

He dropped to his knees beside her and put his hand on her forehead. 'What's wrong, Suzanne? Have you had a turn of some sort? Did you faint and hit your head?'

'No, to all of the above.' She tried to push herself to her feet, but her legs wouldn't hold her, and she slid down the wall again. Mortification filled her as her fingers touched the pool of vomit.

Before she could blink, she'd been scooped up by two strong arms and was being carried along the veranda to the front door.

'Which room is your bedroom?' Peter asked.

'First on the left. No, not in there. I don't want to go there. I'll have a new bedroom from tonight. He'll never share my bed again.' Her voice quavered as more tears filled her eyes; there shouldn't be any left in there. 'Three more doors down the hall to the spare room.'

HIDDEN VALLEY

Her head lolled against Peter's chest as he walked down the hall with her in his arms.

'Is there anyone here I can get to help you?' he asked softly as he pushed the door open with his shoulder.

'No. I'm here by myself. I don't think . . . I don't think Colin will be back tonight.'

'I'm just going to bend down and put you on the bed. Do you want to lie down, or will you feel better sitting up?'

'Sitting up please.' Now that she'd had the big crying jag and screamed it all out to one lone steer on the other side of the house fence, Suzanne was feeling stupid.

How weak am I?

To let another human being bring her to this state. She didn't care if he was her husband; Colin wasn't worth shedding one tear over, let alone the bucketloads she'd cried since lunchtime.

'Is there someone I can call for you?' His voice was kind and Suzanne took in the kindness and let it warm her. It was a long time since Colin had spoken to her like that.

'No, thank you, I'll be fine. I just had a bit of a shock, that's all.'

Peter lowered her to the bed and the guestroom bed creaked. He looked a bit unsure but seized on her words.

'A shock? A cup of sugary tea is what you need. Stay there and I'll bring you one.'

'Thank you. Make one for yourself too. It would be nice to have someone to talk to for a while.'

While Peter was in the kitchen, Suzanne slid off the bed and went to the bathroom. When she washed her hands, a blotchy face and swollen eyes stared back at her from the mirror. She ran the cold water tap, and then soaked a flannel and pressed it against her eyes. It didn't make much of a difference to her appearance, but it helped soothe her sore eyes and nose.

As she walked back into the hall, the kettle whistled, and she headed for the kitchen. Peter stood at the bench spooning tea leaves into the small gold painted teapot she used for her breakfast tea.

He looked up, surprised, as she stood in the doorway. 'I was going to bring it in to you.'

Suzanne managed a shaky smile. 'Now that my legs have got some feeling in them, I don't feel so bad.'

'Are you feeling a bit better?' he asked staring at her.

'I am. I'm so sorry you saw me like that.' She pulled out a chair at the table. 'I just feel embarrassed. I had a bit of a meltdown.' She knew Peter well enough from his part-time work on the station, as well as the tennis nights. He'd always been friendly, and happy to have a chat when he saw her in the garden, but she felt sorry for him now as he stood there and ran his hand through his hair, looking at a bit of a loss.

'I'm sorry,' she continued. 'Were you looking for . . . Colin?'

'I was. I wanted to tell him that there's a problem with the bore out at the weaners' camp.'

To Suzanne's chagrin, her throat closed as she tried to speak, and the ache in her throat came back. She lifted a shaking hand to her mouth and shook her head. 'He's . . . I'm not sure—'

Peter lifted the teapot. 'Milk first or last?'

She waved her hand. 'Doesn't matter.'

'My mum always said you'd have redheaded kids if you put the milk in last.'

Her smile was bigger this time. 'So did mine.'

Without asking, Peter stirred two heaped teaspoons of sugar into the milky mug of tea, and then put it in front of her. 'Drink.'

Suzanne put her head down and did as she was told.

Chapter 35

Darwin.
Thursday, 2.30pm

As they walked along Cavanagh Street to Baker's office, Ryan knew he'd upset Dee. He hadn't wanted to say he thought it was fantastic that she wasn't his half-sister. He felt like a spoilsport, so when she stopped in the middle of the footpath and grabbed his hand he was surprised.

'I've got a plan,' she said. 'And it might just force Baker's hand.'

'A plan?'

'Yep. I reckon we can get him to tell us more now. I mean there's stuff we're allowed to see after six months. So let's see if we can make him change his mind, and we see it now.'

'Okay, spill.' They started walking and Ryan looked down, surprised that Dee was still holding his hand.

'Don't stress. I'm not suddenly coming onto you. I don't need to. I've already got half your cattle station,' she said, her tone brighter than it had been all day.

'So what are you—we—doing?'

'We're practising what we are going to show Mr Baker. Love at first sight and all that. It's got to kick him into a reaction. And we don't tell him about the DNA test, but I'll tell him I've found out who my mother is and see if he has a contact for her. I don't hold out much hope about being told by Catherine or Gerard.'

As they waited to cross the road Ryan noticed a guy watching them from the other side. As he watched the guy pulled out his phone and turned sideways to them. There was something familiar about him; he must have worked at the station as a ringer once.

'Ryan?' Dee tugged at his arm. 'The light's green. Come on, we're just on time.'

He held her arm as they crossed the road, but by the time they go to the opposite corner, the guy had gone. 'Okay, so how are we going to play this?' he asked, quietly impressed with Dee's proactive plan.

'Just follow my lead,' she said.

'Am I going to be sorry if I do?'

'No, and hopefully we might come out of there knowing exactly what's going on.'

***

'Come in.' Mr Baker held his office door open. 'I'm pleased to see you both back so soon.' He ran his gaze over them, and his eyes widened as they settled on their joined hands.

Good, she thought. *Let him wonder.*

'You both look a bit more settled since you were here last week. I assume you've come in to sort out your individual wills today?'

Dee answered for them both. 'Perhaps, after we talk to you.'

'Ah, I see. Would you like some coffee?'

'No, thank you,' Ryan said. 'We've just had some celebratory coffee and cake on the way here. It was a bit early for champagne.'

'Celebratory?' Mr Baker repeated.

'Yes,' Dee chimed in. 'We've had a very busy week, going through Ryan's parents' papers and some old newspapers at the station that his mother saved, and I've been to the registry office up the street from here and picked up a copy of my full birth certificate today. Everything is falling into place.'

'Ah, I see,' he said again. 'So what do you want to tell me?'

Dee shook her head, and leaned across the desk, pinning the elderly man with an intent gaze. His hands were clenched on the desk. 'No, Mr Baker, it's not what we want to tell you, it's what you can tell us now that we've found out most of it ourselves.'

He nodded slowly and moved around to the other side of his desk and sat down. 'So may I ask what you've found out, and what you're celebrating?' His tone was cautious.

'I have discovered who my mother was.' She reached over and touched Ryan's arm, hoping she was not overdoing it. 'And I have found my soulmate.'

Again the eyebrows rose. 'Your soulmate? You've known each other less than a week.'

Dee wasn't game to look at Ryan.

'That's right.' Ryan came in to support her. 'But when you meet the one, you know immediately.'

'The one?' The expression on Mr Baker's face was pure shock.

'Yes, that's correct.' Dee feigned embarrassment and dropped her gaze. 'But as you can imagine, before we take our relationship to the next . . . um . . . the next level, we need to be sure that our assumptions are correct.'

'The next level?' Poor Mr Baker's face went brick red. 'Assumptions?'

'Yes.' Ryan leaned forward. 'Dee and I are going to be living and working together for the next six months as you advised as per the conditions of the will. We would appreciate your honesty in allaying our fears as to who her father is.'

'The logical assumption is to assume that my father was Colin Carey, but we need your reassurance that that is not correct. To my knowledge he didn't know my mother, Bridget Sloane. I would also like to know the contact details for my mother.'

There, she thought, *that way you'll know we have been investigating.*

'I'm sorry, I have no details for your mother at all.'

'So, you are aware of her identity.'

Mr Baker inclined his head, but looked away. He seemed flustered. 'As you have the birth documentation, I see no point in not confirming that for you.'

Dee nodded. 'Thank you. Now I need to know my father's details.'

'Even though my father left half of the property to Dee,' Ryan added, 'we need absolute reassurance that our assumptions are correct.'

Dee kept her attention on the lawyer, and she saw the exact second that he decided to tell them what they wanted to know. He lowered his head, and lifted a shaking hand to his face. His lips tightened and after a moment he let out a breath. 'You have been very busy, and by your investigations and new . . . ah . . . relationship, you have pre-empted some of the things that I was instructed to tell you after six months of Dee remaining at the property. As you know half of them already, I can probably reveal some of the information.' He shook his head, even as he held Dee's eyes. 'As I said, you are correct—or rather your birth certificate is correct. Bridget Sloane is certainly your mother, however'— Dee was grateful as Ryan reached over and took her hand— 'your other assumption is incorrect. Colin Carey was your father, and that's why he left half of the station to you.'

Ryan's hand dropped hers instantly and he stood. Dee struggled to take in a breath as she stared at the lawyer. 'So Ryan and I are half siblings?' She turned to look up at Ryan and his expression was as stricken as hers.

'The DNA test was wrong?' she whispered.

'DNA test?' Mr Baker asked. 'I'm unsure what test you are referring to, however there are certainly DNA records in the documentation for you. Ryan, I regret to tell you, but this is as per Colin's will, that you are mistaken.'

As Ryan stood and looked down at Dee and Baker, a cold feeling spread through Dee's chest.

Ryan was her half-brother.

Mr Baker gestured for Ryan to sit again and he eased back onto the chair.

'I know this will be a shock to you, Ryan, particularly. Colin Carey and Bridget Sloane are indeed your biological parents, Dee.'

'What?' The shock intensified and flooded through Dee in one rolling wave that seemed to consume her whole body. Her ears began to buzz, and she wondered if she was going to faint. Focusing on her breathing, she turned to Ryan; his face was white.

'We are half-siblings,' he said. 'And my father had another child, the same time I was born?' Anger and sorrow melded in his voice.

'No, Ryan, that is not correct.'

'What? What are you trying to say? For God's sake, man, stop stuffing around and get to the point.'

'Ryan, I regret I have to tell you this. I know it will be a shock to you, you are Dee are not half-siblings.'

'But we have the same father,' Ryan protested.

'Colin Carey was not your biological father,' Mr Baker said quietly.

'What the *hell*?'

Dee gasped as Ryan jumped out of his chair. It crashed onto the floor, but he left it there.

'That's bullshit,' he yelled. 'How can you possibly say that? It's a downright lie. You are talking about *my* father.' He turned to Dee. 'I don't know what's going on, but it's not true.'

'It is, Ryan, and now that you have both forced the issue, I can provide you with the documentation to prove it. Including two sets of DNA test results that your father provided to my brother.' Baker's face was red, as perspiration trickled down the side of his face he pulled at his collar. 'One test proving who your parents were, Dee, and a test proving that he did not father you, Ryan. He had that done after your mother passed. He left it all for you with his will.'

Dee was grateful Mr Baker spoke slowly and clearly. The blood was pounding in her ears and she knew Ryan was even more stressed than she was.

'He knew? The bastard knew I wasn't his, my whole life? Why the fuck didn't you tell us all this the other day, instead of going on with that bullshit?'

'No, Ryan, he was unaware that you were not his son until the day your mother died. He told me soon after. He came in straight after her funeral because he wanted to get this will sorted so that both of you were provided for after he passed.'

'So who is my father?'

'I'm sorry, Ryan, I can't tell you that.'

Ryan grabbed the front of Mr Baker's shirt. 'Tell me now. I'm sick of this fucking secrecy.'

'Please sit down. I can't tell you because I don't know, and your father didn't know either. Your mother wouldn't tell him.' Mr Baker stepped back and smoothed his shirt.

'Come on, Dee, we're out of here,' Ryan said.

Dee didn't know what to do or say when Ryan opened the door. She felt as bad as he obviously did. It appeared she had two parents who knew she was their daughter, but neither of them had bothered to contact her. She stood and followed him.

'Wait.' Baker hurried to the door, trying to get them to stay, but Ryan kept walking.

The paralegal sitting at the back desk lifted her head as the went through the foyer. 'Mr Carey, Ms Peters, I was about to bring these in to you.'

Ryan stopped and looked at the envelopes she held out.

'Vivian, what is that?' Mr Baker frowned.

'Letters for Mr Carey and Ms Peters. They were in the safe. I remembered them when you arrived.' She handed one each to Ryan and one to Dee.

'No, wait. I should see them first.' Baker's face was red as he held his hand out.

Ryan took the two envelopes and looked at the lawyer. 'I don't think so, Baker. They're addressed to us.'

He took Dee's hand as they left the office.

They stood in silence as the lift took them to the ground floor.

Chapter 36
Wilderness Station
July 29 1991.

Suzanne sang softly under her breath as she shaped the two squares of cake into a racing car. Ryan loved his cars, and Colin was forever bemoaning the fact that their son would not want to be a cattleman when he grew up.

She jumped as a pair of hands came around her waist, and warm lips nuzzled her neck. 'Can I lick the beaters, Suz?'

She pushed Colin's hands away, but she was smiling.

His lips found their way to her neck again. Suzanne closed her eyes, enjoying the love that Colin had showed her every day since she'd announced she was pregnant. 'You're lucky Ryan's asleep or he would have licked them clean by now.'

'Hard to believe our little champ's three today, isn't it?'

'It is. Now Colin, leave me alone or his birthday cake won't be finished before he wakes up.'

'Are you sure you didn't want to have a party for him?' Colin asked as she walked over to fill the kettle.

'I'm sure. The two most important people in his life will be here to watch him blow out the candles and sing happy birthday to him.'

'Mummy? Cake?'

The subject of their discussion stood in the doorway holding his favourite blue racing car to his chest.

'Could be worse, 'Colin whispered. 'It could be a doll.'

'And if it was, there'd be nothing wrong with that,' Suzanne said. 'Now be a love and either get out of my way while I finish this, or better still, make me a cup of tea and take Ryan out to play while I do the vegies for dinner.'

Colin made a cup of tea for both of them, and put Suzanne's on the bench next to the bowl of blue icing. He winked at her as he took the two almost empty beaters from the bowl with one hand and scooped Ryan up with the other. 'Come on, mate. We'll go and sit outside and see who can lick the fastest.'

'Don't let the flies get on Ryan's, Colin.'

Her husband leaned over and kissed her cheek. 'I wouldn't dream of it, sweetheart.' As they walked to the back door, he turned around and smiled at her. 'Love you, Suz.'

Tears pricked Suzanne's eyes as happiness flooded though her. Since Ryan's birth, their marriage had mended and Colin had gone out of his way to be a good husband and a loving father.

Suzanne stoically refused to look back further than the past three happy years, and vowed that their marriage would stay strong and happy for the rest of their lives together.

With a smile she put the teacup down and started to sing again.

Chapter 37
Darwin Private Hospital.
August 2018.

Ryan locked his ute with the remote, took a deep breath and then smoothed his fingers over his hair as he stared at the manicured lawns of the private hospital. At least the dry weather of August had tamed his curls and given him a semblance of tidiness. The white-breasted wood swallows would be roosting in the trees near the mangroves on the edge of Hidden Valley, and that meant the thunderclouds would start to build soon; Mum loved watching the birds arrive every year, and this week Ryan reckoned there would be hundreds there by now. He straightened his collar and tucked his polo shirt into his jeans.

Swallowing the lump that seemed to be stuck in his throat permanently lately, he wondered if Mum would still be here when the storm season arrived. This time, she'd been in hospital for ten days as the chemo had made her violently ill, and the station was too far away from the hospital to come in quickly when her temperature went up. The specialist's advice that she move to Darwin had been met with a blunt refusal.

'I won't leave my home or my roses,' she'd said.

Ryan bent down and wiped a speck of dirt from the shoes he'd polished earlier. He knew he was delaying going into the hospital; he hated the smell, he hated the bland beige paint on the walls, and he hated the soft music, but more than anything, he hated seeing his mother wasting away more each time he visited.

Steeling his resolve, he put the car keys into his pocket and crossed the car park. Although it was only ten a.m., the heat was shimmering above the concrete. The dry was coming to an end and he needed to get out to the far camps and check the bores; that would be this afternoon's goal.

Pushing open the door of the hospital foyer, Ryan stepped into a different world. Calm and peaceful, even the movements of the receptionists were silent and contained. He walked up the long corridor and tried not to take notice of the sterile smells that assailed him. His stomach began to object, but he knew it was more from stress than the antiseptic smell.

Dad was dozing in the chair beside Mum's bed, and the sight of his usually energetic father asleep—and still holding Mum's hand—made his throat close. The specialist had told them that the chemo would add eighteen months to her life, but all Ryan could see was his mother getting sicker and frailer each time he visited. She'd gone downhill in the last ten days.

'Sweetheart, you must have been up early,' his mother whispered as she lifted her face for his kiss. He leaned over the bed and brushed his lips over her cheek.

Her once soft skin was dry and papery, and he could hear the rasping of her breath as he stayed close to her.

'I was. I love this time of the year. The air is so clean and dry. I went for a wander around the garden and I watered your roses.'

'Thank you.'

'Did Dad stay here with you all night?' He glanced at his father and the sadness deepened. Dad looked so old.

'No, he stayed until about ten, and then he went to the motel down the road. I need to talk to you, Ryan. Dad was a bit upset, and he didn't sleep well.' She looked at her husband and her smile was sad. 'I don't think I've ever seen him sleep in the daytime before. Not once in the forty-three years since I married him.'

Colin's head jerked and he leaned forward, dropping Suzanne's hand. He looked around confused, as though he didn't know where he was. 'Sorry, love, I drifted off.' His expression softened when he saw Ryan on the other side of the bed. 'Morning, son. You're in early.'

'I was worried when you didn't come home last night, or call. I wanted to check you were still here and not broken down on the side of the road somewhere.'

They exchanged a look. Dad knew he'd come in to see Mum.

'You sound like the parent,' Colin said. As he looked back over at Suzanne, his lips set in a straight line and he reached for her hand again. 'Are you okay, love? Have you had your mid-morning tablets?'

'I'm good. Now that I've come to a decision, I feel calm.' Suzanne nodded and she reached her other hand out to Ryan. 'Come and sit on the side of the bed, darling. I want to talk to you.'

Ryan's heart almost stopped when his father's bottom lip quivered. 'Decision? What decision?'

Dad leaned forward, his shoulders hunched over, and he put his free hand over his eyes.

'It's all right, Colin. I'll tell him.'

'Tell me what, Mum?' Now Ryan's heart was pounding so hard it hurt. He sat on the edge of the bed as his mother gripped his hand. Her fingers were thin, her wedding ring hanging loosely near her knuckle.

'I want you to listen carefully. And before I tell you, there is to be no argument, no trying to persuade me to change my mind.' Suzanne cleared her throat and her voice was louder. 'We—Dad and I—had a meeting with the specialist yesterday. The chemo's not working, and he gave me some options.'

'What options? More surgery?' Ryan stared at her. Mum had already had a double mastectomy and it had taken her a long time to recover from the surgery. Then she'd been through a regime of radiation, and now more chemo.

'No, darling. I'm going to stop all treatment.'

'Why?' Ryan's breath hitched as he forced the word out.

'Because it's making me too sick.' She squeezed his hand. 'And it's not working. I want my last days to be pleasant, and not spend them throwing up from some invasive treatment that's only going to give me a few extra weeks. I want to come home and sit in the garden and watch the storm clouds build with the two men I love beside me.'

'How long?' The first tear rolled down Ryan's cheek, but he ignored it.

'Three or four weeks. Dr Alvaro said we can manage the pain at home, and if it gets too hard for you and Dad, we can get a nurse to live in.'

'Three—' Ryan stared at his mother and she smiled at him. 'I don't . . . I can't . . .'

'Hush, Ryan. It's all right to be upset. Once the initial shock wears off, it gets easier. I promise.'

'But Mum . . . what will we do without you?' Ryan gave in to his grief and lowered his face into the pillow beside his mother's head.

'You'll be fine. As hard as it sounds, this is life, my darling boy, and we have to deal with it.' Her fingers touched his forehead gently, just like that had when he'd been a little boy.

Colin stood, and walked around to the bed and placed his hand on Ryan's shoulder 'I've already talked to Cy about getting some more stockmen in and him taking over for a while. That way, we can both stay in the house with Mum every day.'

'And we can talk about all of the things that we are fortunate to have and look back on our happy memories. My only regret is that I won't meet the wife and children I know you'll have one day, but sweetie, I want you to know whenever that happens, I'll be there watching over you. Hold that in your heart for me.'

Ryan couldn't answer, and he stayed still as both his parents' hands stayed on him. Mum smoothed his hair, and Dad patted his shoulder.

Eventually Colin moved away and cleared his throat. 'I'll go and get us some coffee. One for you too, Suz?'

'Yes, please.'

Ryan sat up and rubbed the heels of his hands into his eyes. 'I think I'd rather have a stiff rum.'

'I don't think they serve rum in the cafeteria, but I think that's probably a good idea. While I have a rest, I'd love for you both to go to the pub. Have a counter lunch together.' She smiled up at Ryan and despite the brave front she was putting on, he could see the moisture in her eyes. 'And you can have that rum too.'

All Ryan wanted to do was get out of the bloody room so he could let go of the pain he was holding inside. His voice was thick, and he avoided looking at Mum. 'I've got a couple of chores to do, and I'll meet you there, Dad. About one?'

'Ryan, tell Cy to come visit me too. I won't be coming home for a couple of days. And have you heard from Joe lately? Or is he away droving?'

Colin interrupted. 'I called him this morning and he's on his way back from South Australia.'

Ryan leaned down and kissed his mother, and her hands gripped his. 'I'll see you tomorrow, Mum. I love you.'

'And I love you, sweetheart.'

Ryan managed to keep his emotions under control until he was back in the ute. He put his head on the steering wheel as his chest closed and sobs wracked him.

***

Suzanne lay back on the pillows and let her breathing ease. Now that she'd spoken to Ryan, the tension she'd been holding in for the past two hours began to ease slightly.

'He'll be okay,' she said to Colin as tears filled her eyes. 'He's strong. You're the one I worry about.'

'No need to do that. You're the one we all have to look after.' Colin walked across to the window and stared outside.

'What's wrong? Tell me what's worrying you. Not me and this silly cancer, I mean. I know you well enough to sense you're holding something back, aren't you, Colin?'

When he turned, her husband's face was shadowed. He hadn't shaved today, and the little hair he had left needed trimming. Suzanne put her hand out to beckon him closer. 'Colin, I know we've had some difficult years, but I love you. I've loved you since the first day I saw you. You need to know that. Carry that inside when I'm gone.'

Colin pulled the chair closer to the bed and sat down. He reached for Suzanne's hand again. 'I do know that, love. And I know I've never deserved it. You're a fine woman, and you've been so patient with me. I was an angry bastard in those first years we were married, and I treated you badly. I don't know how you stayed with me. You've done a fine job of raising Ryan, and I want you to know how much I love you. I don't know how I'll go on without you.'

Her eyes were awash with more tears. 'You will, and you'll have Ryan, and you'll have the station to keep you busy. Mourn for me, Colin, and look after my roses, but keep yourself busy. Now tell me what you've been worried about for these past few weeks.'

Colin stared at the floor, but Suzanne was not going to let it go. She had a fair idea what he wanted to tell her.

'I can't bring myself to say the words. I don't want you to leave me, hating me, but I know if I don't tell you, I'll never find any peace. It's not fair, no. I'm not going to say it, because it will upset you too much.'

'I think I already know what you want to tell me.'
'You do?'
'You were unfaithful to me.'

His face blanched and he dropped his face into his hands. 'You always knew?'

'I did. Melbourne Cup Day 1987. The date is imprinted on my mind.'

'It only happened once, Suzanne. I swear it was only once and I've regretted it every day of my life since then. I didn't see her again after that.'

'And that's why you pulled the tennis courts out and put the pool in wasn't it? So we didn't have that crowd around.'

He lifted his face and his eyes were tortured. 'This is my punishment. I'm so sorry, if I hadn't betrayed you, you wouldn't have got breast cancer. I deserve the punishment, not you.'

Suzanne shook her head. 'That's silly. My mother and her sisters all had breast cancer and died in their fifties. I've had almost ten years more than they did. It's not your fault. And Colin, you need to know I forgave you years ago. We've had a good marriage and we have a fine son.'

He reached out and took her hand between his. Her skin was scarred and bruised from the constant injections and catheters.

'I need to tell you something too, Colin. You're not the only one with secrets.'

Colin shook his head. 'Wait. Please let me finish. There's more you need to know.'

Suzanne stared at him as he held her gaze. His eyes were bloodshot, and his cheeks were ruddy with a fine network of veins.

'It couldn't end there and that was my punishment. Bridget had a child. A girl. My daughter.'

Suzanne's breath began as a gasp and then a strangled laugh broke from her lips. 'You have a child?'

He nodded. 'Ryan has a half-sister.'

'Have you ever seen her? Or met her or talked to her?'

'No. And I haven't spoken to Bridget since the day after her sister's wedding, when she called to tell me she was pregnant.'

'I was pregnant at their wedding.' Suzanne looked past him as her thoughts whirled around her head. She put a hand up to her face to stop the dizziness that was threatening. 'So, Bridget was too. She was always curvy, and I hated her for it. Are you're sure you're the father?' Her voice hardened. 'She was very easy with her favours, I believe.'

'I have no doubt. A DNA test was done a few years ago by her adoptive father when I threatened to pull out of our deal. I told him I'd deny everything, and he somehow got my DNA and sent me the proof. He said he'd tell you if I didn't do what he wanted.'

'Deal?' Suzanne's breathing was laboured, and she lay back on the pillows and gestured to the water jug.

Colin poured a glass of water from the jug and held the straw while she sipped and composed herself. If it wasn't so sad, it would be funny. Like one of those twisted movies she'd loved to watch years ago.

'Tell me about the deal.'

'Do you remember Gerard Peters?'

'Yes, of course I do. It was their wedding I was talking about.'

'He and Catherine adopted the child when she was two-years-old and moved away. That's when they sold the mango farm to Peter Porter.'

'Peter Porter.' Suzanne laughed and the sound was on the edge of hysteria. 'And what of Bridget?'

'I have no idea. I never heard of her again, and I had no desire to find her.'

'You need to acknowledge that child. And make provision for her in your will. Promise me you will. She would be a grown woman now, the same age as Ryan. You've provided for her financially over the years? Is that the deal you meant?'

Colin's face took on an unhealthy ruddiness. 'No. Peters blackmailed me. He threatened to tell you and everyone else that I'd had an affair and that Deanne was my daughter if I didn't jump to his demands.'

'Deanne. A pretty name.' Suzanne kept her eyes on him. 'His demands? Tell me what he did. I never liked that Gerard. In fact I never liked any of them except for Peter Porter. I was so happy when he finally fell in love with Sandra. It ended up being a love match, and they were so happy. I can take credit for that,' she said absently, beginning to lose her thread in the complicated past. Her voice softened. 'So many lies. And the guilt I've carried for thirty years because I thought you couldn't father a child.' Suzanne began to laugh until she choked. Colin quickly grabbed her glass of water and put his arm around her shoulder to steady her.

'What do you mean, you thought I couldn't father a child? We had Ryan.'

After taking a few sips, Suzanne blinked and shook her head. 'Later. I'm all right. Tell me about this deal.'

'I signed over the mineral rights for part of the property to him. At the time I thought he was stupid, another one of his schemes, and he did nothing with it. So it was really nothing for me. I mean he's sent geologists in a couple of times, but that's as far as it ever went. There was never any mining. I knew how much you loved that valley, so I called him when you were diagnosed and said the deal was over.'

'My valley? Hidden Valley?'

'Yes. I'm sorry.'

'I want you and Ryan to take me out there next week. I want to see it again before I die.'

Suzanne closed her eyes and let her mind roam back to those days in the late eighties. Those tennis nights, her lovely friend Sandra, that bitch Bridget. And kind Peter Porter who had comforted her in an age-old way the night Colin had betrayed her. Suzanne knew her infidelity had helped her deal with Colin's, and it had begun her journey along the path to forgiving him. The only casualty of that brief, but wonderful, night was her friendship with Sandra. Once Peter and Sandra got together—after that night and on Suzanne's suggestion to Peter—her guilt wouldn't let her stay as a friend to Sandra. Suzanne had used the excuse of a young child taking up her time when Ryan was born, and gradually Sandra stopped calling her.

She drifted for a while until she sensed Colin moving beside the bed and she opened her eyes.

'I'm not asleep. Don't go.'

'What did you mean about thinking I couldn't father a child?' Colin's face had lost its usual ruddiness this afternoon. 'I'm supposed to be meeting Ryan in fifteen minutes. I'll call him and cancel if you want me to stay and tell me.'

'I do. I do need to talk to you.'

Colin made the call and told Ryan he'd see him tomorrow when he came back to visit his mother. 'Yeah, I'm going to stay in town again,' Colin said. 'I'll stay with Mum as long as they'll let me.'

'You mightn't want to,' Suzanne said when he'd put his phone away.

Colin frowned. 'Of course I do.'

'I have a story to tell you too.' She looked past Colin to the window. A bunch of colourful lilies gave her the courage to continue. 'There's something I must tell you. The night you were in Darwin with . . . with . . . Bridget, I was comforted by a friend. Comforted in the biblical sense.' Suzanne lifted her head and flinched when Colin's eyes widened with disbelief. He opened his mouth to speak, but she continued. 'There was no intent, it just happened, and we were both shocked. But you need to know Ryan may not be your child.'

They both sat there in silence as Colin processed the words Suzanne had spoken.

Finally he stood slowly and sat on the edge of the bed. He pulled her up gently from the pillow and cradled her in his arms.

'I love you, Suzanne, and I love our boy. He has been a son to me no matter who—'

Her voice broke. 'Promise me you won't hate him. And promise me you won't tell Ryan. Not yet, anyway. Not until I'm gone, if you must. I couldn't stand it if I spent my last days with him hating me. I don't want to waste precious hours with him.'

'He would never hate you, Suze. He loves you.'

'Ryan is a beautiful son. And he has been a good son to both of us.'

'Will you tell me who it is?' Colin's voice was fierce. 'Because I am his father in every other sense.'

Suzanne turned her head away. 'No, Colin, it only happened once. He was a friend and when I found out about you and Bridget, he was there for me. We were both so guilty afterwards. It won't achieve anything for you to know.' Suzanne put her cheek against Colin's. 'He's gone now, and he never knew. You don't have to worry about that. Ryan is your son in every way that matters.'

Chapter 38
Darwin CBD.
Thursday, 3.00 p.m.

'Yes?' Gerard Peters sat stiffly when he realised who'd called him

'Gerard, it's Frank.' Baker drew in a breath. 'It's hit the fan. They know. They've been running around town doing DNA tests and Deanne got her birth certificate. I can't keep putting them off with this will.'

'Shit, why the hell you ever sent her that letter about the inheritance, I'll never know. If it wasn't for you, she'd still be here, and I'd have two less problems.'

'It wasn't me. The associate took over for a week while I was on leave, and that's how it slipped out.'

'Well, it's been a bloody expensive slipping out mistake for you, Frank. You've been slack, and with that one mistake you've forfeited your share in the deal.' Gerard clenched the phone so tightly his fingers tingled.

'No, you just wait a minute, you can't do that. As much as I don't like it, I know too much about the project, and I still have a copy of Colin's real will. If it wasn't for Reg doing the deeds, you wouldn't have that land. I've changed that will for you so they don't know what's going on. It's okay. You cut me out and I'll go to the police.'

'Are you threatening me, Frank?'

'You guarantee my share from the mining and I'll keep my mouth shut. But if it comes to the crunch, I'll deny any knowledge about wills, land deals or the project. They're both curious and they're digging. And digging deep.'

'I'll think about it. How much do they know?'

'A fair bit. They're not stupid.' Baker's voice quavered.

If there was one thing Gerard hated, it was bloody weakness.

'So why are you ringing me if they don't know about the real will?'

'They might know more when they read the letters.'

'What fucking letters?'

'Letters from Colin.'

'What letters? For Christ's sake, what was in them?'

'I didn't know. They were in the safe and Vivian, the paralegal, gave them to them on their way out today. I tried to stop them, but what could I do? They were addressed to them and marked private.'

Gerard's head started to thump and he loosened his collar. 'For fuck's sake, do you know what this could mean?'

'Probably.'

'You get onto our man out there and you do what needs to be done. Now. Get rid of the pair of them, and I'll consider letting you back in. If you had half the balls your brother had, we wouldn't be in this fucking mess.'

***

Frank Baker was sweating, and prickly heat quivered down his back as he put the phone down for a few minutes and put his head in his hands, not sure if he could go ahead. Perspiration ran down his neck and soaked the collar of his shirt. For the hundredth time in the last two years, he cursed his dead brother, Reginald, his greed and the situation he had left for Frank to handle.

But Frank knew he had no choice. He knew he should have gone to the police two years ago, but greed was in his genes too. He picked up the phone again and his voice shook. 'Joe? It's Frank Baker.'

Chapter 39
Darwin CBD
Thursday 4.00 p.m.

Ryan was numb. Everything he had believed about his life was a lie. His father wasn't his father, and his mother had betrayed Colin. He walked beside Dee as they left Baker's office; he could barely look at her, not knowing how he felt about the man he'd thought was his father being Dee's biological father.

Not his father.

It was too much to take in. He'd scanned the letter Colin had left for him, but had only skimmed it, not taking in all the words as he'd tried to find who his father was. There was stuff about Gerard, and Joe, but Ryan ignored it; he would read it more carefully when he got home. When Baker had said he couldn't tell him, it was not because of any stupid secrecy, it was because he didn't know.

And Colin didn't know either.

'I'll drive you to your ute,' he finally said.

'Thank you,' Dee said as they walked stiffly side by side.

She'd tried to read the letter but had been too emotional, so she'd folded it carefully, and put it in her pocket.

A glimmer of guilt surfaced in Ryan as they approached his Land Cruiser. He'd been bloody rude to Baker, and the situation wasn't the lawyer's fault.

Until he'd processed everything—including the fact that the six month period of Dee living on the station was still a requirement before anyone inherited anything—he couldn't think straight. All he wanted to do was go to the nearest pub and throw back a few rums and get rid of the numbing pain that held him in its grip.

They turned the corner without speaking and reached the Land Cruiser, and Ryan clicked the remote. When Dee was in the passenger seat, he did his seatbelt up with a snap and went to start the engine, but she leaned over and put a hand on his arm. 'Can we talk before we go back to the station?'

He laughed but it was bitter. 'Back to *your* station, you mean. I have no right to it.'

'Stop right now.' Her voice was like a whip and her fingers dug into his wrist. 'Stop that feeling sorry for yourself shit. If you don't, I'll go and get my ute and I'll leave, and I won't come back. Do you think this is easy for me?' Her grip lessened. 'We have to work together to get through this, Ryan. We must.'

When Dee's voice broke, the numbness dissipated. Unbuckling his seat belt, he leaned over and took her in his arms. 'I'm sorry. I'm not coping with this very well.'

She buried her face against his shoulder as his arms went around her and he held her close. 'And you think I am? I might have found who my parents were but it's not a happy situation.'

Ryan held her for a long time and felt the dampness of her tears through his shirt; he was embarrassed when moisture filled his eyes. Gradually calm seeped through him as he rested his cheek on Dee's hair. She was perfectly still in his arms.

'I'm sorry I went off. And I'll call Baker later and apologise to him. It's a bloody awful situation.'

'I can understand why you did. This is a bloody emotional situation. Unbelievable.'

Finally, Dee moved back, and he let her go. She scrubbed her eyes with the heels of her hands and sniffed. 'I'm not going to go to the shops. I'll just follow you home.'

'Okay, I think that's a good idea. I'd decided to follow you anyway. Are you okay to drive?'

'Are you?' she said, smiling though her tears.

'I am. When we get home, we'll sit down and talk this through. I'm not going to say anything to Joe yet. I have a feeling he already knows, from something he said last night.'

'He could, you know, because he'd been pretty ordinary with me. There's a few things I need to tell you.'

'We'll lock ourselves in the study when we get home and read these letters and get our heads around it. I think there's a lot more to this then we thought. Dad—I mean, Colin—must have had a good reason for that six months condition in the will, but I can't figure it out.'

Dee's hand went to his arm again. 'Ryan, he was your father for thirty-two years. Please still think of him as your dad.' She closed her eyes as she realised what she'd said. Just like Gerard had been her father for thirty-two years.

'I'll try.' He snapped his belt back on and started the car. 'Listen, there's a good pizza place at Humpty Doo. How about we get some pizzas and we can heat them up when we get home?'

'A good plan.'

'And a bottle of wine,' he added. 'Red or white?'

'Both,' Dee said, and her eyes met his. Suddenly Ryan knew he would get through this. They both would, if they worked together. Neither of them was at fault, so it was not a blame game.

And he smiled inwardly. The best thing that had come out of today was knowing Dee wasn't his half-sister. He grinned at her. 'You know you couldn't have taken off in your ute, like you said you would.'

'Why not?'

'Because your hallstand is in *our* house, and it would be very expensive to ship it to you wherever you'd planned on going.'

She nodded slowly, but her smile matched his. 'You're right, you know, Mrs Crichton would never have forgiven me. And I love that hallstand. That's a good reason to stay.'

'Who's Mrs Crichton?' he asked, pleased that the rapport between them was back.

'Long story, I'll tell you one day.'

'Okay, and when you do, I think the hallstand should go in the hall near the front door. My mum would have liked that.'

'And my dad,' she said softly.

Ryan nodded and squeezed her hand.

***

Unreality gripped Dee as she followed Ryan's dust-covered Land Cruiser through the outer suburbs of Darwin. She flicked a quick glance sideways as they drove past the Gateway Shopping Centre. Now that she had her ute back, and she had decided to stay at the station for the six months, she would come into the city one day soon and stock up on a few things. With a sigh, she realised she'd have to call Catherine and let her know where she would be living. No matter what her true parentage was, Catherine and Gerard had raised her and provided for her, and she had to remember that. Maybe it hadn't been an ideal childhood, but there had been some happy times. She knew Catherine loved her and had always wanted the best for her. Gerard could go take a flying leap as far as she was concerned.

Dee managed a smile—even though Catherine's and her ideas on what was the best had differed greatly. She glanced down at the long nails where the red polish was growing off. That would be her first job in Darwin next week. Find a nail salon and get back to normal.

Her phone was paired to her ute's audio. Once they got on the highway, she'd try blue toothing a call home before the service dropped out.

Dee tailed Ryan's Land Cruiser closely, always a couple of hundred metres ahead of her, past the turn off to Howard Springs and then they gradually left suburbia behind. Dee smiled as they passed termite mound after termite mound adorned with a variety of clothing. Beanies, straw hats, tank tops and the occasional coloured bra—Ryan had told her on the way in that it was mostly international backpackers who dressed the tall dirt mounds in the colourful clothing. She followed his lead and put on her left indicator as they approached the Arnhem Highway, and then turned onto the main road to Humpy Doo and Jabiru, past market gardens and mango farms.

Ryan, who was not her half-brother. Ryan, the man who when he had held her a while ago, had made her feel more cared for and nurtured than she had in her entire life. From a simple five minutes of being in his arms as they had comforted each other. Tonight would be a night of healing for them both as they supported each other; talking and planning as they finally knew as much as they could. Dee ticked off the unknowns: the reason she had to do six months on the station, the mystery of Ryan's father, and the whereabouts of her mother, but she would demand that from Catherine. She *must* know where her sister was.

Where my mother is.

Dee was itching to sit down and read the letter that Colin had penned for her. The words had blurred when she'd teared up outside Mr Baker's office when she'd tried to read it and she'd put it aside carefully for later when she was by herself.

Ryan slowed in front of her, and she braked. Eventually they drove into the small town of Humpty Doo and he put his left indicator on. She followed his vehicle into the car park of a small shopping centre.

Dee waited in her ute until he came over.

'What's your poison?' he asked, bending down to talk through her window when she opened it.

'Poison?'

He chuckled and Dee was pleased to see the lightness of his expression. His eyes were brighter, and his face had colour in it again. Ryan had obviously been doing some thinking too.

'Pizza. What sort do you like?'

'Oh, anything except chicken. Chicken does not die to go on pizza.'

'Another thing we agree on, partner.' He lifted his hand for a high five and Dee laughed with him.

Oh, this feels so much better.

'I'll go and order now.'

'Okay, there's a bottle shop over there. I'll go and get the wine,' Dee said.

She watched as Ryan bounded up the three steps to the pizza shop, and a warm feeling filled her.

Everything was going to be okay, but the one thing she knew she had ahead of her was learning about the workings of a cattle station. It didn't daunt her—Dee was looking forward to it; she loved a challenge.

Grabbing her purse, she climbed out of her ute, checked that the cars either side had enough room to open their doors without scratching the beautiful new blue paint job. It was so good to have her wheels back; she loved this car, and it also meant she'd be independent once they were back at the station.

A small dark sedan with tinted windows cruised in and parked near the bottle shop. Dee frowned; she'd seen that car before. It was the same as the car that had driven out of the station the day she'd got spooked. Curious, she walked slowly across to the veranda that ran along the front of the four shops, waiting to see if she recognised the person inside the car. A chill ran down her back as she remembered the keying of her ute in the motel carpark, and she hesitated; she might just go back and stay with her car.

Dee went back to her ute and leaned on the tailgate, waiting for Ryan to come out of the pizza store. If he was there while she went to the bottle shop, she wouldn't feel so twitchy. Maybe she was being paranoid, but she knew it was the same car. Was someone following her? Or them? No one got out, and it was impossible to see the driver through the dark tinted windows.

Ryan came out of the shop and came over to her. 'Have you been to the bottle shop already?'

'No, I was waiting for you to mind my ute.' Dee felt silly for being paranoid so she didn't mention the car.

'Mind it?'

'Yeah.' She gestured to the cars either side. 'Make sure they don't open their doors on my paintwork, or God forbid, let a shopping trolley run into the back of it.'

Ryan shook his head. 'You're hopeless. It's only a car.'

'Yes, but it's my car and it's bright and shiny and I love it,' she said throwing him a grin as she headed for the bottle shop. 'Don't you leave it alone while I'm gone.'

'I wouldn't dream of it. If they call my pizza, I'll tell them I've been ordered to guard a car from the general population.'

Dee pulled a face at him but moved fast as she went into the bottle shop. She quickly found and paid for a bottle of each of her favourite red and white wine, and hoped they'd suit Ryan's taste. There was so much she didn't know about him, but despite that, she trusted him.

When she came out of the store, her glance flicked to the left, and relief filled her; the dark sedan had gone. She'd been stressing about nothing.

Ryan was leaning on her ute with his arms folded.

'Don't *you* scratch the paint,' she said with a grin.

'Here, give me those bottles and I'll put them in the esky on the back of my ute. You don't want them rolling around the floor of your perfect ute.'

She handed them over and Ryan put them in the esky before heading back into the pizza store.

Soon, they were on the road again, and Dee looked at the passing landscape with interest as she followed Ryan's Land Cruiser. The highway wound east through scrubby forest, and they drove through the occasional small settlement and passed a couple of turnoffs to crocodile tourist centres. She'd fallen back a little and a couple of cars had overtaken her and were between her ute and Ryan. Dee was confident that she remembered where the turnoff was. She was sure he'd wait there for her anyway. Glancing across at her phone, she turned the ute audio on and ordered Siri to dial Catherine.

To her surprise, the phone picked up immediately.

'Darling, it's so good to hear from you.' Catherine sounded bright and perky, considering it was well into wine time at home.

'Hello . . . Mum.' Dee focused on the highway ahead as she thought of how to phrase what she wanted to say. 'It's good to talk to you too. You sound well.' Dee pulled a face. She couldn't say "sober".

'Yes, it's been an excellent day. I went out to lunch, and I drank soda water. Drinking just makes me feel worse. I'm trying to cut down.'

'That's good to hear.'

'Or it was a good day until five minutes ago. Your father just arrived home and he's in a filthy mood. I'm going to watch Netflix after dinner and leave him to his mutterings.'

Dee chuckled. 'So nothing's changed at home then?'

'No, still the same, except I miss you. When are you coming home, sweetie?'

'Mum, I need to talk to you. Will you promise to listen to me and not hang up?'

A long drawn-out sigh. 'I've been expecting you to call again. I told Gerard it would come to this. What do you what to talk about?'

'I've been to see the lawyer in Darwin and my suspicions have been confirmed. You adopted me, didn't you?'

'No, we didn't.'

'Mum, come on, please. I know you did.'

'We took you in, Dee, but there was never any formal adoption.'

'From your sister, Bridget?'

'Yes.' Catherine's voice trembled. 'From Bridget.'

'Why didn't she want me? Why have I never seen her, even as a pretend aunt?'

'When your father—your real father—wouldn't leave his wife and marry her, she shut down. She gave birth to you; she gave you to me and she took off. I've never heard from her since.'

'So what's my real name? Peters? Or Sloane?'

'We had it changed to Peters before you started school.'

'Oh.' Dee didn't know what to say as emotion clogged her throat. After a while she managed to speak. 'Thanks, Mum. I appreciate you telling me. I'll—hang on a minute. She focused on the road ahead and slowed the ute as a massive road train thundered towards her. The huge left wheels were on the red dirt at the side of the highway, and a cloud of red dust filled the air ahead. Her heart beat faster as the speed of the huge truck created pressure that pulled her ute towards the centre of the road, and she slowed even more as the three sections of the huge truck passed her. The smell of cattle drifted in and she wrinkled her nose as it combined with the red dust.

Once the truck had passed and the dust had cleared, she looked ahead, but the traffic had pulled away and there was no sign of Ryan's Land Cruiser ahead. 'Sorry, a road train just went past. What I was going to say was—'

Dee accelerated slightly and the ute surged forward. She glanced in the rear vision mirror and was taken aback to see a vehicle close behind her. So close it was almost touching her tailgate. She accelerated a little more but kept an eye on her speed; the road was an unknown and she was very aware of the soft red dust on the edge of the highway.

Dee's head jerked as her ute shuddered when the vehicle behind nudged her, and then there was a loud bang as he accelerated into her.

'Bastard, what the hell are you doing?' she yelled.

'Dee, what's the matter? Are you all right?' Catherine's voice screamed through the speakers.

'Yes, no—just hang on.' Dee accelerated again and glanced in the rear vision mirror and her blood ran cold. It was the vehicle from the car park at the pizza store, and as it gained speed, she could see the driver. It was a man, but his cap was pulled low over his face. As she turned her attention back to the road, she realised she was going too fast for the tight curve ahead. She hit the brakes and at the same time the car behind drew close to her again, pulled out onto the wrong side of the road and sideswiped her ute.

Dee wrenched the steering wheel to the right as the car fell back, but it was too late, she'd reached the curve and the wheels of the ute hit the fine red dust at the side of the road. The back of the car lifted, and she wrenched the wheel to the right again. This time, the tyres found purchase on the bitumen, but she was going way too fast to take the curve. Her eyes widened in horror and she screamed as another road train appeared in front of her, and she desperately steered to the left. A telegraph post loomed ahead and the last Dee heard before her airbags deployed was Catherine's keening cry.

Chapter 40

*Arnhem Highway.
Thursday 5.30 p.m.*

Ryan waited at the turn off to Wilderness Station for fifteen minutes before he began to worry. He'd lost sight of Dee's blue ute about half an hour ago, but he knew that she'd see his Land Cruiser at the turnoff and wouldn't go flying past. The traffic heading east was heavy now as those who commuted to Darwin for work from the small settlements along the Arnhem Highway headed home for the day. He looked at his watch and decided to give her another five minutes and then he'd head back and see what was holding her up.

As he waited, a white ute slowed and turned off and parked beside him. Kane McLaren climbed out and walked across to Ryan.

'Gidday, mate. I thought it was you.'

Ryan held out his hand and they shook hands. 'Hey, Kane. On the way home?' The McLaren farm was about another ten kilometres down the highway.

'Yeah, mate. I've been to Darwin to pick up some parts for the tractor. There's always something. Lucky to get through, highway just closed. I was the last vehicle through.'

'Ah that explains it. Dee was travelling behind me, but she must have got caught in the traffic. What's the hold up? Road trains? I passed a few.'

'Nuh, a bad crash. A ute's overturned and ended up in the paddock. Hit a telegraph pole and flipped by the look of things. It looks like it's clipped a road train and gone off the side of the road. Ended up upside down in a paddock. I couldn't stop and help because they were waving the traffic to keep going. There were a few vehicles stopped helping out.'

Ryan's mouth dried as he stared at Kane. 'A ute? What sort of ute?'

'I couldn't see the make from the road, but it was a bright blue one. A Ford or a Holden, not a four wheel drive.'

'Holy shit.' Ryan swivelled around and was up in the ute in seconds. 'That's Dee's ute.'

'Wait,' Kane yelled as Ryan started the engine. 'I'll come with you.'

'How far back, mate?' he asked Kane as he ran around and jumped in the passenger side.

'I'd say about twenty ks,' Kane said. 'Just this side of Wak Wak.'

They were silent as Ryan swung the ute onto the highway. He ignored the speed limit, but there was no oncoming traffic as they headed west back along the highway, and he accelerated more. The sun was low in the sky and he had to slow down a couple of times, squinting as the slanting rays shone onto the windscreen. They didn't pass one vehicle.

'The road must still be closed,' he muttered as worry gnawed at his gut.

'The road train was sideways and one of the trailers had tipped.'

'Cattle onboard?' Ryan asked, his words clipped.

'No, it was empty.'

He nodded and focused on the road and increased the speed more. Kane sent him a glance and grabbed the Jesus bar, but Ryan didn't react.

It wasn't long before they saw the tipped prime mover of the road train ahead, but there were no vehicles queued heading west.

'Looks like the lane to Darwin is open,' Kane said.

Ryan pulled the Land Cruiser to a stop on the verge and jumped out, closely followed by Kane. All he could think of was Dee laughing up at him as he'd teased her about her precious ute.

He strode across to where three men stood beside a man sitting in front of the wrecked prime mover. Ryan assumed he was the driver, but it looked like he wasn't hurt. He looked past the wrecked cabin and caught his breath.

His world stilled. Dee's ute was on its roof about thirty metres into the paddock. A small crowd were standing around it and two men were leaning down looking inside. Ryan's vision blurred as he stared at the scene, but he couldn't see Dee.

'She's still inside. That's not good,' he managed to say. He took off at a run with Kane beside him.

'Calm down, mate.' Kane's voice was low. 'Take it slow. There are people over there helping.'

Ryan nodded, but he kept the pace up. The ute had flipped a fair way into the paddock. It was hard to catch his breath. 'I have to see if she's okay. It'll take ages for the paramedics to get here from Humpty Doo.'

'Ryan!'

Disbelief filled him and he stopped and swung around. Dee sitting on the back of a ute on the side of the road with a rug around her shoulders and her legs dangling above the ground.

'Thank God.' He changed direction and jogged along the road to her and was there in seconds. 'Are you hurt?'

'I'm all right. Don't look so worried. I'm fine,' she said as he reached for her and took her hands.

'Are you sure?' He looked past her to the ute. 'You can't be. Shit, Dee, look at your ute.'

'I know. My beautiful ute. I wonder if the panel beater is still open?' Dee said with a shaky grin.

Ryan shook his head. 'You've scared ten year's growth out of me.' He stared across the paddock. The driver's side was a mangled mess, the roof dented in, and the windscreen was smashed. It would be a write-off.

'Did anyone call the paramedics?' he asked.

The rug slipped off Dee's shoulders as she leaned towards him. The woman sitting beside her lifted it and put it around her again. 'I'm a nurse, and I've checked her over. She seems okay, and she said she didn't hit her head. Said she doesn't want them.'

'I'm not hurt,' Dee said. 'Honestly.'

'It's a bloody miracle if you're not. What the hell happened?'

'Calm down, mate. She's fine. That's all you need to know for the time being.' Kane's voice brought him to his senses.

'The police are on the way,' Dee said quietly. 'I need to talk to them. I was run off the road deliberately.'

Chapter 41
Wilderness Station.
Thursday 7.00 p.m.

When Ryan and Dee finally got back to the homestead, darkness was falling. Dee yawned and tried to keep her eyes open. It was just past seven when they'd dropped Kane at his ute at the gate. He'd paused before he closed the door.

'We'll come over for a drive tomorrow to check on you, if that's okay with you guys?' he asked.

Dee nodded when Ryan looked at her. 'Of course, it'd be nice to see Ellie again, and I haven't met your little boy yet,' she said to Kane.

Ryan was quiet as he drove the ten kilometres along the back road and then turned on to the road to the homestead. He parked the Land Cruiser in the big shed at the back of the house and came around to the passenger side to help her out. 'I'll go down to the donga and get your stuff once I get you settled. From tonight you're in the house.'

'Do I get a say in that?' She burred up.

'In a word, no.' His fingers were cold on her skin as he helped her down from the ute. 'Wait here while I get everything out of the back.'

Dee did as she was told, too tired to find the energy to argue. Being interviewed by the police, and seeing her totalled ute put on a truck had left her mentally and physically exhausted. Dealing with an hysterical Catherine when she'd borrowed a phone—Dee's was still in the ute somewhere—to call her and let her know she was okay, had been hard emotionally. Her elbow was sore where it had hit the door as the ute went over, and her chest was tender from the air bag, but apart from that she was okay. The seatbelt had held firm and she hadn't hit her head as the ute had flipped.

Physically okay, but scared. She knew that guy had been trying to kill her; the air bag and the seat belt had saved her life.

On a scale of one to ten, today would be lucky to get a one; Dee thought of everything that had happened since they'd headed off to Darwin early this morning. Her birth certificate, the DNA results, the meeting with Mr Baker, the letter that was pulling at her to sit down and read slowly, and Catherine telling her that she hadn't see Bridget for years, all followed by the accident that she knew had been an attempt on her life, plus the care and concern that Ryan had shown her, all melded into one big mess in her head.

Once Ryan had unloaded the esky—Dee had been so preoccupied, she'd forgotten about the pizza and wine they'd bought—he came around and took her arm with his free hand.

'I'll show you the main guestroom. You can move in there and make it yours. For good, or until you find one you might prefer, but honestly, it's the best room for you. It's got its own bathroom, and a small sitting room with a desk and it opens out onto the side veranda on the rose garden side. Could be a bit dusty, and we'll have to make the bed up, but apart from that, it's fine.'

She slid her hand down his arm and squeezed his hand. Being looked after was a new experience for Dee. 'Thank you.'

As they walked across to the house, there were no lights on. The dogs ran out to meet them, yapping and jumping at Ryan's legs.

'Are you hungry, fellas? Joe must still be down at the mess,' Ryan said. He turned around with a frown. 'His car's not there, and Cy's ute's gone too. Cy was coming in from the camp tonight, ready to plan the next muster with me. It's good Ellie'll be here tomorrow, we can combine it with work, and save another trip.'

Ryan stopped and stared over at the dongas and the mess building as they reached the verandah. 'The mess is in darkness too,' he said. 'I wonder where everyone's got to?' He took Dee's arm and opened the screen door, and it was a blessed relief to step into the cool and quiet hallway.

'Do you want me to heat up that pizza?'

'Yes, please. I'm starving.'

He led her down the hall and then took a right into another side hall she hadn't been to before.

'Gosh, this is a huge house,' Dee said as Ryan opened the door to a bedroom, and she followed him into a light and airy room decorated in cream and rose pink.

'And that's my excuse for the dust,' he said lightly. 'Being a huge house, I mean. This room's been closed up for a while, so it shouldn't be too bad. I want you to lie down and have a rest while I go down to the donga and get your stuff. I'm still not convinced you're okay. I think we should go into Jabiru Hospital tomorrow and get you checked out. You're a bit pale.'

'I'm okay, honestly. It's more emotional shock than anything else. It's been a strange day.'

'It has been a very strange day.'

'For both of us.' Dee dropped her eyes as Ryan stared at her. 'Does the door have a lock?' she asked moving across to sit on the side of the bed. Her legs were shaking but she wasn't going to admit that to Ryan.

He looked at her curiously. 'My room's in this wing, but don't worry, I won't come in without knocking.'

'Don't be silly. I didn't mean that. I guess being nervous is normal after someone's tried to kill you.'

'You don't think it was an accident?'

'No. Go and get my stuff, and I'll tell you what happened while we eat.'

'You're not too tired?'

'No, I'm not. Now go and do what you have to do.'

'Yes, ma'am.'

Ryan was out the door like a shot. Dee stood and turned the key in the lock before walking over and checking that the door to the veranda was secure. She pulled the heavy curtains closed.

Dee walked slowly across to the bed, and sat on the end. Leaning forward, she dropped her head into her hands as she waited for Ryan to come back to her.

Chapter 42

Jabiru Hotel.
Thursday 9.30 p.m.

Joe belched and took another swig of rum. No matter how much he drank, his anger grew.

'Dad. Go easy on it. You look like you're about to have a heart attack or something. What's got up your nose?' Cy lifted the schooner glass off the table and drained it. 'It's about time we went back to the station. I'm supposed to be talking to Ryan tonight about the muster.'

Joe grunted.

Cy gestured to the bar. 'You want one more before we go back?'

'Bloody oath, I do,' Joe said.

Cy shook his head and walked across to the table where the stockmen and ringers from the station were sitting together. They'd all come into town for the weekly snooker competition. Joe looked over his glass at them.

Stupid buggers. He'd sat in the corner nursing a rum all night while Cy had sat with them for dinner. He wasn't bloody hungry. Just pissed off.

Baker's call had put him a filthy mood.

'We're going to head back now, guys. Don't play up too much, we've got a big day tomorrow.' Cy's voice reached him as he went across to the bar; he came back to the table with a Coke for himself and handed Joe another rum.

'One for the road, Dad, and then we're going.'

Joe's phone rang again and he jerked his head for Cy to leave him.

With a shrug, his son went back to sit with the stockmen.

Joe listened and spittle flew from his mouth as he answered.

'Yes, he's already called me. And Carey? I don't care if he's fuckin' dead. Best day of my life when the bastard carked it. He shafted us, and now you tell me he's her fuckin' father? Why the hell didn't you tell me that years ago?' He listened and his lips lifted in a smile.

'Too right I would have,' he said. 'I would have killed the bastard then.'

The voice on the other end was firm.

'I don't believe it.' Joe said. 'No, not my sister. You're a fucking liar.'

He sat there and shook his head from side to side as he listened. 'Okay, so what do you think is in the letter?' He slumped back in the chair and cursed as he knocked his glass of rum. He caught it deftly before it spilt. 'Right, I've got it. Bloody both of them.'

He put the phone on the table and drained his rum in one hit.

'Cy,' he bellowed. 'We're leaving. Now.'

As they crossed the car park, Joe stumbled and grabbed for his son.

'What's going on, Dad? What have you got yourself into now?'

'Don't you worry about it, boy,' he said. 'I'm going to do something that I shoulda done years ago. But the good news is, it's going to set you and me up for life.'

***

Gerard disconnected the call, disgust burning his throat. He should never have got involved with bloody Joe. He was a fucking loose cannon. Once Joe had dealt with Deanne and Carey's son, he was dispensable too. He was too much of a threat to the deal.

Gerard was angry; he should have moved on the land in the Territory sooner; they could have pulled all the pegmatite out years ago, and Carey couldn't have stopped them, not with Reg Baker in their pocket. Gerard knew he'd been greedy, but that was a risk he'd been prepared to take. Christ knew, he'd taken a few of them in his life and they'd always worked out before.

Bloody hell. Carey had died last year. If he'd known, they would have moved onto the land straight away, bugger waiting for the share price to go up.

Fuck Joe. He should have told him Carey was dead last year. It would have given him time to get out there before fucking wills had been read; it would have stopped all this shit with Deanne and young Carey.

Joe was not going to have a cent of this deal. If it went to shit, it would be his doing.

Carey had been such an easy mark back then. He'd been more interested in getting into Bridget's pants than thinking straight back then. He'd Gerard had bided his time, and waited, knowing the share price would go up again. He'd had his fingers in many other deals, keeping him occupied and seeing his investments rise. But this one, this was the big one that would make him millions, he knew it would. He'd known the share price would take off one day; he'd considered it a long term investment.

And now the share price was starting to move, just as bloody Deanne and Carey's son had come into the picture. Just as the market was lifting out of a two-year slump that had knocked about fifty percent off the battery metal's prices, China had been hit hard by the coronavirus outbreak.

Gerard had a Chinese company ready to bankroll him and they could start mining at Hidden Valley immediately. They'd paid the first two million deposit in cash; the first problem was laundering the cash deposit. Thanks to bloody Dee, Rodney's cash purchase of the farm wouldn't go ahead.

***

Wilderness Station
Thursday 9.30 p.m.

Dee's energy and focus returned after a short rest and a shower, and sharing the pizza with Ryan. She held her hand up when he went to fill her wine glass for the second time. 'One was enough, thanks. I don't want to be sleepy when we read all this stuff.'

They ate in the formal dining room, another room she hadn't seen. Sadly the cedar dining table and sideboard held the same patina of dust as the rest of the house. Dee smiled when Ryan opened the box and handed her a paper serviette.

'I've never eaten pizza out of the box with my fingers,' she said when they'd finished.

'You haven't lived.' Ryan grinned at her and her stomach did a little skip. Indigestion, she told herself.

'I'll make us a coffee and then we'll go to the study. Is that okay with you?'

Dee nodded, and stood to clear the table.

'Leave it, I'll do it later.'

'Would you please stop treating me like an invalid!'

'Sorry.' Ryan lifted his hands in the air and nodded. 'Okay, I will.' He turned to go to the kitchen but stopped and walked back to where she stood by the table. 'Listen, Dee. It's not about treating you like an invalid. When I saw your ute all smashed up this afternoon, I thought I'd lost you. Lost you, when I've just found you, and today with everything we've discovered, I finally knew I could now do something about it. I didn't have to worry about you maybe being my sister anymore.' His smile was shy, and a rush of warmth chased away the last of her tiredness.

'I'll come to the kitchen with you and help you carry the coffee.' Ryan nodded and she knew he'd picked up on her nervousness about being alone. She was still jumpy, and this house was too unfamiliar for her to feel safe. Too many rooms, dark corners, nooks and crannies, and doors to the verandas.

Ryan glanced at her when they came into the study and he crossed to the large window and drew the curtains closed. She settled on the sofa near the boxes of newspapers, and Ryan passed her a mug of coffee.

'Thank you,' Dee said. 'For the coffee and for being thoughtful.' She gestured to the closed curtains.

'It's okay. I won't leave you by yourself.' He sat down beside her. 'Now tell me what you told the police.' Ryan had waited with Kane while she had spoken to the police when they'd finally arrived.

'When you were away on the muster, someone came into the house one afternoon. I knew it wasn't Joe, because whoever it was, was creeping about. When they drove off, I took note of the car. I didn't mention it to you because I thought it might have been someone coming to feed the dogs, and I felt a bit silly, but it did spook me at the time. I worked down in the donga that night. I didn't come up to the house in the dark.'

'You didn't see who it was?'

She shook her head. 'I hid behind the study door when they opened it.'

'No one feeds the dogs except for Joe and Cy and they both have white utes. And they both know the study is my private space anyway. What sort of car was it?'

'I don't know the make, but it was a small dark sedan with tinted windows.'

'Bloody hell.' Ryan pushed his closed fist into his hand.

'What?' Dee sat up straight.

'Remember that night last week at the hotel and that guy there who gave you a bit of a chat up?'

'Yes.'

'It obviously wasn't a coincidence; he's been following us. I saw him on the corner opposite the park before we went in to see Baker this afternoon and he was watching us.'

Dee wrinkled her forehead. 'But why? Why would he be interested in hurting me? Because I brushed him off? Surely not.'

'No,' Ryan said slowly. 'I think it's got something to do with all this legal stuff. We're being watched, and I don't know why.'

'Well, let's get into it and read these letters and see if there's any clues.'

Chapter 43

Wilderness Station.
Two years earlier.

Colin Carey sat at the leather-topped desk and looked at the computer Ryan used for the accounts. Shaking his head, he turned to the drawer and pulled out a foolscap pad, and a fountain pen Suzanne had given him when they were first married. She'd been in his mind constantly over the past few days.

The phone call with Reg Baker, the family solicitor had shaken him. As he'd got all the legal files in order after the funeral, he'd rung Reg Baker to rescind the deeds—for Hidden Valley—he'd shared with Gerard Peters in 1987.

The deal that would keep Gerard quiet about the paternity of Deanne Peters. The bastard had blackmailed him, but now that Suzanne was gone, Colin didn't care if the truth came out. He also had to change his will; he'd promised Suzanne he would look after his daughter, the daughter he had tried to forget about for thirty years.

Most of the time he had been able to forget, but some nights the guilt had overwhelmed him and he'd not been able to sleep as he wondered what she looked like, and what she was doing. He knew she'd be well provided for, but had always worried what sort of father Peters would have been. Catherine was all right, but Gerard was a slime bag.

There was no point worrying now. It was too late.

And now he was caught.

Hidden Valley was lost to the family unless he could find a way out of the deal that Peters had blackmailed him with for the past thirty years. Over the years, Colin had sometimes forgotten about it as time had passed and the Peters—and Bridget—had disappeared from the locality and his life.

Reg had just explained to him that the papers he held at his office would stand up in a court of law and give Gerard ownership of the land.

'No, it was an interest in the mineral rights, not the land.' Colin corrected him.

'No, Colin, the papers I have here show the majority shareholder in the Hidden Valley Mining Co and thus that section of land, is one Gerard Peters. His solicitor lodged the papers with us . . . ah, let me see . . . in December 1988.'

'No,' Colin argued. 'It was only the mineral rights, and it was nothing to do with shareholders. He wanted the land at the time and I said no.'

'No, Colin, that is not what you instructed us to do. I have the notes in front of me.'

'It is, Reg. I signed nothing to that effect. There's been a mix up somewhere. I know exactly what I did. He has done nothing with the mineral rights, and I am going to rescind the gift. There must be a way I can do that.'

'No, that's not correct. I'm very sorry. It is watertight. He owns the land.'

'Reg, I beg your pardon, but that is bullshit, I did not make Gerard a majority shareholder. There was no money exchanged or shares bought, it was the simple deeding of a mineral rights to a section of the land that I am now rescinding. I also want to change my will now . . . now that Suzanne has passed.'

'That I can do for you. We will discuss the question of the land next time you come into the office. Is it a major change to the will or can you give me the information over the phone? I'll draft it up for you.'

'Yes, the property will be divided evenly between my son, Ryan, and my daughter . . . Deanne Peters. There will be conditions attached.'

'Deanne Peters?' Reg's confirmation of the name was fast.

'Yes, that's correct.'

There was silence for a few moments, and Colin got the impression that Baker was wondering if he'd lost the plot. 'Next time you're in Darwin, come in so we can discuss this in the office.'

'I will. When would suit you?'

'Righto, come in and see me next Friday, say four-thirty, and after we sort it all, we can go to the club.'

'Right. See you then.' Colin hung up, confused. There was nothing wrong with his memory, and he had never agreed to anything of the sort.

There was something very wrong there. Colin pulled the pad across to him and began to write.

An hour later he sealed four envelopes and wrote on the front of each of them. In two of the envelopes were letters to Ryan and to Deanne, the daughter he had never met. In the third was a copy of the new will that he had written—he didn't trust Reg Baker—and taken down to the mess, witnessed by two of the permanent stockmen. In the fourth, was a copy of the will to be lodged with his solicitor.

He wrote on the front of each envelope and then placed them in a larger envelope, and addressed it to the paralegal he knew at Baker and Baker. He marked it private and confidential.

He penned a quick note, and attached it to the fourth envelope.

Dear Vivian, I would be grateful if you would place these letters in the company safe and not in my file. Please ensure that this copy of my will goes in my file. Many thanks.

He signed it with a flourish, *Colin Carey.*

Leaving the envelope on the table at the front door, he returned to the study and pulled out the third drawer of the filing cabinet and put the signed copy of his will in the last file at the back of the bottom drawer, as he had outlined in the letter to Ryan.

Ryan, his son, in every way but blood.

Colin put his head in his hands. He had much to be thankful for, but he deserved none of it. He hoped he had made enough reparation.

One stupid mistake and he had ruined so many lives.

Chapter 44

Wilderness Station.
Thursday 10.00p.m.

Ryan and Dee stared at each other in disbelief as they finished reading the letters Colin had left for them.

Dee's face was white, and for a moment, Ryan pushed his anger aside, worried she was going to faint.

'Gerard blackmailed your father,' she said.

'It appears to be the case.'

Dee put her hand to her head. 'I don't understand. Why?'

'Dad . . .' Ryan hesitated saying the word. 'He told me in my letter that he didn't know he wasn't my father until the day Mum died.' He took a deep breath. 'He didn't know who my birth father was either.' Ryan stared down at the patterned carpet. 'So many secrets,' he said quietly. He jumped when Dee moved closer and reached out and took both of his hands in hers. He was almost too numb to register the spark that jolted the nerve endings in his arm.

'I'm sorry, Ryan. With me finding out who my parents are, it's created a huge mess for *you*, and left you wondering now.'

'Don't be sorry.' He gently squeezed her fingers. 'I'm happy for you, and if it helps you deal with it, despite what he said in the letter to me, Colin Carey was a good man. He treated my mother like a princess when I was a child, and in the letter, he said he didn't tell her about you until the day she passed away. I remember that day so clearly. He was supposed to meet me at the pub near the hospital for a counter lunch, and he rang and said he couldn't come. He must have found out that afternoon.'

He removed his hands from Dee's and spread one hand over his face, embarrassed by the emotion that was overwhelming him. 'We were going to bring Mum home that week, and make sure we took her out to Hidden Valley. I got a call when I was halfway home to go back to the hospital, but by the time I got there she'd passed.'

'I'm sorry, Ryan.' Dee's hand was on his shoulder, and the gentle movement of her fingers soothed him.

'I sat with her for a while and held her hand, and I remember how loose her rings were. She'd been so brave when she was ill. The nurse came in and wanted to take her rings off and give them to Dad, and that's when he broke down. He wanted them buried with her.' His shoulders shook as the memory hit him, and it was a few moments before he realised Dee's arms were around him and his face was against her neck.

His face that was wet with his bloody tears.

Ryan sat up and wiped them away angrily. 'Whatever is going on with this blackmail, I know it's got to do with Hidden Valley. Ellie took me out there in the helicopter the other day, and someone's been out there, digging around the salt pans. There's white pegs and metal markers covering a huge area. She told me she'd seen vehicles out there, but they'd shot through by the time we got there.'

Dee spoke quietly. 'Do you think it's something to do with Gerard?'

'Dad indicated that in the letter.' Ryan shrugged. 'You know him better than me. What do you think?'

'I'd say there's a good chance of it.'

'It sounds like it. But I can't understand why you've been followed, and why that guy ran you off the road.'

'I'd like you to read the letter your father left for me. He said he was sorry that he didn't acknowledge me, but Bridget disappeared and then Gerard contacted him. He didn't want to hurt your mother, and he said he was so sorry that he left me with Gerard and Catherine because he knew what Gerard was like.'

'I sure don't like the sound of him. What I'm trying to do is figure all the connections. I need to get my head straight.' He lifted his head and held Dee's gaze. 'As well as giving Gerard a serve, Dad also said he didn't trust Reg Baker.'

'The lawyer?' Dee frowned. 'If you can't trust a lawyer, who can you trust?'

'Dad says there's another will.'

'A different will to the one with all the conditions that Mr Baker had? The one with all the secrets we're not supposed to know.'

'We won't know until we read it. We just have to hope that the one he made and had witnessed on the station, like he said in our letters, is still here.'

'Where?' Dee's eyes were wide.

'He told me where he put it. In the filing cabinet.' Ryan stood and crossed to the metal filing cabinet beside the desk. He slowly pulled open the bottom drawer and reached to the back and pulled out a vertical file. He flicked though a dozen envelopes, and then smiled as his eyes settled on the one he was looking for.

He walked across and put it on the coffee table in front of Dee.

She screwed her nose up, and he smiled. 'You look like a kid when you do that.'

She pulled another face at him, and his smile widened as she read the front of the envelope. 'Cattle weight trends 1965-1986?'

'He told me where he put the will. Dad obviously didn't trust anyone. Have you got your phone handy?'

'No, it's in my ute somewhere, remember?'

'Sorry, I forgot.' Ryan stood and crossed to the desk and came back with his phone. 'Here's mine. I'll hold the pages up and get you to take a photo of each.'

'Photograph it? Why?'

'Because I want to get a copy of this. I'm afraid after reading Dad's letter, we can't trust anyone. Until I understand what's going on here, we're going to be very, very careful.'

Dee held the phone as Ryan opened the flap on the large buff-coloured envelope. There was a sheaf of papers and he flicked through them, until he reached the middle of the pile. He nodded as he held out four pages stapled together. 'It's his will and it's dated a month after Mum died.' He frowned.

'What's wrong?" Dee lowered the phone that she held at the ready.

'I'm just thinking about the other will and all the legal stuff in it, and the special requirements and the secrecy. It just doesn't ring true. It's not something Dad would have done, I'm sure of that.'

'And if it was, rather than do this and hide the fact that it was written in a letter to you, surely he would have gone back to the Bakers and simply redrafted a new will?' Dee agreed.

'Exactly. I wouldn't be surprised if Dad had lodged this one with them too.'

'So what are you going to say to Mr Baker?'

'I'm still thinking about that. And you know what else I find a bit pushy about him?'

Dee looked at him. 'No.'

'Why was he so keen to get us to do new wills right now? Through him? Especially as the probate can't go through until the end of the year until you've been here six months. There's something not right. I'll be finding myself another lawyer. Sorry.' He shook his head. '*We* might find ourselves a new lawyer. What do you think?'

'I'll follow your lead.' Dee let out a sigh. 'It's all doing my head in. More so than the day I met you in Baker's office. I thought that was complicated, but this—it's hard to understand. Okay, read it. What does it say?'

Ryan held the thin foolscap sheets covered with neat handwriting, and Dee watched as he quickly scanned them. Eventually he lifted his head. 'Very simple, and so very Dad. Plus it's witnessed by Harry Chittick and Des Myers, two of our permanent stockmen. I have no doubt it's a legal document. The property has been left to you and me in its entirety and spilt equally down the middle. No mention of any conditions or you here six months. There's no need for us to worry about wills at this point regarding the station, because if anything happens to either of us, Dad said the remainder of the property is to go to the other. That's something, I guess.'

Ryan was sitting beside her again and Dee looked up and caught his gaze on her.

'Just as well we trust each other,' she said.

His brow wrinkled. 'You do trust me, don't you, Dee?'

'I do,' she said quietly. They both looked away at the same time, and then Ryan held the pages up to be photographed.

Chapter 45
Wilderness Station.
Friday 2.00 a.m.

Dee woke suddenly as a loud boom shook the house. Footsteps thudded outside on the veranda and she froze as fear iced her veins. Her heart was beating slow and heavy as she lay there listening, waiting for someone to burst into her room. Her legs were shaking, but she was poised for flight, and found the courage to move silently from the bed and feel around for the clothes she'd left hanging over the back of the chair last night. The room was pitch dark, and not game to turn a light on and draw attention to herself, she felt around with her hands trying to find the chair in the unfamiliar room.

A couple of distant bangs sounded from outside, and she wondered if they were gunshots. Finally, the soft back of the padded chair was beneath her hands and she quickly pulled on her jeans and a T-shirt over her PJs. It had been after eleven when Ryan had put the will back in the filing cabinet, and escorted her to the guestroom, then checked the bedroom and the bathroom for her, as well as checking the outside door was securely locked.

Her heart had swelled as he'd put his arms around her and brushed a kiss on her forehead. 'I won't say sweet dreams, because I think both of us will have some trouble getting to sleep. I'll see you in the morning. Lock the door behind me.'

Crossing to the window now, Dee opened the curtains a crack, and her eyes widened. The night was lit up by an orange glow, dark shadows flickering on the mess building in the macabre light. For a moment she wondered if it was a storm, and the red dust was swirling, but as her eyes became accustomed to the dark, she could see figures running around the outside of the building. Voices called urgently as more figures appeared and her heart rose into her throat as she realised it was a fire.

The donga she had spent the last week in was well alight, and now she could see the flames shooting into the night sky. She stood gripping the curtain, instinct telling her not to show herself or go outside, grateful that Ryan had brought all her stuff up to the house before dinner.

Her hand shook as she gripped the curtain, and she watched until the flames had died down, and about half an hour later, the figures had all disappeared, except for one who was walking towards the house. She drew a breath and waited.

***

Ryan hadn't been able to sleep, as thoughts and doubts filled his head. Eventually he'd given up and come out to sit on the veranda to look at the brilliant starlit sky. Watching the stars had always soothed him. Mum had been a deep thinker and had taught him how small humans were in the scheme of the universe, and how your problems would pale into insignificance by simply watching the movement of the stars.

He yawned and was about to go inside to bed, when he'd noticed someone moving around down near the mess. His eyes had narrowed as he'd watched, and he'd stood and moved into the shadows at the end of the veranda where he could get a better view of whoever it was skulking around and

HIDDEN VALLEY

carrying something. After the events of yesterday his suspicions were immediately aroused.

He would swear it was Joe—the shadowed figure was tall and bulky like his uncle and he wondered what the hell he was doing. He'd heard Cy's ute come in late, and then he'd called to apologise for not catching up with him about the muster.

'I'll see you tomorrow, mate,' Cy said. 'We went down to the snooker comp and Dad's had a skinful.'

There was the sound of a window breaking, and then as he watched, Joe walked quickly back to his caravan and disappeared inside. Ryan had turned to go back inside as an ear-shattering boom shook the house and a flash of white light lit up the night sky. He grabbed the fire extinguisher from beside the front door and raced down to the mess.

Two of the camp crew rushed out of the dongas on the opposite side of the building, followed closely by Cy, and then Joe came out of his caravan.

'What's going on?' Joe called, as though he had only just seen the fire.

'You bastard,' Ryan thought. 'You lying, murdering bastard.'

'A donga's gone up,' one of the ringers called.

As Ryan got closer, he could see it was Pete and Steve who'd come out to help. Each of them held an extinguisher, but as they approached the donga ahead of him, there was another explosion from inside. The flames billowed and black acrid smoke billowed around them.

'What's the stupid bitch got in there? She'll be toast,' Joe yelled.

Ryan pushed back the anger that rose in him at Joe's words and came to a snap decision, hoping against hope that Dee would stay where she was. 'I don't know,' he yelled in return. 'But at least she's not in there. I left her in Darwin.' He watched Joe carefully; his face was lit up by the flames and he didn't miss the filthy expression that appeared briefly before Joe turned away.

'Thank God for that,' Cy said. He'd run to the bore next to the yards and dragged the big hose up and now he turned the stream of water onto the fire. It only took a short while, until the flames died down enough that they could get close and put the rest out with the extinguishers.

'There's no one else in this block, is there?' Ryan checked with Pete and Steve.

'No, boss,' Pete confirmed. 'There's only Steve and I here. The rest of the guys stayed in town. That boom must have been the gas bottle next to the stove going up.'

'Good. Thanks for your help, guys. Appreciate it.' Ryan turned to Joe and kept his voice civil as Steve and Pete headed back to bed. 'What do you think caused it?'

'She must have left something turned on it there and had something that caught fire. Nail polish or something. I saw those long red nails. What a ditz,' Joe said with disgust in his tone, but he didn't meet Ryan's eyes.

'Okay, I think it's all good now. Just as well it didn't spread.' He enjoyed giving the instruction. 'Joe, I'll get you to watch it until dawn. Make sure it doesn't start up again. I'd hate it to spread to the mess and the rest of the accommodation. Cy's got a big day tomorrow, and you won't have any meals to cook because everyone will be out at the camps.'

'What about you?' Joe asked tersely.

'Me?' Ryan stared at him. 'When Dee arrives, she and I are going out to Hidden Valley. We've had some unwanted visitors out there. And besides, I guess I haven't told you pair yet, she's Colin's daughter and she's inherited half the property. Split evenly down the middle with me.' With that, he turned and went to head back up the drive.

'Half?' Joe called. 'What about me?'

Ryan shook his head. 'Sorry, mate. There's no mention of you in the will.' He turned again and strode back to the house.

Chapter 46

Wilderness Station.
Friday 3 a.m.

Dee waited in the guestroom for Ryan to reach the house, not brave enough to go outside to see what was happening. She knew there'd been a fire, and she knew it had been brought under control, but she didn't know the how or why of it. She heard the screen door to the veranda close, and then a moment later, footsteps came up the hall to her room. Still unsure and not brave enough to open the door, she waited until there was a tap on the door and Ryan's low voice reassured her.

'Dee, it's me. It's safe to open the door. I'm the only one in the house. I've locked the front door too.'

As she opened the door and when Ryan stepped into the room, the acrid smell of smoke surrounded her.

'What happened?' she whispered. 'Is everything okay. No one's hurt?'

'There was an explosion and then a fire,' he replied as he crossed to the window and checked that the curtains were closed tightly, before reaching over and turning on the lamp on the small antique desk beside the window.

Fear stayed with Dee as he stared at her, and she could see the concern on his face. Concern and what else?

Despair? Disappointment?

'And?' she asked, knowing there was more.

'It was the donga you stayed in, and I'm sorry to stay I'm pretty sure Joe set the fire. I couldn't sleep and I was sitting out looking at the sky, and I saw him creeping about.'

'The one I stayed in? He set fire to it? On purpose?' Her voice was quiet.

'Yes, I'm pretty sure that's the case.' Ryan began to pace the room. 'Anyway, I told him that you'd stayed in Darwin, and he looked bloody angry.'

'Two attempts on my life in one day?' Dee sat on the end of the bed as her legs gave out. 'What the hell is happening here?'

'I don't know, but Joe's involved.' Ryan stopped pacing and sat beside her, his leg brushing hers. As the dim light caught the perspiration glistening on his chest, Dee registered he wasn't wearing a shirt. She averted her eyes, as a totally unwanted and inappropriate thought sprang into her head.

And what a fine chest it was.

Despite her fear, and the shock that someone was trying to kill her, she was aware of Ryan, and it took all of her self-control not to reach out and run her fingers over his bare skin.

Finally she cleared her throat. 'So what are we going to do? Do you have any proof? Should we call the police now?'

'I've set a trap for Joe. I told him we were going out to Hidden Valley tomorrow. If he's involved in whatever is going on out there—and whatever it is, it's big enough for him to commit murder—he'll follow us out.'

'Won't that be dangerous?'

'No, because you won't be there. You can stay here at the house. I'll get Ellie to come over and stay with you.'

'No.' Dee folded her arms.

'No? Would you rather go back to Darwin?'

'No, as in no, I'm not staying here or Darwin. I'm coming with you. We're in this together, Ryan. This property will be half mine, and I care about the right thing happening as much as you do, plus I don't want to be treated like some wimpy girl who gets babysat at home.' She stared at him, her voice low and tight. 'Gerard is involved in this.'

He stared back and didn't speak for a long time. 'I was going to get Kane to come with me,' he finally said.

'No.'

'Let me finish, but if you come, we can leave before light, and be out there early, check it out and come back.'

'If that's what you first intended why did you tell Joe you were going there?'

'You're too clever by half, aren't you?' Ryan lifted his head and stared past her. 'I was going to confront him.'

'Oh, that would be nice,' Dee said sarcastically. 'I can see two scenarios there.'

'Two?'

'Yeah. One, you end up dead and I get the whole property, or two, you end up dead, and probably Kane too, and then he comes back to me, or gets his mate in the car to come back and finish me off, and they have open slather and can do what they want out there.'

This time Ryan folded his arms and stared at her. 'So what's your plan?'

'What you were going to do, but I'll be there too. If we go out early, is there somewhere out there to hide?'

'Yes.' He nodded slowly. 'There's plenty of small caves in the cliffs.'

'And we get Kane to come out too, as extra security. Do you trust Kane?'

'I do.'

'And we tell the police what we're doing, and tell them our suspicions about the will and Baker. Plus we send the photos I took of your father's . . . of Colin's will to a solicitor friend of mine as security. Sally lives in Byron Bay and is far removed from all of this, but I trust her.' Dee turned to him as she sat beside her. 'So what do you think?'

'I think you can refer to Colin as your father without worrying about my reaction.'

'I don't mean that. What do you think about my plan?'

'There's one thing I'm concerned about. If we run into trouble, there's no phone service out there.'

'Okay, we email everything we discussed to the policeman who interviewed me. We'll document what's happened, and our suspicions, and name them. The sergeant gave me his card with a direct email contact. I'll also send him a text to say I've emailed him.'

Ryan was shaking his head. 'You're unstoppable, aren't you?'

She merely smiled up at him, trying to avoid looking at that bare chest.

'I can't wait to get you out with the cattle. They won't be game to do the wrong thing.' He covered a yawn with his hand.

'I'm looking forward to it. You'd better get some sleep. What time will we leave?'

'The sun gets up about quarter to six, and first light's around five. So before five. What time is it now?'

'Just after three. So go to bed for an hour or so. I've had some sleep so I can draft the emails, and the text.'

'I'll sit in the chair here and doze. I'm not leaving you here. I wouldn't put it past Joe to come snooping.'

Dee shook her head. 'Get on the bed. I'll get on the computer. I'll wake you up at four-thirty. What about Kane?'

'I'll call him when we leave.'

Dee sat at the computer and tried to keep her gaze away from the bed. Ryan had stretched out on the same side she'd slept on, and his face was buried in her pillow. His back was smooth and tanned and within minutes, rose and fell gently as he slept. A rush of warmth settled in Dee's chest, and she closed her eyes. It was only because they had been through so much together in the last week.

Nothing more.

How hard was it going to be living and working on the station with Ryan if she was attracted to him? Dee turned her attention to her laptop, there was a lot to be sorted before that happened. It took half an hour to document everything and email the police as well as downloading the photos and sending them to Sally with a copy of the email she'd sent to the police sergeant. She glanced at the time on the computer and yawned. There was still forty-five minutes before she had to wake Ryan. She set the alarm on his phone for four forty-five and put it next to the bed. To fill in the next few minutes, she dug out a set of cargo shorts and a clean T-shirt and her boots and socks to wear when they left. Tiredness tugged at her and she looked longingly at the bed.

If she lay on the far edge, Ryan wouldn't even know she'd caught some sleep. She turned the desk lamp off, closed her laptop and tiptoed around the side of the bed and slid onto the edge without a sound.

Within minutes Dee was fast asleep. As she drifted off she was vaguely aware of the rattle of a diesel engine as a vehicle left the station.

Chapter 47
Wilderness Station.
Friday 4.40 a.m.

Ryan woke as something pushed into his back; the room was in pitch darkness and for a few seconds he wondered where he was. He frowned as he became aware of a solid warm bulk against his back. As he slowly rolled over, he woke fully when Dee murmured in her sleep, and remembered he was in her bed in the guestroom.

Holy hell, she was pressed up against him, sound asleep. His immediate reaction was very physical and out of his control; he inched away slowly before he woke her up. He lay on his back and put one hand over his eyes wondering what time it was and enjoying the feel of her beside him.

Yesterday had been a big wakeup call. The thought of anyone hurting Dee had terrified him, and he knew that even though they'd only known each other such a short time he cared about her.

Hell, how could he not? They'd been through the emotional wringer together over the past few days. Once they got the will sorted and ended this Hidden Valley shit with Gerard Peters and whoever else was involved, he was determined to get to know Dee properly and see what developed.

He jumped as the tones of David Bowie's *Starman* came from his phone as the alarm kicked in. It had been his mother's favourite song, and she had introduced him to Bowie's music as they'd sat out stargazing at night.

Dee rolled over and murmured again as he turned the music off, and then Ryan reached over and shook her shoulder gently. He still wasn't comfortable taking her to the valley with him, but if he crept out, he'd be equally worried about leaving her here alone. He was still trying to come to grips with Joe's actions. If he hadn't seen him leave that donga with his own eyes, he would have had a hard time believing it of his mother's brother. Starting a fire, believing that Dee was inside; Ryan felt sick as he thought of what the outcome could have been.

'What? What's the matter?' Dee whispered as he gently touched her face to wake her up. As much as he knew he shouldn't, Ryan let his hand linger on her cheek, and she turned her face into his palm.

'That's a nice way to wake up,' she whispered, her breath warm against his skin.

God help him, he couldn't help himself. His brain had joined the lower half of his anatomy. Ryan closed his eyes, fighting the battle between the desire to lean over and kiss her awake, and the knowledge they had to get moving, not to mention the fact that he had no right to kiss her.

Not yet anyway.

In the end the kiss won out, but he only intended a light brush across her lips, but as his lips brushed hers, Dee raised her hand and held his head close. The kiss deepened and when he moved away she let out a small sigh.

'I'm sorry. I couldn't help that.' Ryan sat up and put his feet over the side of the bed, rubbing his hand over the rough stubble on his cheeks. The next time he kissed Dee, he would be showered and shaved . . . and not stressed about taking her into what could be a dangerous situation. His heart kicked up a beat when she replied.

'Neither could I,' she said softly.

'Come on, time to get moving. I'll have a quick wash and get the ute keys and my boots and a shirt. Lock the door behind me.'

Ryan was quick, he didn't turn any lights on and once he'd used the bathroom and dressed, he came back via the kitchen. Picking up half a dozen bottles of water, a couple of apples and a box of muesli bars, he prepared for a long day out there if it was needed. He was determined to find out what was happening, and who was involved. By the time he tapped on Dee's door, and she opened it, she was dressed and ready, boots on and her hair pulled back into a braid.

'You'll need your phone,' she said handing it to him. Her voice and movements were brisk, and Ryan relaxed. He was worried he'd overstepped the mark with that brief kiss.

'I didn't mean to go to sleep,' she apologised. 'Before I lay down, I emailed the police at Humpty Doo, and I sent the photos of the will to my friend, Sally.' Dee gestured to the phone. 'I've found Kane's number, ready for you to text him when it's not so early.'

'Great. I won't put any lights on, and I'll roll the Land Cruiser to the gate. There's enough of a hill to get us down there. I don't want Joe to hear us leave.'

They were silent as they walked to the ute, and Ryan loaded the water and food into a crate on the back. He opened the passenger door for Dee, and when she climbed up, he snicked the door closed quietly. He caught a look at her face as the interior light came on briefly, and he could tell by her set expression that she was as churned up as he was. Once he was in the ute, he reached over and squeezed her hand. 'We'll be fine, as long as we see Joe out there, and I get some photos of him near the mining posts, it's enough proof he's involved.'

'What are you going to do then?'

'I'll front him and tell him he's no longer welcome here. The police can deal with the fire stuff. Then we'll get the new will sorted out, and our lives can get back to normal.' Ryan released the handbrake and put the ute in neutral; it rolled backwards down the very slight incline past the rose garden, and towards the gate. Once the homestead was between him and the mess, he started the engine and let it idle along quietly until they were over the cattle grate. 'Keep an eye out behind us and see if any lights come on.'

Dee swivelled around, but the dongas and the mess stayed in darkness.

'No, all good.'

He glanced across at her and could just see her face in the glow of the dashboard lights. 'I'm looking forward to showing you the property and having you work beside me.'

'No bad feelings anymore?' she asked quietly.

'No, Dee, it didn't take long after I met you to know that you were genuine, despite my initial reaction.'

'I understand, it would have been a shock seeing me in the lawyer's office.' He caught the movement in the dim light as she shook her head. 'There's been a lot more shocks since then, though.'

'And I want you to know that now that we've discovered Colin was your father, I think the property split is a fair solution. Although maybe not so fair to you that I've inherited too.'

Dee's hand gripped his thigh and Ryan jumped.

'I don't ever want to hear you say that again. As you said, he was your father for your whole life in every other way.'

'Thank you.' Ryan was quiet when she removed her hand and he accelerated along the back road towards the turnoff. He'd meant what he'd said to Dee, and he appreciated her reply. But he knew over the next few months, not knowing who his father was, was going to do his head in.

Joe might know. He would tread carefully, and try to get it out of him, before . . .

Before what? he wondered. What would be the consequences of Joe's actions?

He shook his head; there was no point speculating. He reached for his phone sitting on the dashboard and passed it to Dee.

'Can you text Kane now, please?'

Dee took the phone and opened the screen to messages. 'Okay, got him. What will I say?'

'Just ask him if he can come out to Hidden Valley as soon as he can this morning. Ask him to let us know when he reads the text. I'd like to talk to him first.'

Dee's fingers flew over the keys. 'Done.'

They both jumped when the phone rang immediately. Dee glanced down at the screen. 'It's Kane.'

'Can you answer, please? I don't have Bluetooth in this old ute.'

'Hi Kane, it's Dee. Ryan's driving. That's good. I'll let him know. Hang on.' She moved the phone and turned. 'Kane said he can come out whenever it suits. He said nothing's too early for them because James has been up since five a.m.'

'That's great. Tell him if he could come now, we can meet him at the road that comes down from the highway. And if he comes early, I won't take up too much of his day.'

Dee thought to put the phone on speaker before she answered. 'Kane, Ryan said—oh good, you heard him,' she said as Kane's voice came over the speaker.

'Okay, on the way. Mate, what's going—' Static hissed and the call dropped out.

'Damn,' Ryan said. 'We've dropped out. I wanted to tell him to be careful. See if you can call him back.'

Dee tried but there was no service. 'No luck.'

'Okay, we'll wait until we meet him at the turnoff and I'll tell him what's going on then.'

Dee put the mobile phone back on the dashboard and looked through the window. To her left, the sky was a pale apricot, and the day was getting light enough to make out the landscape the road wound through. The stands of trees growing from the red earth surprised her; she'd imagined it would be more desert out this way. Tall grass at the edge of the road swayed as they drove past, and as the sun cleared the horizon, she could see the dozens and dozens of termite mounds of various sizes right through the bush.

'Are we still on *Wilderness Station*?' she asked.

'We are. It goes for . . . shit!' Ryan swerved slightly to avoid a small wallaby that bounded out of the long grass ahead of them. 'Sorry. I was worried about that. Not a good time to be on the road out here.'

'It's really different to what I imagined,' Dee said. 'A lot greener.'

'You think this is green. Wait until we get into our valley—it's magnificent. Hidden Valley is one of the outliers of what they call the stone country in Kakadu. They were cliffs in the ancient seas that covered the land here millions of years back. The rock platforms are full of hidden gorges and valleys from when the cliffs eroded. And to answer your question, we could drive for another three hours along this road and still be on *Wilderness*.'

Dee's eyes were wide. 'I could drive right around our plantation in less than twenty minutes. I am so excited about seeing the whole station. When can we start?'

Ryan grinned across at Dee just as the sun peeked above the horizon. 'Count today as the first tour. Once we get this sorted, I'll take the scenic route back home.'

Chapter 48
Wilderness Station.
Friday 6.00 a.m.

Joe reached the saltpans just on sunrise. Anger pumped through him and he pulled out the hipflask he'd filled with rum before he'd left the station.

It was all that bloody woman's fault. Until she'd turned up poking her nose into things, everything had been going to plan. Bloody Frank Baker had stuffed up then and Gerard would have to deal with him. And what Ryan had dropped on him after he'd put the fire out and he'd discovered that the bitch wasn't even in there, he'd almost lost it. The mention of a new will had fuelled his rage. So Ryan finally knew that Colin had a daughter, and he wasn't the blue-eyed only bloody child.

Ryan had done his dash; he could bloody well die along with the bitch. Poetic justice to leave them both out here in the valley.

It was all so incestuous; Joe was just so thankful that Suzanne had never known about the daughter, and she'd had as happy a life as she could, married to that unfaithful prick.

Joe's biggest worry had been that Bridget Sloane would break up his sister's marriage. When he'd heard she was pregnant, he'd known straight away it was Colin's.

He'd made sure as soon as the kid was born that Bridget was no longer a threat. She hadn't even wanted the baby; handed the kid over to her sister as though she was a bag of groceries.

If he'd suspected that Colin would leave the daughter a share of the station he would have killed the bloody kid at the same time. He was just sorry that Colin had lived most of his life not knowing what had happened to the bitch. But he'd known at the end. *His* end.

Joe laughed as he picked up the flask and took a long swig.

But Suzanne had loved the bastard, and she'd been pregnant with Ryan when it had all happened, so Joe had bided his time.

Bloody Karma, it was. He laughed now as he thought about how he'd been out on the station with Cy and Colin when Colin had his heart attack. Telling Colin that the bitch had died in a cave out here in his precious valley had been one of the most satisfying moments of Joe's life. He'd sat back and watched the life go out of the bastard's body. Cy had been out on the boundary fence, and by the time he'd come back to camp, Colin was dead. Joe had pretended to grieve when he'd told Ryan of Colin's death.

He parked the car behind a stand of eucalypts and threw a hesitant glance up the cliff to where he'd left Bridget's body thirty years ago. He hadn't been put here again until Gerard had sent him out to meet the geologists.

Every time he met them here, that friggin' cave spooked him. He'd pick a vantage point well away from there this morning. It would be easy to pick the pair of them off from another cave up the cliff.

Joe grinned.

Then again, he could man up and put the bitch in there with her mother.

Yeah. Full circle.

He nodded, he liked that idea.

Going around to the back of the ute, Joe lifted out his .243 rifle and a couple of boxes of bullets. He leaned the rifle with the scope against the side of the ute and reached through the window for the sat phone. He had a few hours until they arrived if she was coming from Darwin, and he had some calls to make. He looked at the flask and hesitated briefly before he grabbed it and shoved it into his shirt pocket.

He was a damn fine shot, and a bit of rum wouldn't change that. He headed for the cliff and carefully navigated the climb to a cave halfway up the face where a couple of trees grew from the cliff face covering the entrance.

Perfect.

He settled in for a long wait and turned on the phone.

Gerard answered first ring. 'Joe.'

'Hey, mate. Today's the day.' He belched. ''scuse me.'

Gerard's voice was as cold as it always fucking was. 'What do you mean?'

'Things have got out of hand up here, and I'm dealing with the problems this end. You have to deal with Baker.'

'What problems?'

'Ryan let slip last night that Colin made another will. They've got it.'

'What!'

'You heard me. You need to deal with Baker. I think he's got cold feet. I've waited bloody thirty years for this. I am not going to see all that money go west now. You deal with Baker, and now.'

'Right, I'm on it. Have the guys from Jianfeng been back to the valley yet? The final proposal's in, and they want to do some more surveying. The good news is they've signed a three year deal with the US company to supply the lithium for batteries for the electric vehicles, and we're their main source. They're keen to start immediately.'

'Who needs bloody coal these days, hey?' Joe lifted the flask and took another swig. 'I'm meeting them here the day after tomorrow. I'll have dealt with our two problems by then.' He didn't see a need to mention that he'd stuffed up last night, but that had given him all the more determination to get it right this morning. 'I'll deal with them. You deal with Baker.'

'I will today. My bloke in Darwin can go pay him a visit.'

'Okay. I'll let you know when I'm done here.' Joe leaned back against the cold stone, his rifle across his knees, waiting for Ryan and the woman to turn up.

Suzanne had gone; and in his mind Ryan embodied every hurt that Colin had ever inflicted on his sister. Killing Ryan Carey would be the punishment Colin had deserved.

***

'He was quick.' Dee was surprised to see Kane's Land Cruiser station wagon already parked at the turnoff ahead.

'It's much closer to their farm from that back road from the highway than it is to us.' Ryan changed back a gear and slowed down. 'Shit, no!'

'What's wrong?' Dee sat up straight and peered ahead. The sky was climbing in a cloudless sky, and bright rays were slanting off the windscreen.

'Ellie's with him. Our call dropped out too soon.' Ryan turned to Dee. 'Listen, I know you're going to resist, but I'd like you to get in the car with Ellie and go back to their place until we get this sorted. It's not safe.'

'I'll sit in the middle and Kane can come with us. Ellie can go back.'

'Bloody hell, are you always this stubborn?' Ryan muttered under his breath. Dee folded her arms and shot him a glare. He pulled the ute up behind Kane's car, and she followed him out onto the dusty road.

They walked over to Kane's window. Ellie smiled, and waved a greeting to them from the passenger side.

'Gidday,' Kane said 'I saw the tracks. I wasn't sure if you'd already gone ahead.'

Ryan turned to look at the narrow road that headed off to the east. 'Damn, there's been a vehicle through already.'

'Yeah, I was going to give you another half hour and go in. I thought you'd decided not to wait for us. What's happening?'

Ryan looked in the back and nudged Dee. 'Look, there's been a vehicle here already, and James is in the back. It's not safe. You're going back with Ellie.'

Kane looked at Ellie and gestured outside, and they both got out of the vehicle.

'I'm not,' Dee said.

Ellie frowned and walked across to Dee. 'What's going on?'

'Ryan thinks it's not safe. He didn't expect you to come and bring James. He's been trying to talk me into going back with you, but I'm not.'

Kane put his arm around Ellie's shoulder. 'What's going on, mate?'

They listened quietly as Ryan quickly went through the events of the past week, and when he got to his suspicions of Joe trying to burn down the donga he'd thought Dee was in, Ellie paled.

'That's shocking.' Ellie moved away from Kane and stood beside Dee. 'Are you okay?'

'I am, and yes, it is shocking,' Dee said.

'And that's why I don't want you anywhere out here. Please, Dee, now that you can go to Ellie and Kane's farm, you'll be safe.' Ryan stared at her and his expression was grim.

Ellie was the first to object. 'That's not an option, Ryan. I'm not going back with James. If what you say is true—sorry, I don't mean I'm doubting you, I believe you—there's a chance we could meet someone on the road back to the highway. There's safety in numbers and we have two vehicles.'

Kane and Ryan looked at each other.

'The other option is we could all go back together,' Kane said.

Ryan shook his head. 'I want this sorted today. You go back with Ellie and you can take Dee with you.'

'Oh, for God's sake, Ryan. For the tenth time I'm staying with you.' Dee folded her arms and glared back at him. The brief kiss they'd shared earlier was far from her mind.

In the end, Ryan gave in, and Kane and Ellie decided to go into the valley with them on the agreement that at the first sign of any trouble, they would all leave together.

Ryan was quiet, his attention focused on the road as they set off with Kane and Ellie's Land Cruiser close behind. As they entered the valley, Dee looked around, taken by surprise at the lush green grass that grew up to the edge of the towering red cliffs.

'It is magnificent.' Her voice was hushed as she stared at the beauty surrounding her. 'And this is part of the station?'

Ryan nodded, seeming to thaw. 'This is where Mum wanted to build a new homestead.'

'It's beautiful. All the more reason to keep it as it is.'

'Yes.' The road stretched out straight before them, and there was no sign of any other vehicle. 'The area where the markers Ellie and I saw last week is just up ahead. I'm going to park over in the shadow of the escarpment where our vehicles won't be obvious. We can wait here and see if Joe comes in.'

'Would they have been his tracks, we saw, do you think?' she asked.

'I doubt it. More likely to be from the campers Ellie saw from the air the other day.'

Dee narrowed her eyes and peered ahead. 'Look! Isn't that a ute over there? Behind that clump of tress at the base of the cliff.'

Ryan slowed and shoved his hand out the window gesturing for Kane to do the same.

'It's—' Suddenly there was a huge bang, and the windscreen shattered, peppering them both with shards of glass.

'The bastard's above us,' Ryan yelled. 'Get down on the floor, Dee. Now!' She put a hand to her head, and it came away wet. She stared at her fingers as blood dripped through them.

'Ryan . . . um . . . I'm bleeding.' Her head spun as she wondered if she'd been hit because she was sure that they were being shot at.

Ryan looked across at her and the look on his face scared her. He wrenched the wheel to the left and headed towards the base of the cliff. 'Where are you bleeding? Have you been hit in the head? Take your shirt off and press it hard to stop the bleeding. Then get on the floor. As soon as we get beneath the cliff, I'll stop.' He used his fist to push out the shattered glass in front of him so he could see where to go.

'Be careful.' Dee's head spun as she did as he said and pressed her shirt against the wound. 'I'm okay, I think it's just a piece of glass.'

'We're almost there.' The ute bounced over roots and rocks, and they were almost to the cliff when two more shots sounded from above. Ryan glanced in the rear vision mirror and his voice sent chills through Dee. 'Kane's been hit.'

There was a narrow chasm in the cliff ahead of them, and Ryan drove the ute into it. Either side of them were sheer walls of rippled sandstone. 'He can't get us here if he is above us, and I'm pretty sure he is.'

'What about Kane and Ellie, can you still see them?' Dee's voice was husky as fear held her in its grip.

HIDDEN VALLEY

'No, I can't. But there's more openings like this where he can hide his vehicle. By the time Joe comes down the cliff we'll be ready for him.' Ryan cut the engine and reached down to where she sat on the floor of the ute and lifted the shirt away from her head. Dee winced as it stuck for a few seconds, but he worked it away slowly and nodded. 'It's a flesh wound where the glass has cut you. Keep the pressure on, it's going to need a stitch or two.' Leaving her, he opened the door and ran around to the back of the ute, and Dee's blood ran cold when he appeared beside her window, holding a rifle. He opened the door and held his hand out to her.

Dee took it and Ryan helped her down. 'I want you to crawl under the ute. Lie down in the middle and don't move.' He pressed his fingers to her mouth. 'Don't argue with me, please, sweetheart. Just do it. Trust me. I'm going after him. If he comes down here, lie still and don't move. Okay?'

She nodded, shaking so much she was unable to speak. Ryan grabbed her and kissed her hard. 'Don't move, no matter what happens.'

Dee scrambled beneath the ute, too scared about what was happening above to worry about whatever creatures might be in the dirt beneath her. Time passed slowly as she lay there on her stomach, her face pressed into her hands. Something crawled over her bare back, but she didn't move. The world was silent, and she closed her eyes as her forehead began to ache at the hairline.

'I can see you, Joe. Come down, you gutless bastard.' Ryan called in the distance.

Dee jumped and bit her lip as there was another loud shot, and then silence again for a few minutes. A moment later, there were two shots in quick succession and then the noise of a car approaching.

Then another three shots.

She lay there trying to stop the shaking as fear held her in its relentless grip. Her scalp contracted with goose bumps as a car door opened and footsteps crunched on the rocks behind the car. Holding her breath, Dee lifted her head slightly and bit her lips hard, holding back a cry as a pair of dusty work boots stopped beside the car a metre from where she was.

Her skin crawled with fear as someone opened the door above her head.

'Dee, where are you?' Ellie's voice called quietly.

Dee was torn, Ryan had told her not to move for any reason, and she screwed up her face, and kept her lips together.

'Dee, where are you?' Ellie's voice was a whimper. 'Please be okay.'

Suddenly all hell broke loose. Another shot and Ellie's scream, and then a motor starting and revving hard.

'No.' Ellie's second scream chilled her blood, and Dee couldn't stand it any longer. She pushed her boots hard against the back tyres and crawled to the edge of the car and peered out.

Ellie was bent double keening, and Dee just caught a glimpse of the back of their white station wagon as it disappeared down into a gully. She scrambled out and grabbed Ellie. 'I'm here. What is it? Are you hurt? Where's Kane and Ryan?'

Ellie's eyes were wide and vacant as she whispered. 'Joe followed me. I didn't see him until he jumped off that ledge.' She put her hand on her chest as she tried to inhale with deep gulps punctuating her words. 'Took our car. Got James. Oh God, no.'

Dee's eyes widened in horror as she understood. 'James? James is in the car?'

'Yes, oh God, oh God, he's got my baby.'

Dee held Ellie's arms to try to get through to her. 'Quickly, get in the car. We'll go after him.'

Stuff whatever Ryan told her to do. If it was dangerous, so be it. A child's life was in danger.

Ellie nodded and flung open the door of the ute. Dee climbed up into the driver's seat, praying that Ryan had left the keys in the ignition. She nodded as her fingers closed over them and started the motor, put it into reverse and backed quickly out of the narrow chasm.

She threw the ute into a turn and pointed it towards the road they had come in on, as Ellie pointed ahead. 'Look, I can see him ahead about a kilometre.'

Dee took a deep breath and planted the accelerator. It was hard to see though the small hole that Ryan had punched in the windscreen 'Is Kane all right? Ryan said he'd been hit.'

Ellie's voice was stronger. 'No, Joe hit the car, shot one of the back tyres out. He won't get far. Oh God, as long as the wagon doesn't roll if he goes fast.'

'Ellie, listen to me. We'll catch him. He can't drive and shoot at the same time. We'll have your little man back soon. I promise you.'

How the hell she was going to do that, Dee didn't know, but while ever she had breath in her, she wasn't going to let that creep get away with Ellie and Kane's little boy.

Ellie sat up straight and looked at Dee for the first time. 'There's blood running down your cheek.'

'I'm okay. It's only a glass cut where he shot the windscreen out.'

Dee focused on the dirt road ahead. The wheels hit a stand of long grass and a flock of birds rose in a raucous flurry. In the distance ahead, dust rose behind the station wagon.

'I'm sorry I lost it back there,' Ellie said. 'I know we have to stay calm.' Her fingers were white where she gripped the dash.

As Dee stared ahead, the gap closed between the two vehicles. As they slowly closed the distance, the vehicle ahead stopped suddenly a couple of hundred metres in front of them.

'What the hell is he doing?'

She peered ahead as Joe got out of the car, and walked around to the other side. Dee slowed the car near a large stand of rocks. She was able to position the ute so it couldn't be seen from ahead. Ellie opened the door and jumped out and ran across to the last rock. Dee climbed down and hurried across behind her, the sun hot on her bare shoulders. The cut on her forehead wasn't stinging anymore, but her head was aching like a bastard.

'What's he doing?' she asked as she reached Ellie.

'He's opened the back door. Oh God, he's lifting James out. Come on. Quickly!'

Dee put a hand on her arm. 'No, wait. We can't spook him. Not while he's holding your boy.'

She peered around the rock as the cries of a screaming toddler reached them. Joe was holding him.

'He's bleeding. His head and neck. Joe, I mean,' she quickly corrected. 'He's been shot.'

Ellie gasped and put her hand across her eyes. 'I can't do this again,' she said. 'I can't do it.'

'Quickly, Ellie, come on! It's okay. He's put James down on the road and he's driving away.'

They both raced to the ute and Dee had the motor going before Ellie's door was shut. It seemed to take forever to travel the distance to where the car had stopped. She approached slowly, and Ellie yelled and pointed. 'There he is. He's sitting in the dirt.'

Dee parked on the edge of the narrow road, and Ellie was out and across the dirt in seconds. She scooped James up and held him tightly to her chest, her tears creating red tracks on her face where his little dust-covered hands touched her cheeks.

'Mumma,' he said clearly.

'He's okay, Dee. He's okay.' Ellie smiled though her tears. 'My brave boy wasn't even crying. He was sitting there playing in the dirt.'

'I wonder what's going on?' Dee said staring at the dust as the car disappeared into the distance. 'What's he doing?'

'I'd say he didn't even notice James was there straight away. All he was interested in was getting away, I think. Kane shot out both tyres on the front of his ute, that's why he took our car. I didn't see him coming behind me when I came looking for you. I should never have left James in the car.'

'Come on, we'd better go and see if we can find Ryan and Kane.' Dee didn't let herself think about the other three shots she'd heard.

She drove back slowly as Ellie held James on her lap. She'd looped the seat belt around him and held him tightly, but Dee was aware of him not safely secured, and she didn't speed, even though she was desperate to get back to their men.

When they reached the base of the cliff, Dee pulled up and she and Ellie jumped out, Ellie holding James to her tightly, but to their growing consternation, there was no sight or sound of either Ryan or Kane.

They both stood scanning the cliff, and the myriad of caves and chasms dotting the sheer sandstone face. The air was still, the only sound was the piercing scream of a hawk as it circled high above them riding the thermals. To their right, the ground shone silver and Dee frowned. 'Is that water over there?'

'No, it's salt pans. It's where the markers were.' Ellie said distractedly as her gaze raked the cliffs from top to bottom. 'Oh, God, where are they?'

'Do you know which way they went up?'

Ellie nodded and pointed to a tree about fifty metres away. 'There's a track up there, it goes up to the pool at the top of the cliff. I saw it from the air when we flew over here the other day. Joe came down over there.' She pointed to a rough track with ledges making steps.

'I'll get you a tarp to sit on with James, and some water and food from the back of the ute, and then I want you to sit somewhere out of sight just in case he comes back. Or in case someone else comes out here. He's not the only one involved in this.'

'Where are you going?'

'I'm going to climb up there and see if I can find them.'

'Is your head okay?'

Dee went back to the ute and got a couple of bottles of water, an apple and two muesli bars. She wouldn't give any room to the thoughts that were trying to crowd into her head.

She couldn't bear to think of Ryan—and Kane—hurt, or worse up there.

Once Ellie and James were settled on the tarp beneath a stand of trees past where the track started, Dee drank from one of the water bottles. 'I'll go and find them.'

Ellie reached up and squeezed her hand. 'You be careful. Watch out for snakes.'

Dee nodded and set off up the track, small rocks rolling beneath her boots. When she was a hundred metres up, she cupped a hand to her mouth and called. 'Ryan! Kane!'

There was no reply, apart from the echo of her call bouncing off the cliffs.

Dee fought back tears as her imagination kicked into overdrive. Nausea roiled in her stomach and her head ached. If Joe had shot them, it could take hours—or days—to find them up here. If they were hurt and couldn't call out, she wouldn't know where to look. The expanse of the cliffs was huge.

'No.' She forced herself to be positive. 'They must have gone to the top.'

But if they were all right, they would have seen Joe drive off, and come back down to check on us, the negative voice in her head insisted.

As the track got steeper, it narrowed and Dee stopped and put her hand out for balance as a wave of dizziness rocked through her.

She closed her eyes for a second as the world spun, and when she opened them, a flash of movement had her jumping back away from the cliff. A large striped snake slithered into a small cave at her eye level. She looked over her shoulder and realised that she was only one step away from the edge, but she wasn't game enough to put her hand back on the cliff face now.

Slowly and with determination, she stepped forward and climbed higher. 'Ryan,' she called again as loudly as she could. There were three cave entrances above her.

Dee ducked as small rocks fell past her from a ledge above her head. Checking she had room to move back, she took a couple of steps backwards and slowly tipped her head back so she wouldn't get dizzy again.

'I told you to stay under the ute,' a voice said, and then two heads appeared over the ledge above.

Dee clutched at her chest, and her legs gave way and she sat down hard on the track. 'Why didn't you answer me when I called?' she said indignantly.

'We didn't hear you. We were in a cave.'

'Are you both all right? You're not hurt?'

'Yes, we're fine. Where's Ellie and James?' Kane asked urgently. 'Are they safe?'

'Yes, she's down there under those trees with James.' Dee pointed down to the trees.

'Stay there.'

'What the hell are you doing wandering around? Joe's still here somewhere,' Ryan said when he reached her and wrapped his arms around her. Kane kept going down to the bottom of the cliff. 'Have you seen him? I think I clipped him with one shot.'

'He's gone,' Dee said.

'I shot out the tyres on his ute,' Kane called up to them.

'He took your wagon.' Dee said. 'James was in it, but he put him out on the road. We followed him and hid when he stopped. And yes, he's bleeding.'

'Jesus, Dee.' Ryan held her close for a moment longer.

'What were you doing in a cave?' she asked.

Ryan's face was set, and he looked away. 'We found something. I'll tell you about it later, but first I want to get you off this cliff and to Jabiru to get your head stitched. We got enough of what we needed to know from Joe.'

'How do you mean?'

'He couldn't keep his mouth shut. He was so damn sure he was going to kill us until I shot him. It's a wonder you didn't hear him yelling down there.'

'All I heard was the gunshots. What did you find? Tell me.'

Ryan pulled her close. 'Dee, there's no easy way to tell you this. Joe killed Bridget. Her remains are in the cave.'

Dee widened her eyes and her legs almost gave way. 'Are you sure?' she whispered.

'Yes, the bastard was bragging about it.'

Dee clung to Ryan for a long moment, before she lifted her head. 'I was so scared I'd lost you,' she said.

'It's going to take a lot more than that to lose me,' he said.

Dee closed her eyes as he lowered his head, and this time it wasn't simply a mere brush of his lips on hers.

Chapter 49
McLaren Mango Farm.
8.30 a.m.

Somehow, they all crammed into Ryan's ute, aware of the danger of being on the road with Kane sitting on the tray, his back against the cabin, and James unsecured on Ellie's lap. Ryan drove the twenty kilometres out to the highway slowly, keeping a close eye out for the McLaren station wagon that Joe had escaped in, but there was no sign of him.

When they turned onto the Arnhem Highway, Ryan kept to the left of the road and kept the speed low, but he kept glancing at Dee as she leaned against him. He was worried that the piece of glass had lodged in her skull. The bleeding had stopped too quickly.

It only took ten minutes to get to the farm, and Ellie broke the silence as they drove up to their house.

'Mum's here, and another car. God, I hope nothing's wrong. I don't think I could take any more stress today.' She put her face against James' head and Ryan saw the sheen of tears as she lowered her head.

Dee sat up and looked around, but didn't speak.

Ryan parked the car outside the shed a short way from the house and went around to help Ellie out with James. By the time he got there, Kane had the door open and held his arms out for the toddler. Ryan helped Ellie down, and then held his hand out for Dee as she moved across the seat.

'Feel okay?' he asked.

She nodded. 'Just a bit of a headache.'

Ellie held Kane's arm. 'Come up to the house and I'll make a cuppa. I think we need to debrief.'

'Yes, and we need to call the police at Humpty Doo,' Dee said. 'And I want to know what Joe said to you.'

Ryan put his arm around her, and Dee leaned into him as they followed Kane and Ellie up to the house.

He frowned as Ellie let out a cry. 'Oh, Kane. Look. It's Emma and Jeremy. They're here a week early.'

Ryan and Dee stayed at the bottom of the stairs as Ellie and Kane went up to greet the couple on the veranda.

'Do you want to stay or go straight to Jabiru to the hospital? Or home?' he asked quietly.

'Stay for a while, a cuppa would be good,' she said. 'I don't think I could face more driving for a while. Besides, I'm worried that Joe will be back at the station.'

'Okay,' he said, leaving his arm around her. 'We'll call the police and get them to come here. I'll tell them what Joe's driving.'

'Come on up, you pair. Mum's got the kettle on.'

When they reached the veranda, Ellie came over to Dee. 'Mum's been a bit fragile, so come with me and I'll show you the bathroom so you can wash your face, and I'll get you a clean T-shirt.' She lowered her voice. 'I've taken James in to her. We're not going to say anything about what happened; it would freak her out.'

Kane stepped forward. 'Dee and Ryan, this is Emma and Jeremy, Ellie's sister and her husband.'

Ryan was pleased when Emma came over after Jeremy shook his hand. 'Hello, Ryan. I haven't seen you since we left school.' She stood on her toes and kissed his cheek.

'Good to see you again, Emma.' Suddenly he remembered that Ellie had told him that Emma was a doctor. 'Can I ask a favour? Could you go with Dee and check out her head? I'm worried there's a piece of glass in the wound.'

'Sure, come on Dee, we can get to know each other while I check.'

'I'll come too. I'll ask Mum to bring the tea tray out when she's dressed James.' Ellie's laugh was shaky. 'I got into trouble for getting him so dirty so she's giving him a tub in the laundry.'

The three men moved across to the outside table and sat down.

Kane and Ryan sat there quietly, still in a state of shock after what had happened. Jeremy looked at them curiously but didn't ask any questions.

Emma and Dee were back quickly, and Emma reassured Ryan as he stood again and came across to Dee. 'It's all good, just a nick on the hairline that bled a lot. No glass, and I don't think it will even need a stitch.'

'I think the headache's got more to do with lack of sleep and stress,' Dee said with a small smile as he put his arm around her. She leaned into him and he held her closer.

Ellie came out onto the veranda followed by an older woman close behind her, carrying a tray with cups and a large teapot.

'James has gone down for a sleep,' she said with a smile at Ellie. 'Poor little mite was worn out. Kane, can you take the teapot, please, love.'

'Mum,' Ellie said. 'This is Ryan and Dee from *Wilderness Station* where I've been doing the mustering. This is my mum, Sandra.'

Sandra handed the teapot to Kane and followed Ellie to the table. Before she put the tray of cups down, she lifted her head and smiled at them. 'Hello, Ryan, I knew your pa—'

She stopped suddenly and the tray fell from her hands, teacups falling to the floor and smashing on the veranda tiles. Her eyes were wide, and her face had lost all its colour. Her mouth opened and closed, as she put her hand out in front of her.

'Oh my God, Peter,' Sandra cried, as her eyes rolled back, and she pitched forward in a dead faint. Ryan jumped forward and caught her before she hit the floor.

***

Dee was still shaking ten minutes later. Sandra had come out of her faint as Ryan held her, and when she'd looked up into his face, she burst into tears. She could barely talk between her sobs.

'It was you I kept seeing at the shopping centre. I thought it was Peter,' she said over and over again. 'I thought you were Peter. I don't understand. Why do you look so much like Peter?'

Emma and Ellie stood either side of Sandra and supported her as they took her into the bedroom. Jeremy followed them in.

Ryan walked to the table and sat there quietly, his face as pale as Sandra's. Dee held his hand, unsure of what had transpired. All she could think of was the photo at Gerard and

Catherine's wedding when Bridget had been pregnant with her, and Suzanne pregnant with Ryan

What the hell was going on?

Kane went inside and came out with a bottle of whisky and put a glass in front of Ryan. 'I thought you might appreciate a shot of this instead of a cup of tea.'

'Thanks, mate. I won't say no.' Ryan let go of Dee's hand and ran a hand through his hair. 'I can't figure it out exactly, and I don't know how, but I think your mother-in-law has just solved part of our mystery.'

Emma came out, and crouched down beside Ryan's chair, placing a photograph on the table in front of him. 'Mum asked me to show you this. None of us have seen it before.'

Ellie came out and stood behind Emma as Ryan picked up the photograph. Dee leaned forward and he held it out so she could see it too.

'I always knew you reminded me of someone,' Ellie said. 'Not so much your looks now, but the way you walk and the way you run your hand through your hair. It's my dad.'

'Look at the photo,' Emma said. 'It's one taken when Mum and Dad were first going out. It could be you, Ryan. You're almost Dad's double when he was your age.'

Ellie clutched Emma's hand and stared at Ryan. 'You know what this means? You're our half-brother.'

Epilogue

Six months later.
McLaren Mango Farm.
Friday 7.00 p.m.

Dee lifted her damp hair from her neck as she walked from the kitchen to the barbeque on the veranda. Emma's husband, Jeremy was in the kitchen with Sandra helping with the salads as the four Porter siblings took James down to the dam for a swim.

'Steak's almost cooked.' Connor—husband of the youngest Porter sister, Dru—called out as he manned the barbeque with Kane. The smell of frying steak and onions wafted down to the front dam where Emma, Ellie, and Dru were sitting with Ryan, watching James splash at the edge of the water. Clouds were building in the west, hinting at the promise of a thunderstorm later.

'Sandra sent a tray out for the cooked meat,' she said, placing it on the table. 'Smells good. I'm starving.'

'How are you, Dee?' Connor asked. 'Used to this ferocious build-up to the monsoon season yet?'

'I am. I think I must have acclimatised more quickly, being born here. I consider myself a true Territorian.'

'I hear you've settled into the station life very well. Ellie's always talking about how good you are with the cattle,' Kane said.

'I love working out there. And I love being up here in the Territory. Being part of a family is a new experience for me, and I'm loving that most of all.'

'Everything's been sorted now? All the legal stuff?' Connor, with his investigative background, had been a great support to them through the investigation and the legal process. Joe had been arrested and charged with Bridget's murder, and the attempted murder of Dee and Ryan. Gerard Peters had been arrested as an accessory to both charges. His companies had been under close scrutiny by the Australian Securities and Investments Commission of his affairs, and with the discovery of money laundering, and false companies, it looked like Gerard was going to go to prison for a long time.

'Joe and Gerard are in custody, but Baker is proving more elusive to the investigators,' Dee replied. 'He's denied any involvement, and placed the blame for the bogus will on his dead brother, Reginald.'

Dee walked across to the railing and looked out over the mango farm. The edges of the towering clouds were turning silver at the edges as the sun sank towards the horizon.

Kane came over to stand beside her and rested his elbows on the railing as they looked out across the trees. 'Life's come full circle, hasn't it?'

'It has when you think I probably played out on that lawn as a toddler,' Dee said.

Ellie and Kane's farm had been owned by Gerard back in the eighties, before he'd sold it to Sandra and Peter Porter. When Peter had been murdered, Kane's stepfather Panos Sordina had bought it, and on his death, Kane had inherited the property. The documents giving ownership of Hidden Valley to Gerard Peters thirty years ago had been found to be fraudulent, and after an investigation Rodney had denied any involvement and had managed to avoid any charges. Gerard had given the police the name of the small time criminal who had followed Dee in Darwin and broken into the lawyer's office, and caused her accident on the highway.

'And how are you coping with it all, Dee?'

'Surprisingly well. Everything has been tied up neatly. Bringing my mother's remains out of the cave and having a proper service and burial gave me closure, as it did for Catherine.' She smiled and pointed to the black BMW coming up the drive. 'Speaking of who, here she comes now.'

Dee stood with the three men watching Ryan and his half-sisters laughing together. The four Porter siblings had decided to drop the "half" tag when the DNA test had confirmed that Peter was Ryan's father.

Sandra carried the salads out as Catherine ran lightly up the steps. Dee still couldn't believe how much the woman she had thought of as her mother for her whole life had changed since she had left Gerard to the police and moved to Darwin.

Catherine came over to Dee and kissed her cheek. 'Hello, darling. All ready for your pre-wedding dinner?'

'I am.'

Sandra came over and embraced Catherine. 'Hello, Cat. It's good to see you again. It's been a long time.'

Happiness flowed through Dee as she stood and watched them laugh like a pair of teenagers. Sandra had never once doubted that Ryan was Peter's son—even before the DNA test—and that knowing when Suzanne fell pregnant, it had been a couple of months after that when she and Peter had got together, so she had no problem with it. Ryan was four months older than Emma; it had taken him a bit of adjusting for him to accept that his mother had not been faithful to Colin. Dee had sat and talked with him many nights outside the homestead, looking at the stars, and he'd finally accepted he couldn't judge his mother. The knowledge that his true father had been a good man had helped him heal.

The only thing that Dee had wanted to know was why Gerard had taken her in when she was a baby. Catherine had held her close. 'As hard as it might be for you to understand now, sweetie, Gerard did love me back then. He wanted to see me happy.'

Sandra firmly believed that Peter hadn't known that he was Ryan's father and would not be swayed. She put it simply. 'He was such a good man, he would have acknowledged Ryan, no matter what Suzanne wanted, but I understand now why Suzanne let our friendship lapse. She must have carried a burden of guilt her whole life. Letting Colin think he was Ryan's father.'

'Come on, you lot,' Jeremy called down to group at the dam. 'Dinner's ready.'

Dee moved to the top of the steps and Sandra came over to stand beside her as Ryan lifted James onto his shoulders and walked up to the house flanked by his sisters: Emma, Ellie, and Dru. They were all laughing as James kept yelling out, 'More horsey rides, *Unca* Ryan.'

Sandra put her arm around Dee's waist. 'You know, sweetie, I never thought I would ever feel this happy again. We've been through some hard times—and you have too—

but look what we have now. She beamed down at her three daughters, her stepson, and her grandson. 'A beautiful family, three wonderful sons-in-law, and tomorrow I will have a new daughter-in law. Are you excited?'

Dee smiled. 'I'm happier than I have ever been in my life, Sandra. So happy it almost hurts.'

'That's the best kind of happiness, love.'

##

Saturday, October 10, 2020

The wedding of Deanne Maree Peters and Ryan Porter-Carey was held in the rose garden at *Wilderness Station* the following afternoon. Dee stayed the night after the pre-wedding dinner at Ellie and Kane's with Catherine, and Ryan went back to the station.

As the bridal car, Connor's black Jeep—polished to a high gloss, and bedecked with red ribbons—approached the front gate of the station, Catherine reached over and took Dee's hand. 'Nervous, darling?'

'No, just very, very happy, Mum.'

The Jeep pulled up at the entrance to the garden and Dee's eyes widened. An arch wound with red ribbons and white roses formed an arbour for her to walk through.

Ellie, Emma, and Dru were waiting for her, all dressed in ruby red dresses matching Dee's bouquet. They helped her from the car and lifted her wedding dress until they were off the red dirt and on the lawn where Ryan waited with Cy, his best man.

Dee's eyes filled with happy tears. It was a testament to Ryan's good nature that he had asked Cy to be his best man.

HIDDEN VALLEY

His cousin had been distraught and offered to leave when Joe had been arrested.

A soft westerly wind carrying the same promise of rain as the clouds last night carried James' excited cries across the lawn. Four rows of chairs with red satin bows formed two semi-circles at the edge of the rose garden. In front of the chairs, Ryan waited with Cy and his three brothers-in law.

Dee walked across the lawn and paused beside Sandra. She smiled at Sandra when the older woman stood and kissed her gently.

'You look beautiful,' Sandra whispered.

The celebrant nodded to the DJ hired for the occasion and the music swelled as Catherine led her to Ryan.

Joy flowed through Dee. If anyone had told her the day she set off for Darwin with an antique hallstand on the back of her blue ute six months ago that before the year was out, she would be in a rose garden marrying the man she loved, she probably would have turned tail and fled.

They stepped towards the celebrant and Catherine waited while Ellie lifted Dee's veil and Dru reached for the bouquet. Catherine took both of Dee's hands and placed them in Ryan's. As he held them, she looked up and was moved by the sheer joy and love in her heart. The same love and happiness was mirrored in his expression.

'I love you,' Ryan whispered as music faded, and the ceremony began.

Five minutes later, after the formalities had been met, the celebrant smiled. 'You may kiss the bride.'

Ryan's arms pulled her close and he lowered his head slowly. He pressed his lips against hers, and Dee smiled as his lips tilted against her mouth. She had been smiling since the night beneath the stars three months ago when Ryan had proposed.

'Ladies and gentlemen, please join me in congratulating Mr and Mrs Porter-Carey,' the celebrant said when they finally broke apart.

Ryan held her hand as they walked across the lawn to their family. Above them, one golden ray of sunshine pierced a towering white cloud and formed a rainbow. The low rumble of thunder presaged the oncoming monsoon season.

Her husband stopped and held her close. Dee's gaze followed his eyes to the beautiful colours above.

'A season of renewal, my love,' Ryan's words vibrated against her cheek. 'A new beginning.'

'A rainbow sent by those who've already left us.' Dee said. 'And a new beginning for all of us here.'

'Come on.' Ryan stepped back and took her hand. 'We have a family over there waiting to see us.'

They stepped forward as Emma, Ellie, and Dru held their arms open to greet their brother and his wife.

THE END

Acknowledgements

I had thought the stories of the Porter sisters were complete two years ago when Dru and Connor found their happy ever after as they solved the mystery at the diamond mine, however insistence by readers, especially Maria Finlay-Frenken and Trish Welsh, that they wanted to read more of the Porters planted the seed for another story.

As I said when I wrote Kakadu Sunset, Kakadu National Park is one of Australia's special places—World Heritage listed for both its environment and its living Indigenous culture. In 2013 on the way to the Northern Territory, we crossed the vast outback, travelling through ancient landscapes. Many of these landscapes have been scarred by various types of mining. Visiting Kakadu and experiencing the spirituality of the land made me wonder what would happen if mining occurred in that pristine environment. The story of *Hidden Valley* continues to raise the awareness that we must think very carefully before we destroy our pristine environments.

As always a huge thank you to my writing buddy and editor, Susanne Bellamy, for your thoughtful comments and ability to steer me in the right direction when I get stuck on a plot point. Also to Roby Aiken, who I believe is the best proof-reader in the world!

A special thank you to my editor, Libby Turner who has had faith in my work since the first book in the Porter Sisters series was submitted six years ago. Again, Libby has polished my story to make it shine.

And to you, the reader: Thank you for choosing this book. I hope when you read, that you love it and talk about it, and that maybe you will want to visit this wonderful part of Australia. I hope you enjoy Ellie. Emma, Dru, and Sandra's stories. Drop me a line at annie@annieseaton.net. I would love to hear from you.

Reviews on Goodreads are always welcome and much appreciated!

All Annie's books are available in print at Annie's store

eBook links:

https://www.annieseaton.net/books.html

Print Store:

All books are available in print at Annie's store

Free postage

https://www.annieseaton.net/store.html

Look for Annie's next series: **THE AUGATHELLA GIRLS**

About the Author

Annie Seaton lives near the beach on the mid-north coast of New South Wales. Her career and studies have spanned the education sector for most of her working life, including a Master's degree in education and working as an academic research librarian, a high-school principal and a university tutor until she took early retirement and fulfilled a lifelong dream of a full-time writing career. Annie's books have been very well received and she has won several awards:

Book of the Year (Whitsunday Dawn)
Ausrom Readers' Choice Awards 2018.

Finalist (Whitsunday Dawn)
ARRA romantic suspense.

Finalist - NZ KORU award 2018 and 2020.

Winner - Best Established Author of the Year 2017 AUSROM.

Longlisted - Sisters in Crime Davitt Awards 2016, 2017, 2018, 2019.

Finalist (Kakadu Sunset) - Book of the Year, Long Romance, RWA Ruby awards 2016.

Winner - Best Established Author of the Year 2015 AUSROM.

ANNIE SEATON

Winner - Author of the Year 2014 AUSROM.

Each winter, Annie and her husband leave the beach to roam the remote areas of Australia for story ideas and research. She is passionate about preserving the beauty of the Australian landscape and respecting the traditional ownership of the land. For those readers who cannot experience this journey personally, Annie seeks to portray the natural beauty of the Australian environment—its spiritual locations, stunning landscapes and unique wildlife.

The Northern Territory—the setting for the fictional Hidden Valley—is one of the world's last *Wilderness* frontiers.

THE PORTER SISTERS

I hope you've enjoyed Book 4 of the Porter Sisters series

Here are Books 1-3,5 and 6

These books and many more available from Annie's print store:
https://www.annieseaton.net/store.html

Signed copies, free postage.

Book 1:

Between Ellie's damage and Kane's secrets, can they find a way to open up to each other before the shadowy forces shut her up...for good?

Book 2

While some come to the Daintree to find shelter, others are here to exploit the rainforest's riches. And they will stop at nothing to get their hands on its bounty.

ANNIE SEATON

Book 3

As Dru's past catches up with her, their instant, mutual dislike threatens to blind them to the true danger lurking in the mine, one which could leave them both at the mercy of the desert.

Book 5

Can they survive the wilderness in the heat and the rugged conditions, and can they both keep their hearts intact as they learn to rely on each other?

Book 6-Kakadu Dawn… June 2023

Printed in Great Britain
by Amazon